Women
in the
Canadian
Mosaic

Women in the Canadian Mosaic

edited by
Gwen Matheson

Peter Martin Associates Limited

To our mothers and foremothers

Canadian Shared Cataloguing in Publication Data

Women in the Canadian mosaic / edited by Gwen Matheson

ISBN 0-88778-125-X ; 0-88778-126-8 pa.

1. Women - Canada - Addresses, essays, lectures.   2. Women - Canada - History - Addresses, essays, lectures.
I. Matheson, Gwen.

HQ1453.W6   301.41'20971

Design: Diana McElroy

PETER MARTIN ASSOCIATES LIMITED
35 BRITAIN STREET, TORONTO, CANADA   M5A 1R7

United Kingdom: Books Canada, 1 Bedford Road, London N2, England.
United States: Books Canada, 33 East Tupper St., Buffalo, N.Y. 14203.

Contents

Acknowledgements:

I gratefully acknowledge the assistance of the following people in the form of advice, information, and general encouragement: Angela Miles, Lynne Teather, Kathy Vanderlinden, Marcia McClung, Krista Maeots, Marylee Stephenson, Leslie Towers, June Callwood, Jill Conway, Patricia Cook, Frieda Forman, Judy LaMarsh, Sandra Pyke, Johanna Stuckey, Helen Tucker, Joy Wilson, and others too numerous to mention.

I would also like to thank the Ontario Arts Council and the Ontario International Women's Year Office for their financial assistance.

Introduction

*"Women from the motherland have come to Canada to advocate the cause of suffrage, but their words have not exactly fitted the case on this side of the water. The need was for the awakening of a consciousness of reform from within, and not so much for advice from without. Canada in this matter as in others was intended to work out her own destiny, and the need was for leadership."** *

If the first sentence of this commentary by an observer of the early Canadian women's movement were altered to read, "Women from the *United States* have come to Canada to advocate the cause of *women's liberation,* but their words have not exactly fitted the case on this side of the *border,*" the whole passage would more or less accurately describe the situation for Canadian women at the beginning of the seventies. The need for Canadian women to achieve a "consciousness of reform from within, and not so much for advice from without" began to be recognized four years ago at a time when there was almost no feminist literature being produced in Canada, and we had to depend chiefly on the efforts of American (and sometimes British) writers. This book was intended to help remedy that deficiency.

It is a collection that has grown organically with the women's movement in Canada over the last few years. The selection of topics and of potential writers was the result of my own role as both participant in and observer of this movement through various organizations, hundreds of meetings, and the general pursuit of women's studies.

All the contributors have in one way or another been

*From V. Strong-Boag's introduction to *In Times Like These* by Nellie McClung (Toronto, 1972).

committed to the feminist cause. They have known the difficulties as well as the tremendous satisfactions of this kind of work: the countless meetings and conferences, the organizational details, the experience of working with other women—in some cases for the first time—and learning to overcome the age-old barriers which separate us. They have experienced the many stages of development both within themselves and in the movement as a whole—the conflicts, the resolutions and compromises, the shifts in points of view—all of which they have attempted to come to terms with and record.

Throughout the many months spent gathering the material and searching for a publisher I was sustained by the support and encouragement of the contributors. My relationship with them has helped to preserve my faith in women and in their ability to work together despite some of the setbacks and disillusionments experienced in the movement itself. I have become convinced that female brain-power is probably the greatest unused resource in this country.

My main regret in looking back over the long association with these and other women writers is that not all articles submitted could be included in the book. My original plan of attempting to present the entire situation of women in Canada in microcosm soon proved to be far too ambitious. The collection gradually resolved itself into two groups of articles: those investigating various aspects of the history of women in Canada, and those dealing with the more personal experiences of women engaged in a particular area of contemporary life. No attempt was made to present a uniform viewpoint. Indeed, the authors' wide variation in approach, analysis and style is representative of the "mosaic" quality which characterizes the women's movement in Canada today.

"People must know the past to understand the present and to face the future," wrote Nellie McClung in 1943. Since the intention of this book is to offer Canadian women some knowledge of their past and a greater understanding of their situation in the present, it is appropriate that the article dealing with this great Canadian feminist should occupy first place in the anthology. If there has been any primary influence on the whole tone and approach of the book it has been hers. I first encountered her *In Times Like These* in 1972 during the early stages of my work. This powerful feminist manifesto, published thirty-four years before Simone de Beauvoir's *The Second Sex* and nearly half a century before Betty Friedan's *The Feminine Mystique,* was a revelation to me. Its author had lived in Canada and yet was almost unknown. With increasing excitement and dismay I discovered that almost everything McClung had to say in *In Times Like These* as well as in her two autobiographical volumes, *Clearing in the West* and *The Stream Runs Fast,* can still be applied to women in Canada today. It was not difficult to find in her work appropriate epigraphs to introduce each article in this book.

McClung's theory and the energy with which she sought to actualize it were based on a firm faith in the future and in the ability of women to change the world for the better. This kind of feminism which saw in women a potential to "serve and save the race" is sometimes strongly attacked by feminists today. Their feelings on the matter have considerable justification, since such a philosophy can be misused to keep women "in their place" as martyrs and sacrificial victims, roles they have played for thousands of years. But whether through biology or conditioning (and probably both) women have always displayed a greater concern for the preservation and nurturing of life than have men. Rather than being denigrated, these "feminine" attributes should be encouraged as qualities which must no longer be considered the special property of women. This is ultimately what feminists mean when they say, "Women's liberation is human liberation."

In Canada as elsewhere we seem to be entering a new period of self-searching, doubt, and attempts to find new directions. In our attempts we must avoid succumbing to well-meaning but overly simplified philosophies. By retaining a respect for the individual personality we must keep ourselves free from the sort of dehumanized categorizing to which those devoted to a cause are often inclined. Those people, both women and men, who are able to take a radical stand and yet maintain a comprehensive point of view are very much needed in our society. In this respect perhaps Canadian women will have a special contribution to make. Before we reach that "Better Country" dreamed of by the suffragists and other visionaries, we can try to be among those who, according to one of Nellie McClung's favourite quotations, "in time of storm held the ridgepole up and spiked again the rafters of the house".

G.M.

"The world has suffered long from too much masculinity and not enough humanity."

—Nellie McClung

The Past

V.E. Lang is a citizen of both Canada and Ireland and has a doctorate in pre-Shakespearean drama from University College, Dublin. Besides feminism she is interested in Bronze Age archaeology in Ireland and freelance writing. She teaches theatre arts in Mississauga and is currently researching an article on the Scottish emigrants of Ste Anne on Cape Breton island.

Gwen Matheson is a lecturer, free-lance writer and doctoral student in English literature. In 1961 she received a master's degree at McGill University and in 1966 a Phil.M. degree at the University of Toronto. She has taught a number of English, Canadian and American literature courses at McGill, Waterloo and York Universities as well as women's studies courses at York and Seneca College. She has published several articles and reviews of films and books and in 1973 researched a program on Nellie McClung for the CBC's "This Country in the Morning". Her interest in feminism and in utopian literature has resulted in a number of publications on topics as diverse as women in the Soviet Union, Nellie McClung and the work of Aldous Huxley.

Nellie McClung:
"Not a Nice Woman"

Gwen Matheson and V.E. Lang

> *"By nice women, you probably mean selfish
> women who have no more thought for the
> underpaid, overworked women than a pussycat
> in a sunny window has for the starving kitten on
> the street. Now in that sense I am not a nice
> woman, for I do care."*

"I've always wanted to know you. I knew you would improve on acquaintance." These words were addressed to Nellie Letitia McClung by Martha Black, a Member of Parliament, upon their first meeting. Such reactions to "Calamity Nell", an early figure in the Canadian feminist movement, were not uncommon. Even today some find her explosive mixture of idealism and rebelliousness disconcerting. But being controversial was Nellie McClung's trademark. She once wrote that people wanting to hurt her feelings would have to submit their case in writing, and her motto was, "Get the thing done and let them howl."

Nellie McClung's picture on a Canadian stamp (an honour accorded few of our deserving women) indicates just how important those "things" were. Few Canadian women realize, for instance, that their legal rights as "persons" and their right to vote are in considerable part due to her efforts. A daughter of hardy pioneers, she devoted her life to breaking new ground for women. She was the first woman to represent Canadian Methodism at the World Ecumenical

1

Conference, the first woman member of the CBC's board of governors, and in 1938 was a Canadian delegate to the League of Nations. Her many achievements are all the more remarkable in view of her background, sex and period.

Nellie was born the sixth child of an Irish father, John Mooney, and a Scottish mother, Letitia McCurdy Mooney, at Chatsworth, Ontario in 1873. At the age of seven, she moved with her family to the better farming country of Manitoba where they settled near Wawanesa at the junction of the Assiniboine and Souris Rivers.

The childhood described in her two-volume autobiography, *Clearing in the West* (1935) and *The Stream Runs Fast* (1945), is a distinctly Canadian experience. She recalls prairie farm life of the late nineteenth century with warmth, sympathy and a strong feeling of nostalgia. Though the life was hard and demanding, it was suffused by a sense of unity with the natural world. But even as Nellie lived it, she realized that this life was passing. Years later she summed up her feelings by saying how glad she was to have known the farm in the days of the horse, before "the dominance of the machine".

While Nellie saluted beauty, courage and endurance, she was equally aware of the crushing drabness and monotony of pioneer life—the soul-and-back-breaking work that had to be done over and over again. The very farms themselves, she thought, had "a demanding look, a clamorous imperative voice". She realized, too, that the heaviest burden fell on the pioneer women. It was the women who fed, healed, clothed and sheltered all that demanding life and, in their spare time, raised their children. She felt driven by a need to bring some sort of vitality, pleasure and real enjoyment into these lives.

This instinct was reinforced by the young reformer's reading of Dickens. She longed to do for her people what he had done for his—to illuminate the commonplace, to give dignity to the ordinary. Always proud that her parents belonged to the "common people", she felt she had a special mission to help the "innumerable host . . . who carry on from day to day, without applause, unconsciously keeping alive the best traditions of humanity".

In her childhood and youth Nellie McClung's unorthodox personality at times baffled even her own parents. It was with her good-natured father that she felt the closest affinity of spirit. Often she slipped out to exchange jokes with him—jokes that she well know would not be appreciated by her mother. Although her relations with her mother were always respectful and deeply affectionate, they were also often strained.

Letitia McCurdy Mooney frequently misunderstood her unconventional youngest daughter. A stern Scottish moralist, she had a highly orthodox sense of duty and respectability and a traditional "old world reverence for men". According to Nellie, her mother attributed qualities of wisdom and foresight to her menfolk that would have surprised them.

If Mrs. Mooney had strong opinions on the role of men, she had equally firm opinions on the place of women. As a child Nellie was forbidden to run in races because her legs might show, chaperoned on all outings and repeatedly warned against being too bold. Once, moved by sympathy for the colourful rebel, Louis Riel, she and her sister spoke out in his defence at a Christmas party. After making several telling remarks to the astounded assembly, the daring sisters were hustled off by their mother with the admonition, "It's a woman's place to help the man, to keep out of public matters and out of public notice."

It was this attitude of her mother's that was a major factor in channelling Nellie McClung's reforming spirit towards a feminist point of view. Too often, she felt, women acquiesced in silence and adopted the "handmaiden" role which society prescribed for them. "Women who place a low value on themselves," she later wrote, "make life hard for all women." And at sixteen she determined to prepare herself for what she considered to be her mission in life—to open doors for people, especially for women.

But she felt strongly her own lack of preparation for such a task. In the isolated prairie community there was no school before Nellie was ten years old and even though she read voraciously from that time on, the book supply was limited. She was desperately aware of being "fettered by ignorance".

For a girl in Nellie's position, education usually meant one thing—Normal School, the teacher's college in Winnipeg. So in 1889, after having passed the Second Class Teacher's Examination, Nellie set out for Winnipeg, one of the youngest students to be admitted to the Normal School. Schoolteaching was at that time a profession with many taboos and restrictions, but Nellie determined to succeed and eventually graduated with honours. She secured her first teaching post in Manitou in 1889, earning the grand sum of $40 a month.

As might be imagined, this new teacher's methods were not precisely orthodox, either for those times or our own. Her first school was in a community riven by old hatreds and feuds which poisoned even the school atmosphere and erupted into continual fighting between students. Convinced of the unwholesomeness of such an environment and the need for a healthier channel for youthful energies, Nellie spent her first pay cheque on a football. She and her pupils, she decided, would play football together, and any time a fight broke out the ball would be confiscated for the day. The plan was highly successful, and although there were the inevitable few in the neighbourhood who objected to this "unladylike" approach to school discipline they were soon won over by the diplomacy and charm of which Nellie was always so capable.

It was while teaching in Manitou that she first met Mrs. McClung, the local minister's wife and an early leader of the Women's Christian Temperance Union. Nellie was captivated by her progressive philosophy and announced enthusiastically, "She is the only woman I have ever seen whom I should like to have for a mother-in-law!" The friendship was to have a deep effect on the course of Nellie's life.

Through the minister's wife she met her future husband, Wesley, the McClungs' son. The relationship which began when she boarded in the McClung home continued when she returned to Winnipeg to study for a higher teaching certificate. She and Wes corresponded regularly and at length, and Nellie described her emotions as a feeling that all the candles of her mind had been lit. And yet she had doubts.

Marriage, she feared, could have a terrible finality about it. It might mean the end of all ambition, hope and aspiration for the wife. Neither was marriage the vocation of every woman. She felt that too often society "taunted" women into marrying, refusing them respect or fulfillment outside the home. She wanted women to have a genuine choice between marrying or not, and to be able to achieve success in many areas outside of marriage. But at the same time she felt that the family was the most important element in society. It was in the family that true happiness was found; it was to the family that one turned in distress and it was the family who gave help most readily and abundantly.

Fortunately Wes was the product of his mother's progressive philosophy and would be considered a liberated man even today. He did not, Nellie pointed out, think that "his wife should always be standing behind his chair, ready to spring to attention". In fact, he was insistent that Nellie give equal consideration to her own interests and ambitions, and agreed with her unorthodox concept of the family. She firmly held that husband and wife should be equal partners in the home, even advocating shared financial responsibility. She also felt that no family should have an unwelcome or unwanted child, nor should mothers have so many children that they would not have time to enjoy and know each one. These beliefs led her to become one of the first Canadian supporters of birth control.

Wes McClung and Nellie Mooney were married on August 24, 1896, in a Presbyterian church on the banks of the Souris River. After the wedding they moved into a four-bedroom apartment over the drugstore in Manitou where Wes worked.

Although she had once feared that marriage and the advent of motherhood could turn a woman exclusively in on her own family, she herself had exactly the opposite experience. After having gone through a period of temporary rebellion against the discomfort and inconvenience of pregnancy, she described that moment when she held her first-born son Jack in her arms as the "most exquisite" of her life. The great overflow of protective, almost fierce maternal love that the twenty-three-year-old Nellie experienced in that June of 1897 turned outwards, out to all women and children everywhere. There must be a way, she determined, to harness this "woman-power", to make it the most effective force in the world.

Following her mother-in-law's lead, Nellie's first impulse was to join the Women's Christian Temperance Union, which she felt was one of the most progressive Canadian organizations of the time. The WCTU was imbued with a genuine reformist fervour, a factor which appealed to her own brand of active, concerned and socially committed Methodism.[1] There, she discovered her talent for public speaking and the satisfaction of working together with other women towards a common goal.

In Nellie McClung's mind religion, temperance, and female emancipation were closely allied. Alcohol, often the only "diversion" available in the harsh frontier society, had particularily destructive powers. Her mother had always favoured prohibition, and Nellie's first impression of the effects of alcohol came from a terrifying childhood incident when an enraged ox, goaded by the spurs of its drunken rider, charged straight towards her and the small baby she was minding.

It was impossible for these early reformers to conceive of a woman drinking. Whatever "fun" and profit there might be in alcohol belonged exclusively to men. But it was women's maternal instincts that led them to "look after" the country and impose prohibition. The WCTU women were too aware of the effects of drunkenness on families, too horrified by statistics like the one that claimed three thousand women had been murdered by their drunken husbands in one year in the United States. And the whole situation was made worse by the fact that women had no legal rights over their children.

It was as a positive and not a negative movement that

---

[1] Nellie once in fact aspired to become a member of the Methodist clergy (revealed by her son Mark in an interview in the *Ottawa Citizen*, August 28, 1973). Of course she received no support for such an unorthodox plan. This frustration of a high-spirited young woman with a passionate sense of justice must have rankled deep. (She was later to write in *In Times Like These* that "the antagonism of the church to receiving women preachers has its basis in sex jealousy".) Although she was always loyal to the established church she was also bitterly critical of some of its attitudes, especially with regard to women.

Nellie saw prohibition. Its purpose was to give, not to take away. This point of view was closely linked with her conviction that Christianity was meant to provide a more abundant life. The church ought, she believed, to quicken people's imaginations and sympathies so that they turned to true and vital pleasures, not to the opiate of alcohol.[2]

Yet even when Nellie was in deadly earnest, as with her temperance concerns, she never lost her incomparable sense of comedy. Mrs. Louise Dean of Calgary who knew Nellie McClung for many years as "an inspiration to all of us" recounted on a CBC interview (spring, 1973) an experience that the great reformer had at one of the schools she was visiting as a temperance speaker. She had used the customary demonstration of showing the class two glasses—one filled with water and the other with whiskey—into both of which a dew worm was dropped. After this slimy martyr to the cause of temperance had performed its act of surviving briskly in the water and then curling up and dying in the stronger stuff, Nellie asked the children what "lesson" they had learned. To this one little boy put up his hand and brightly replied, "We learn that if we drink lots of whiskey we'll never have worms." This little joke which, according to Mrs. Dean, Nellie enjoyed telling on herself, confirmed her friend's opinion that to Nellie humour was indeed "very precious".

Although during the first few years of her marriage Nellie was actively involved with the WCTU she still main-

[2]Many people today fail to realize that the support of prohibition by Nellie McClung and others like her was rooted in a radical social consciousness which was deeply opposed to the commercial exploitation of individuals. The liquor industry did indeed have a dark side, being linked not only with class oppression but with the further abuse of women in the form of prostitution. James Gray has vividly illustrated this in his recent book *Booze* (Toronto: MacMillan, 1972), in which he writes of prostitution as "a subsidiary of the booze problem", and describes the international distillery empire built up by the Bronfman family as being aided by "governments as booze pushers".

tained a certain resistance to what she called "these flashes of crusading spirit". Her first job at that time, she felt, was to raise a healthy, happy family. Jack was not yet two when Nellie's only daughter Florence was born, and less than two years after Florence, Paul joined the family circle. The McClungs moved from over the drugstore into a larger, rented house.

Fortunately for Nellie, however, her in-laws were still living in Manitou. And her gentle but determined mother-in-law who held advanced views on the potential of women had plans for the young Mrs. McClung. One day she marched into her daughter-in-law's kitchen, took over the housework for the day, and disposing of Nellie's protests sent her off to write a short story for a competition in *Collier's* magazine.

The story that Nellie produced didn't win, but it became the opening chapter of a romantic comic novel about earlier Canadian family life, *Sowing Seeds in Danny*. Published in 1908 with distribution in both Canada and the United States, the book sold over 100,000 copies and made its author close to $25,000. It was the first of nine other best-sellers and of her total output of seventeen volumes, including collections of short stories and essays as well as novels. Her literary talent alone, especially for humour and effective rhetoric, ranks Nellie McClung among the most outstanding English-speaking feminists.

The novel also launched its author into another new field of adventure when her mother-in-law persuaded Nellie to give public readings. This turned out to be quite successful, although Nellie had to bolster herself for her first engagement by an excursion into what she called "Applied Beauty". After buying a new blue dress, she had her hair done at a hairdresser's, and had a manicure and facial; she also had her first encounter with commercial rouge, having hitherto used a rose leaf from an old summer hat.

Nellie never did feel the need to sacrifice any of the traditional "feminine" pleasures for what she called "common justice". One of the truest things that can be said about her is that she always seemed to believe that it was possible to have the best of all good worlds.

Although Nellie was now the wife of a prosperous young druggist with a full-time, live-in maid and a mother-in-law always willing to lend a hand, she never forgot the hard lot of the farm woman. It was the story of one of these women as recorded in a country newspaper that later in 1914 inspired one of Nellie's most satisfying literary successes. This was the versified story of Jane Brown, a farm wife and mother of six who died at the age of thirty-three, worn out from too much child-bearing and the strain of keeping her husband's farm running on "woman power". This piece received widespread acclaim, and "was recited at many Women's Institutes, socials and other gatherings". It was to these women, to the Jane Browns everywhere, that Nellie felt she had something to offer. She could somehow show them that there was more to life than monotonous, repetitive slaving.

Nellie continued to work for the WCTU, lectured, wrote, and was even asked to contribute to the *Winnipeg Free Press*. A new baby, Horace, was born in 1900, and there were two assistants now in the drug store. But the hours were long, and Wes began to feel the strain. Finally in 1911 he became an agent for Manufacturer's Life Insurance Company, and the family moved to Winnipeg.

Nellie who was then thirty-eight was a famous author and rather less well-known as a reformer. The family had scarcely settled into their new home on Chestnut Street when Mark, the last and youngest son, was born. But Nellie's world was now beginning to expand far beyond home and family.

The Winnipeg move had, in fact, brought about some of

the most important changes in her life. She joined the Canadian Women's Press Club, a group that was deeply impressed and inspired by the visit in 1912 of the British militant suffragettes, Emmeline Pankhurst and Barbara Wiley. But although Nellie admired these women, she herself was to employ somewhat different tactics.

All her life Nellie remembered her first flame of anger and resentment when she learned that women could not vote. She had little faith in the competence or, indeed, the willingness of most male politicians to bring about the new Canada she envisioned. Men, after all, she observed dryly, had had long enough to demonstrate their ability as the arbiters of human destiny. "Women have cleaned up things since time began," Nellie once wrote, "and if women ever get into politics there will be a cleaning-out of pigeon-holes and forgotten corners, on which the dust of years has fallen, and the sound of the political carpet-beater will be heard in the land."

It was an immediate concern for the appalling conditions of women factory workers that inspired fifteen Press Club members to form the Political Equality League dedicated to the enfranchisement of women. This led to their first direct confrontation with the Conservative Manitoba government, under the premiership of Sir Rodmond Roblin. In Nellie's own words, Sir Rodmond was a "Gentleman of the Old School", and her portrait of him in *The Stream Runs Fast* is perhaps her most devastating satire. Sir Rodmond felt that "nice" women did not visit factories, did not even know about such things and, above all, did not want or need the vote. But Nellie was now used to dealing with this particular objection, and during a dramatic interview she let him know her feelings:

> By nice women you probably mean selfish women who have no more thought for the underpaid, overworked

women than a pussycat in a sunny window has for the starving kitten in the street. Now, in that sense, I am not a nice woman, for I do care. I care about those factory women, working in ill-smelling holes, and we intend to do something about it, and when I say "we" I'm talking for a great many women, of whom you will hear more as the days go on.

It was a manifesto and had Sir Rodmond been an imaginative man he would have quaked in his shoes at hearing it.

Ironically, it was Sir Rodmond who supplied the material for the Political Equality League's greatest success. He had dismissed the suffrage movement as the concern of "short-haired women and long-haired men". His doom was sealed. On January 28, 1914, a delegation from the League appeared before the Assembly, petitioning for female franchise. Sir Rodmond was "at his foamy best". He eulogized his mother, declared that the noble women before him were proof that society was good enough as it was, and ended with a ringing declaration that he could not permit such nobility and purity to be sullied by political contact. Nellie was in the delegation, listening with absorption and growing glee. She observed Sir Rodmond minutely, for the next night she was to present her own interpretation of his speech in the "Women's Parliament".

"The Women's Parliament", presented the following night in Winnipeg's Walker Theatre, was a burlesque of the encounter with Sir Rodmond—an assembly of *women* received a *male* delegation petitioning for the vote. Great pains were taken to reproduce the setting of the Legislative Assembly, even to providing correctly dressed page girls (one of them Nellie's own daughter Florence). The highlight of the affair was "Premier" Nellie's parody of Roblin's speech which she addressed to the male delegation, praising their masculine beauty and declaring her satisfaction with any society which could produce such specimens of perfect manhood.

This performance which was described by the *Winnipeg Telegram* as "productive of mirth of the highest degree" emphasized the League's conviction that chivalry was no substitute for "common, old-fashioned justice". A pedestal, as the star of the show had once remarked, was no place for a healthy woman and is a difficult thing from which to descend when one has to chop the wood. This burlesque which played three times to a packed theatre won enormous success and financed the Political Equality League Campaign in Manitoba.

Carried along by the exhilaration of making history, Nellie wrote that "every day felt like the day before Christmas". Public opinion was now with the suffragists, and it was only a matter of time until women got the vote. Universal suffrage was granted by Manitoba in January 1916, followed in the same year by Alberta, Saskatchewan, and British Columbia. They were joined by Ontario in 1917, and Nova Scotia and the Dominion government had espoused full franchise by 1918. Women in New Brunswick had to wait for the vote till 1919, in Prince Edward Island until 1922, and in Quebec until 1940.

Wes was made manager of his company's branch in Edmonton and the family moved there in the fall of 1914. Nellie welcomed the change for she was aware of the rumours that the new Liberal government might ask her to run and perhaps be Minister of Education. At the same time she felt hesitant to take on the burden of such an office. If she succeeded her success would belong only to her as an individual, but if she failed it would be "for all women everywhere".

Edmonton seemed to Nellie and her family "a city of glamour", to the north of which "lay the great white world of mystery, the land of dog teams, northern lights and undiscovered treasures". In the atmosphere of this new frontier city which was "young, hopeful and full of surprises" she felt more keenly alive than ever and worked day and night. But always at the back of her mind was the war and her dread of her eldest son Jack's enlistment.

It was in this state of mind that she wrote *In Times Like These,* her most radical feminist work and the one by which at present she is becoming best known. Disgusted and enraged by war, which she regarded as a product of the "masculine, military mind", she provided the fullest elaboration of her feminist theories. The tone of the book is perhaps best conveyed by a chapter heading: "What do women think of war? (not that it matters)". Within this grimly realistic context, she expounds "women's claim to a common humanity", a claim originating not in male chivalry but in a sense of justice and fair play. The world, she felt, had suffered long from too much masculinity and too little humanity.

Yet *In Times Like These* is not the work of a "man-hater", an epithet often falsely applied to the suffragists by their opponents. It was Nellie's conviction that men and women could not exist in isolation from each other; for good or ill, their fates were indissolubly linked. What she did want, however, was to see the old prejudices against women "fall like the leaves in autumn when a wind shakes them down and blows them into fence corners".

When war was declared Jack was old enough to enlist and in December 1915 he set out for Europe. To keep herself from brooding his mother threw herself into war work, fund-raising, lecturing, and writing. Jack survived the war and went on to a distinguished legal career, but Nellie knew after he came back that he had "seen the negation of everything he had been taught", and he would never be the same.

The end of the war gave Nellie an opportunity to enter politics. On the ticket of the Liberals and United Farmers she was elected to the Alberta Assembly in 1921. In the next five years she sponsored such social legislation as dental and medical care for school children, married women's property rights, and mothers' allowances.

But Nellie had never followed a party line before and she couldn't start now. Although she enjoyed her five years in Parliament (1921-26) she later came to feel that the results were too little for the amount of effort involved. It was the "bonny fight—the knock-down and drag-out battle" that the indomitable reformer enjoyed, not the nit-picking tedium involved in so much of parliamentary work. For this reason her defeat in the 1926 election was not too severe a blow.

"The middle years of life come on like thunder" Nellie wrote of this period in her life. The family had moved to Calgary in 1923 where Wes's company had sent him, and the children were beginning to scatter. Paul had gone to Texas, Florence was married and living in Regina, and Jack was at Queen's College, Oxford.

Nellie, however, was still in fighting trim, and she and Judge Emily Murphy, the first Canadian woman magistrate, were soon off on a new crusade—the famous (or infamous) "Persons Case".

In their fight Nellie and Emily Murphy were joined by Mrs. Irene Parlby, a member of the Alberta Cabinet, Mrs. Louise McKinney, ex-MLA, and Mrs. Henrietta Edwards, author of a book entitled *Laws Relating to Women.* It was Judge Murphy who discovered that, by an 1876 enactment in British law, women were not legally persons. "Women," the law declared, "are persons in matters of pains and penalties, but are not persons in matters of rights and privileges." A petition was drawn up by the "Alberta Five" and presented to the federal Senate, from where it was referred to the Supreme Court of Canada. In April

1928 this august body turned down the case, thereby denying the personhood of one-half of Canada's population. Undaunted, the Alberta Five pressed their suit on to the Privy Council in England, where, in October 1929 it was announced that women were, after all, persons. Nellie observed dryly that when newspapers all over the British Empire carried the black headlines, "Privy Council Declares That Women Are Persons!" it came as a surprise to many Canadian women who had not known they were not persons until they heard that they were.

Throughout this and her numerous other activities Nellie proved with eminent success that she could combine family and career. Even Will, her favourite brother, had urged her to stay quietly at home and devote herself chiefly to her five children and husband. He was not the only one to feel this way, and the fighting feminist was conscious that she was, as she put it, "vulnerable in five places". During the height of her suffrage campaigning she telephoned home just before each lecture, and then would begin her talk with the reassuring remark, "Settle down now and don't worry about my children. They are all well and happy, clothed and fed. The baby is in bed and all is well." Her children themselves were aware of their responsibility, and Nellie liked to tell how her youngest son, disheveled and covered in mud, had been hurried home by an older brother with the words, "Quick now! It's a good thing I got you before the *Telegram* got a picture of you—Nellie McClung's neglected child!"

It was, paradoxically perhaps, the security and happiness she felt in her personal life that spurred Nellie on to act in other spheres. She felt that her own happiness gave her a special responsibility towards women who were not so fortunate. She took a genuine personal interest in the succession of young immigrant women who helped her to run her household, teaching them English and learning about their native cultures. One of them, a Finnish woman, was the inspiration for a successful novel (*Painted Fires*).

Nellie McClung who spent much of her life fighting for women, the world's largest minority group, also had an abiding concern for the rights of other minorities—from Ontario Indians to British Columbia Hindus. One of her most painful memories arose from an incident during the Ecumenical Conference she attended in London, England in 1920 when a delegate from the southern United States objected to sitting beside a black delegate. Significantly, she found herself later being exposed to the same treatment when a male member of the Alberta Legislative Assembly expressed anger at having to sit next to her because she was a woman.

Nellie believed passionately in the future of Canada as one of the world's great nations. Commenting in 1914 on the "wonderful plans" that she and women like her had "laid for our country's welfare", she wrote:

> We would re-write our history. We would copy no other country. We would be ourselves, and proud of it. How we scorned the dull brown Primer from which we had learned Canadian history! Written as it was from the top down with no intimate glimpses of the people at all.[3]

She saw Canadian women as having a definite and powerful role to play in creating that "better country" of her dreams.

This vision was not limited to Canada, however. Nellie was always well aware, for instance, that Canadian feminism was linked with the world-wide sisterhood of all women. Her international outlook in other matters had taken her as a Methodist delegate to the World Ecumenical Conference in London in 1921. And in 1938 at the age of sixty-five she

[3]*The Stream Runs Fast.*

made another trip abroad, this time as a delegate to the League of Nations in Geneva. She always had a universal point of view.

Saddened by the league's inability to act and by the outbreak of yet another war, Nellie returned to Canada. Yet her faith was never broken, and even when she was an old lady her eyes twinkled with irresistible humour and hope. In her comfortable home, "Lantern Lane", which she shared with Wes at Gordon Head near Victoria, B.C., the veteran of many struggles finally found time during her last years to devote herself more completely to her writing and to become acquainted with her grandchildren. Her sense of the continuity of human life along with her belief in the "fellowship of the soil" and her deep religious faith enabled Nellie McClung to live with courage and good humour until her death, after a series of heart-attacks, in her seventy-eighth year.

She once remarked in her old age that if she could re-live her life she would like to spend it teaching young children, showing them the delight and importance of being planters, builders, makers, and menders. "Children are great idealists," she said, "until the stupidity of their elders puts out the fires of their aspirations." Her apparently utopian visions were in actuality quite realistic, for they were derived from a belief in inner values rather than in mere material progress.

The "new liberalism" of contemporary society which applies theories of *laissez-faire* and rugged individualism to human social codes would have been described by Nellie as "the easy-going shallow tolerance of the unconcerned". And a key to her whole philosophy is contained in a comment she once made on the subject of "personal liberty":

> If there were only one man on the earth, he might have personal liberty to do just as he liked, but the

advent of the second man would end it. Life is full of prohibitions to which we must submit for the good of others.

Nellie McClung and other outstanding Canadian women of the past have just now begun to receive the recognition they deserve. Many of her ideas as well are only now becoming fully appreciated, for she was not only ahead of her own time but was also in many ways ahead of our time. Harmony among nations and religious groups is more than ever an urgently sought goal. The land still stands in need of ecological protection, and what has been termed Nellie's "agrarian bias" is seen now to be not so irrelevant after all. The liberation of women is still far from being won. Nellie believed that there is a natural "curative power" in human life and in the fact that "evolution when blocked and suppressed becomes revolution".

It was Nellie McClung's great distinction that she was not content merely to enjoy her own success. Her faith, which stressed action rather than dogma and creeds, gave her feminism a distinct spiritual aspect. It was, she felt, a compelling obligation on all of us "not to eat our bread alone".

When she started her work in the fields of social reform and the emancipation of women, it was not considered a "nice" thing for a "lady" to do; it was not the sort of thing that made her an easy guest. But if Nellie's Irish background made her seek out laughter, her Scottish derivation made her tenacious. These qualities along with the influence of her environment resulted in a particularly Canadian brand of feminism—acknowledging the complexity of human problems rather than reducing everything to a single issue, not tolerating fools gladly and yet being on the whole good-humoured rather than rancorous, preferring the bite of wit to the vehemence of denunciation. Hers was the undeterred perseverance and over-mastering endurance of the Northern breed. And it is perhaps no accident that one of her favourite biblical quotations was the one about the virtuous woman "who was not afraid of the snow for her household".

It was a common household activity that once gave Nellie McClung the opportunity to sum up her general attitude towards life. "I would not like," she declared, "to pull through life like a thread without a knot." She need not have worried. There are still a good many McClung knots helping to hold together the fabric of Canadian society.

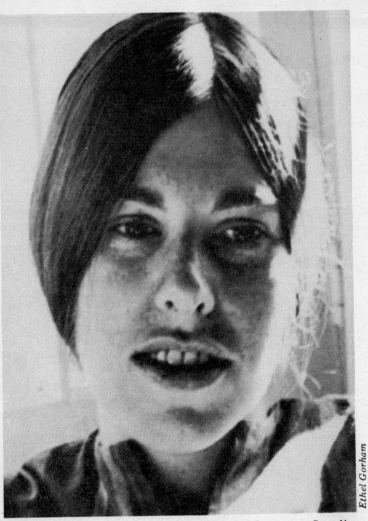

Ethel Gorham

Deborah Gorham was born in New York and became a Canadian citizen in 1967. For the past five years she has taught a number of women's studies courses at St. Patrick's College, Carleton University and is working on a study of the Canadian feminist, Flora MacDonald Denison. Her article "English Militancy and the Canadian Suffrage Movement" appeared in the first issue of Atlantis: A Women's Studies Journal, published at Acadia University, Wolfville, Nova Scotia.

The Canadian Suffragists

Deborah Gorham

"The anti-suffrage attitude of mind is not so much a belief as a disease."

Outside the Senate Chamber in Ottawa there is a bronze plaque commemorating the historic decision of the Judicial Committee of the Privy Council of Great Britain which declared that Canadian women were legally "persons" under the terms of the British North America Act. The date of that decision was October 18, 1929. In this declaration the British Empire's highest court of appeal overturned a decision handed down the year before by the Supreme Court of Canada. Its immediate practical effect was to make women eligible for appointment to the Senate, but its symbolic significance was equally important. Although the framers of the BNA Act had not in truth considered that women should be part of Canada's political community the Privy Council decision made them full participants in the constitution of the Dominion. And although in 1929 the Canadian woman's struggle for legal and institutional equality was not yet over (the major piece of unfinished business being the granting of the provincial suffrage to the women of Quebec) the successful conclusion of the Persons Case is a landmark in the history of Canadian feminism. When the law recognized women as "persons" a major undertaking begun by Canadian feminists in the nineteenth

23

century, the task of achieving full citizenship for women, was symbolically completed.

In the late nineteenth and early twentieth centuries, Canada was experiencing a period of social and economic change characterized by rapid urbanization, the pressures of immigration from non-Anglo-Saxon countries, increased industrialization and labour unrest, and changes in the pace of agricultural development. Major changes in women's social, political and economic roles were an important factor during this period, a factor which has been given too little consideration in the accounts of historians. This omission not only leaves the woman reader with the all-too-familiar feeling that her history has been left out of "Respectable" (male) History, it also distorts male history itself. The women's emancipation movement in Canada came about partly as a result of these social and economic developments but it was also a factor which served to shape them.

The women's suffrage movement, symbol of nineteenth- and early twentieth-century feminism then and now, was the most visible manifestation of women's emancipation, but it was merely the tip of the iceberg. Those who attacked women's suffrage were attacking much more than the idea that women as well as men should enter the polling booth. Unlike the opposition to a wider male suffrage, resistance to women's suffrage was everywhere based not so much on fear of the effects women might have as voters but on the fact that the woman voter challenged the ideal of womanhood which formed an essential part of a social order that many saw slipping away from them. As one conservative Canadian voice put it in 1909:

Nature has assigned to us all our duties in life. To the man has been given the task of supporting the woman, of sustaining the home, of fighting the battles and of governing the family, the clan or the nation. To woman has been committed the charge of the home and the duty of exercising a moderating influence over all its occupants. The Suffragettes . . . are at war with nature. They want the women to be too much like men.[1]

More often than not, Canadian feminists gave wholehearted support to the idea that women had special duties. However, they insisted that these very duties made it essential that they participate fully in public life. Only then could they carry out their special mission: the protection of the home, the family, and of women and children. Thus they used in their own defense the view of womanhood expressed in the above extract quoted from a *Toronto Mail and Empire* editorial.

Feminists in the United States and Britain used the same tactics. But this approach may have been a tactic of argument as much as it was a deeply felt belief. One of the most thoughtful commentators on the American movement has suggested that the U.S. suffragists' arguments were shaped not at their own initiative, but more often in response to the arguments of anti-suffragists.[2] Tactically it was wise, at least in the short run, to emphasize the woman's maternal role because this technique turned the arguments of the opposition against itself. But tactics are one thing, inner beliefs are another, and many American and British feminists were ambivalent about both their literal and their figurative maternal roles. If this was true in the United States (and in Britain) perhaps it was also true in Canada. Only as we come to know more about a larger number of Canadian feminists will we truly be able to judge.[3]

[1] *Toronto Mail and Empire,* October 23, 1909, p. 16. An editorial commenting on the arrival of Mrs. Pankhurst in North America.

[2] A. Kraditor, *Ideas of the Woman Suffrage Movement* (New York, 1965).

[3] One of the most useful recent analyses of Canadian feminism is V. Strong-Boag's introduction to the recent reissue of Nellie McClung's *In Times Like*

In any case, there were Canadian women who advocated equal rights for its own sake, and who made it their primary reason for insisting that women must have a wider place in society:

> Why should women, who represent half the human family, not have equal rights and privileges . . . or all the *natural* conditions of their brothers, or civil conditions made by the laws of their country . . . for the benefit of the human family in general?[4]

asked Flora MacDonald Denison, an activist in the Toronto movement.

Denison and others like her firmly insisted that as human beings they had a *right* to full citizenship. They fought for their rights as individuals and not only because they felt a duty to expand their maternal role into the public sphere. But Denison herself used maternal feminist arguments when it served her purposes. Canadian feminists of the period cannot be categorized as belonging to one or another clearly delineated group; both equal rights feminism and maternal feminism were realities in Canada.

If the Persons Case marks the symbolic end of the nineteenth century woman's struggle for equal rights in Canada, where did that struggle begin? The struggle of nineteenth-century Canadian feminism has its origins in the European society out of which the new Canadian society developed. The most important institutions which formed the attitude of Canadian society toward women were those which were common to all of North America and were a direct result of the influence of the parent cultures on their colonial

---

These. Strong-Boag argues that maternal feminism was dominant: I suggest that she may have overemphasized it. See McClung, Nellie, *In Times Like These* (Toronto, 1972); reissue in the *Social History of Canada* series (general editor Michael Bliss), with introduction by V. Strong-Boag.

[4] This quotation is from a speech on "Political Equality" in the Flora MacDonald Denison papers, Box 2. Denison's papers are at the University of Toronto.

offspring. European society was patriarchal, and the patriarchal nature of that society was upheld by those twin
institutional pillars, the church and the law.

Of the two, religion was probably the more important
because it shaped attitudes—attitudes of women as well as
men. From its beginnings, Christianity has offered women
both a negative and a positive message. This double message
is nowhere more openly expressed than in the Pauline
Epistles. From Paul we learn that slave and free, male and
female are equal in God's sight; but we are also told that
wives are to obey their husbands and to remain silent in
church. Institutionalized Christianity has tended to reinforce the negative message. It has been patriarchal, its
central figures have been male, and its ritual has been controlled almost exclusively by males. Throughout the history
of Christianity, only the more radical heresies and sects
have offered scope for the democratic Christian message.

Although the conflict between religious belief and feminism is less important today when few feminists are religious
(in the church-going sense) and when religious institutions
themselves are more open to change, the sexism of religion
posed a problem for many religious feminists of an earlier
era. Devout feminists attempted to resolve it by stressing
the democracy of Christ's message, as Nellie McClung did
when she insisted that "Christ was a true democrat" but
"the Christian Church has departed in some places from
Christ's teachings—notably in its treatment of women".[5]
Unfortunately this sort of statement did little to alter
the fact that religious belief was used to justify sexist legal,
social and political structures and was in fact one of the
most powerful agencies of a patriarchal society.

The legal structure of European society certainly reinforced the inferior position granted to women by religious

[5]Nellie McClung, *In Times Like These*, pp. 68-9.

ideology. This legal structure was transported to the New World when the new colonies were established. The legal position of women in Canada as settlement began reflected the legal position of women in France and England, and it is important to remember just how onerous the law was. The legal structure grew out of the patriarchal nature of society, and there is no question that the subservient status of women in the eyes of the law appeared to its supporters to be sanctioned by the patriarchal Christian tradition. The genuinely oppressive provisions of the law in both French and English Canada applied only to married women, but, since most women married, the freedoms allowed to un-married adult women under the law were of minor impor-tance.

What was the position of women under English common law at the beginning of the nineteenth century?

> The theoretical basis for the married woman's loss of legal rights was the feudal doctrine of coverture. Based in part upon biblical notions of the unity of flesh of husband and wife, the doctrine was described by Blackstone as follows: "By marriage, the husband and wife are one person in law; that is, the very being or legal existence of the woman is suspended during the marriage, or at least is incorporated and consoli-dated." In modern times, the doctrine has been de-scribed with greater candor as resting "on the old common-law fiction that the husband and wife are one . . . [which] has worked out in reality to mean . . . the one is the husband".[6]

In concrete terms, what this meant was that a married woman had only a limited control over her own actions, and could not own property. Any property she brought to the marriage belonged to her husband, and any wealth she acquired or produced was also his. Moreover, a mother had

[6]L. Kanowitz, *Women and the Law* (Albuquerque, 1969), p. 35.

no rights whatever concerning her children: " . . . a mother
had no more legal relationship to her children than a stranger . . . the father was the sole guardian of his children until
they reached the age of 21. He could educate them how and
when he pleased, give them in adoption or bind them out
as apprentices, and he was entitled to all their earnings."[7]
No woman could vote in nineteenth-century English Canada and the married woman enjoyed no right to a voice in
the law courts. (It should be remembered that the issue of
the suffrage was less important as it applied to women before the late eighteenth century, since the suffrage was
confined to a small class of men, and was associated with
property rather than with individual rights. Indeed, in some
cases women, by virtue of being property owners, could
exercise the suffrage. This was true in Quebec, for instance,
in the late eighteenth and early nineteenth centuries.) In
summary, then, in Canada, at the time of settlement, a
married woman's "only basic legal right was the right to
support by her husband with the necessities of life, according to his means".[8]

Given these institutional constraints on their activities it
is not difficult to understand that nineteenth-century
Canadian women, like their American and British counterparts, had to begin by attacking the legal structures which
hampered them. They could not begin by attacking the
social and psychological barriers to women's freedom that
the women's movement sees as central today, even though
many nineteenth-century women were also concerned with
these more subtle constraints.

When and where did the Canadian fight for equal rights

[7] Margaret MacLellan, "History of Women's Rights in Canada", in *Cultural Tradition and Political History of Women in Canada,* study no. 8 of the Royal Commission on the Status of Women (Ottawa, 1971), p. 2.

[8] *Ibid.,* p. 1.

for women begin? In Canada, the feminist movement was shaped by regional factors, although there are certain shared characteristics which manifested themselves in all areas of the country. The movement began in Ontario, but achieved the symbolic success of equal suffrage first in the prairie provinces. An active movement developed in British Columbia, but at a relatively late date. In the Maritimes it appears that only small numbers of women were involved in public activities and few indeed were concerned with the equal rights issue. In Quebec, French-Canadian women were slow to involve themselves in any activities outside the home, and it appears that in the period before the achievement of the Dominion suffrage, the equal rights movement in that province was in the hands of a small number of English-speaking women in Montreal.

Women were active in Ontario in the last decades of the nineteenth century and at the beginning of this century, but most of their activity was not focussed directly on equal rights. By the 1870s the province was rich enough to support a significant number of middle-class women with sufficient leisure to devote themselves to concerns other than the immediate ones of raising a family and of managing a home. With this new-found time many women devoted themselves merely to a more elaborate social life.[9] Those women who did seek other channels for their energies usually applied them to social welfare causes, thus fitting the model of "maternal feminism". This activity extended from Women's Institutes to temperance organizations and found a central focus in the 1890s, with the founding of the National Council of Women.

But as early as the 1870s there was a small band of dedicated women who saw that the equal rights issue was

[9] For a description of the social life led by such women, see L. Creighton, *The Elegant Canadians* (Toronto, 1967).

one of central concern. The equal rights women were also concerned about temperance or slum clearance, or the evils of prostitution, but they were distinguished from others by the fact that they saw equal civil, economic and educational rights as a cause of primary importance. Largely because of their efforts other socially concerned women, notably those for whom temperance was the major social issue, would gradually see that they too had to make a positive commitment to their own rights as citizens.

The equal rights advocates launched a Toronto suffrage society at a public meeting held in the city council chambers in 1883, but the origins of this suffrage society go back to a private club, the "Toronto Women's Literary Club" founded in 1876 by Dr. Emily Howard Stowe, Canada's first woman physician. Catherine Cleverdon in *The Woman Suffrage Movement in Canada* dates the beginnings of organized Canadian feminism from the founding of this club,[10] and it is becoming commonplace to use this date as a signpost. Like the Seneca Falls Convention of 1848, which is usually taken to mark the beginning of an organized movement in the United States, the date of the founding of the Literary Club should be seen as a convenient landmark but should in no way be taken as a rigid or definitive starting point for the whole feminist movement. However, it is likely that it does mark the first attempt to publicize the equal rights issue.

Its founder, Dr. Emily Howard Stowe, is a genuinely interesting and important figure. She was one of those nineteenth-century professional women who made her way to a career (in her case in medicine) in the face of severe practical and psychological opposition. Faced with a career-versus-motherhood dilemma, she proved herself committed

[10]C. Cleverdon, *The Woman Suffrage Movement in Canada* (Toronto, 1974), p. 20.

enough to a career to leave her children in the care of a sister while undertaking her training.[11] Forced to receive her training outside the country (no medical school in Canada would admit her) she was exposed to feminist ideas during her stay in the United States. On her return to Toronto she felt the need to advocate the advancement of women in Canadian society. The Literary Club's innocuous name was apparently chosen intentionally, the founders believing that any overt mention of that chief of feminist causes, the suffrage, would arouse too much hostility.

The Literary Club in its early stages hardly represents a movement: only a few women were involved and it was primarily an individual educational experience for those who did attend its meetings. However, as we have seen, the Toronto Women's Literary Club did provide the nucleus for the first Canadian suffrage society, the Toronto Women's Suffrage Society, which was launched at a public meeting in March 1883, and this society also provided the base for the development of an attempt at a national organization, the Dominion Women's Enfranchisement Association (later the Canadian Suffrage Association). But the national society appears to have been national in name only, and remained largely a Toronto organization.

The equal rights movement in Ontario in the 1880s and 1890s seems to have been directed to two main areas, the suffrage and increased educational opportunities for women. It scored some notable successes, including the admission of women to the University of Toronto. The Ontario legislature's response to the demand for political rights met with qualified success. The right to vote for school trustees had been granted to women with the necessary property qualifications in 1850. In 1884, the legislature

[11] Joanne Thompson, "The Influence of Dr. Emily Howard Stowe on the Woman Suffrage Movement in Canada", in *Ontario History*, Volume LIV, no. 4, December 1962, p. 254.

granted the municipal franchise to unmarried women with the necessary property qualifications. In 1872 Ontario passed the first Married Women's Property Act in Canada. The pattern of granting local franchises, or of franchises specifically concerned with education, had parallels elsewhere. In England, for instance, the franchise for the school boards set up by the Education Act of 1870 was granted to women. In the 1870s women were permitted to be poor law guardians and under the County Councils Act of 1888 they were admitted to participation in local government. Why were male legislatures so willing to grant these concessions? Because these tasks and responsibilities were housekeeping tasks and thus it was considered that women could participate in them without violating the accepted Victorian image of women.

When it came to granting the suffrage in jurisdictions which involved less restricted areas of activity, the Ontario legislature was to prove less open to women's suffrage. In spite of the fact that there was an active petition campaign in the 1880s (largely dominated by the temperance interests) and in spite of the fact that the women had gained a supporter in the legislature, the Liberal John Waters, who sponsored several suffrage bills in the 1880s and 1890s, these bills met with no success and little debate. There was not enough of a movement in the province to bring pressure on a legislative body most of whose members found the idea outlandish and ridiculous and continued to do so for some time to come. The provincial suffrage was in fact not achieved in Ontario until 1917 and is said to have been a direct result of women's participation in the war effort.

Why did the struggle take so long in Ontario? Although Ontario was the first place in Canada in which sentiment for women's rights emerged, there is little doubt that those interested in women's rights were not able to secure mass public opinion in their favour, nor were they able to arouse sufficient numbers of women for sufficient lengths of time. Although they were earnest and dedicated, women like Emily Howard Stowe and the second-generation women like her daughter Augusta Stowe-Gullen and Flora MacDonald Denison appear to have been if not content, at least resigned to wait for public opinion to swing their way. In the first years of this century, most of them watched the progress of the English militants with benevolent interest, but with a sense of detachment,[12] and they seemed to accept the views of their male supporters that although women's suffrage was "inevitable", in Canada it might be a long time in coming.

It was a characteristic of male supporters in Canada to qualify their support for the suffrage with comments about women's "apathy", and to insist that the suffragists garner an unrealistic amount of visible support: the *Toronto World*, for instance, which was a friend of the cause (Flora Mac-Donald Denison wrote a column for the Sunday edition), urged the "apostles and evangelists of the movement [to] get the women of Ontario together and confront the provincial premier [Sir James Whitney] with a requisition signed by a majority of their number calling on him to fulfill his pledge". Whitney had agreed to support the suffrage if he saw "sufficient" public demand. When Augusta Stowe-Gullen, as president of the Canadian Suffrage Association, wrote to the paper praising the editorial, she did not point out that this demand on the part of *The World* was both unnecessary and virtually impossible to fulfill.[13]

[12] This sense of detachment concerning militancy was true of most but not all the Canadian suffragists. A few of them (Flora MacDonald Denison was one) felt not only sympathy with the suffragettes, but a strong sense of identification with them, even though they did not adopt militant tactics in Canada. For a full discussion of this question, see my article "English Militancy and the Canadian Suffrage Movement" in the Fall 1975 issue of *Atlantis: A Women's Studies Journal.*

[13] *The World's* editorial appeared on page 1 on October 23, 1909. Stowe-Gullen's letter appeared on November 6, 1909, on p. 6.

In Ontario, although the equal rights women played an essential role in providing a forum and a focus for the issue, the long time span of the movement in the province appears to have served to institutionalize non-success. By the early 1900s, support by enlightened voices in the province had become a substitute for full citizenship and only the success of the movement elsewhere brought the issue to a final conclusion in Ontario. And perhaps it was social and economic change which finally made success inevitable. Especially important was the rapid development of women's occupational roles that took place in Ontario in the last decades of the nineteenth century and the first years of the twentieth century. Women established themselves in teaching, they began to enter office work and factory work, and the percentage of women gaining more education and entering professional fields increased considerably. Although they were still second-class citizens in the labour market, their increased participation did make them more visible and gave them more power. This was the case even before the experience of World War I, during which women were employed in occupations and used in the military in greatly expanded areas.

From what we know of it at present, the Ontario women's rights movement would appear to have been largely middle-class in origin, allied to the temperance movement and centered in Toronto. When we turn to the prairie provinces, we find a picture which is notably different in several ways. It has already been suggested that the Persons Case marks a symbolic end to the equal rights struggle in English Canada. In the context of a discussion of feminism in the prairies, it is significant that all five of the women whose names appeared as appellants in the Persons Case suit were residents of Alberta.

Although one of the five was Nellie McClung, she was not in fact the leader of this particular struggle.

The prime mover behind the Persons Case was another Alberta woman, Emily Murphy, who like Nellie McClung had been born in Ontario but had found full scope for her energies in the west. Emily Murphy, who moved to Alberta in 1907, distinguished herself as a journalist and in social service work and in 1916 she was appointed police magistrate for Edmonton. This was the first such appointment to be made not only in Canada, but in the British Empire.

Canada's first woman judge was appointed by an Alberta government; the first province to grant the suffrage to women was Manitoba, followed quickly by the other two prairie provinces. Feminism in the prairies won the whole-hearted support of important interest groups including the farmers' organizations. Women were active in the political and social life of the prairies, in the radical movements, in the temperance movement. The use women made of their position in a new society is perhaps the most outstanding difference between North American feminism and the European context to which it owes its origins. In Canada, historians have tended to see a regional division which relates to this factor: the suffrage came first in the prairies because the prairies were still a new society in which women and men worked together.

The equal rights movement in the Canadian prairie provinces did not follow a completely uniform pattern. The movement had an early phase in Manitoba, almost as early as the first stage of the movement in Ontario. In Saskatchewan and Alberta (which achieved provincial status only after the turn of the century) the movement really began after 1910. Those who have examined the prairie movement point out that in Saskatchewan it was rural and small-town, whereas in Manitoba, Winnipeg was clearly the centre of the movement.[14] It has also been pointed out that whereas

[14]Christine MacDonald, "How Saskatchewan Women Got the Vote", in *Saskatchewan History*, Volume I, no. 3, October 1948.

in Manitoba, during the second phase of the struggle, women
had real opposition in the form of provincial Premier Roblin
who was a personal opponent of women's suffrage, in
Saskatchewan women were faced with "support" from
Premier Scott,[15] but in the same form that we have seen it
manifested in Ontario. Scott agreed that women should
have the suffrage, but only if they could mobilize a widespread campaign to overcome "apathy". This sort of technique was actually much more difficult to deal with than
outright opposition. The Manitoba women could answer
Roblin's anti-suffrage arguments,[16] but how were women
to answer the demand that they overcome "apathy"? Why
should it have been necessary in any case? If *some* women
wanted the suffrage clearly any "supporter" of the suffrage
ought to have been committed to giving it to them, even if
they were in a minority.

Since Nellie McClung, an inspiration for this book,
was a leading figure in the feminist movement in Manitoba,
it seems fitting for us to examine the progress of the suffrage
movement in that province in some detail.[17] The suffrage
movement in Manitoba began in the 1890s. The first organized attempt to work for the suffrage in the prairies was
launched by a group of Icelandic Manitoban women some
time in the early years of that decade. From these beginnings the Icelandic community in Manitoba apparently continued to work for the franchise from the 1890s until
success was achieved in 1916. Although they communicated
with English-speaking advocates, they maintained a separate
campaign. English-speaking Manitoban women became involved in suffrage organizations through the Women's

[15] June Menzies, "Votes for Saskatchewan's Women", in N. Ward and D. Spafford, *Politics in Saskatchewan* (Toronto, 1968), p. 84.

[16] See Matheson and Lang's article in this book.

[17] This account of the early movement in Manitoba is drawn largely from Clever-don.

Christian Temperance Union which also began actively advocating the suffrage in the 1890s. It was the WCTU which staged the first mock parliament in the history of the Canadian suffrage movement in Winnipeg in February 1893. A year later the Manitoban Equal Franchise Club was founded.

However, in spite of these beginnings the suffrage movement in Manitoba made little headway in the nineties or in the first decade of this century. It was really only after 1910 that the movement began to gain momentum once again and it was only with the founding of the Winnipeg Political Equality league in 1912, with Lilian Beynon Thomas as its first leader, that real progress began to be achieved. But from then on, until January 1916 when Manitoba became the first Canadian province to enfranchise women, the movement progressed steadily towards success.

There are several interesting elements in this period of feminist history in Manitoba, and several explanations for the movement's success there after 1912. The chief explanation lies in the fact that the women who were involved in the suffrage cause and in allied movements in Manitoba were also very much involved in other movements which had a broad and firm base in the affairs and concerns of the province. This was true from the beginning of the movement in Manitoba: E. Cora Hind, for instance, a journalist and agricultural expert whose determination earned her a post on the *Winnipeg Free Press* after twenty years of persistence, was active in the WCTU from the 1890s and out of her temperance interests became committed to women's suffrage.[18] Suffrage was never her main concern, but the support of such a widely respected figure did much for the cause. The later group of feminists, including Nellie McClung herself, was similarly involved in a

---

[18]Mary Innis (ed.), *The Clear Spirit* (Toronto, 1966), has an article by Kennethe Haig on E. Cora Hind.

wide range of problems. This was also true in Ontario, but it appears that in the prairies a commitment to equal rights was more widely disseminated among socially active women and, of equal importance, the women involved in social concerns had close connections with powerful forces in the region.

It was vital to the feminist campaign in all three prairie provinces that the women had the support of the most influential of the farmers' groups, the Grain Growers Associations of Manitoba and Saskatchewan and the United Farmers of Alberta. The *Grain Growers' Guide,* the organ of all three of these organizations, was a strong and influential supporter of women's rights from its beginnings in 1908. However, the support of the farmers' organizations was qualified, and the qualifications indicate the limits the progress of women's rights had made in the Canada of the early twentieth century. The farmers' organizations were men's organizations, but both men and women were, after all, farmers in the prairie society, the women being vital to the farm economy. Yet although the farmers were willing to give support to "their women" in their cause, it was only in 1915 that the Manitoba association offered women entry into full membership in the association. As a concession, the women were to be admitted at half the dues paid by men. The women, realizing more fully than the men the limitations imposed by such a concession, accepted membership but insisted on paying full dues.[19]

A major base of support for the women's movement throughout Canada was the temperance movement, and specifically the WCTU. As a social cause, temperance seems rather unappealing in the mid-twentieth century and it is easy today to forget how deeply imbedded the temperance cause was in nineteenth- and early twentieth-century reform

[19] *Grain Grower's Guide,* January 20, 1915, quoted in Cleverdon, p. 61.

movements, not only in Canada but also in Britain and the United States. Temperance was a central issue for reformers whose other concerns covered a very wide spectrum, from Sunday observance (the Lord's Day Alliance) to socialism (J.S. Woodsworth). There was good reason for this interest in temperance: the abuse of alcohol was recognized as a severe social problem in the nineteenth and early twentieth centuries. Although in England, drunkenness usually appears as a problem connected with urbanization and industrialization, in Canada it was also perceived as a rural problem. And, as many temperance reformers pointed out, it was a problem which bore with particular severity on women. As Nellie McClung put it, "No one could deny that women and children were the sufferers from the liquor traffic; any fun that came from drinking belonged to men exclusively, and the men themselves would be the first to admit that."[20]

Given the circumstances of life in rural Canada, it is easily understandable that a specifically female temperance movement should have emerged. As with its counterparts in the United States and Britain, the temperance movement in Canada had strong links with evangelical religion and especially with the Methodist movement. It has also been pointed out that the movement had strong "nativist" elements—elements hostile or at least suspicious of immigrant groups that were not Anglo-Saxon, and that the nativism of the prohibition movement in general and of the WCTU in particular may have limited the suffrage movement as well.[21] The movement began in Canada in the 1870s and by the 1880s the WCTU had become a national organization. For many individual WCTU members and for the

[20]Nellie McClung, *The Stream Runs Fast* (Toronto, 1965), p. 59.

[21]M.G. Decarie, "Paved With Good Intentions", in *Ontario History*, Volume LXVI, no. 1, March 1974.

organization as a whole, the interest in temperance led them, sometimes unexpectedly, to the support of other reform causes—most notably, the cause of woman's suffrage, which many temperance advocates, male as well as female, began to see as a necessary step towards the achievement of prohibition.

Nellie McClung took an active role in the suffrage movement during the last years of the campaign in Manitoba. She was interested in the suffrage not as an empty symbol, but because she saw it as a means of achieving the kinds of social changes to which she was committed: the temperance measures, the protection of women workers, an end to corruption in government, a more sane, non-violent foreign policy.

The tone of the suffrage campaign in Manitoba, during these last years leading to final success, reflects the tolerance and the aversion to conflict that were such a strong part of McClung's character. Both the character of the suffragists and the character of their opposition determined that in Manitoba hostile confrontation simply was not necessary. Typical of the sort of technique that was used was the staging of a "mock parliament" in 1914. This piece of gentle theatrical satire perhaps represents the high point both of McClung's career as a suffragist and of this last phase of the Manitoba suffrage campaign.

This attitude of determined reconciliation was employed through to the end of the struggle in Manitoba. During the 1914 election campaign in the province the opposition Liberals strongly endorsed the principle of woman's suffrage. Nellie McClung and Lilian Beynon Thomas as representatives of the suffrage cause spoke to their convention and were a resounding success. The Conservatives, on the other hand, made their opposition to the suffrage a major part of their campaign. "Wifehood, motherhood and politics cannot be associated together with satisfactory results," said their campaign literature.[22] The Conservatives won by a small margin in 1914; however, their government was short-lived. They were forced to resign because of a construction industry scandal in May 1915 and the Liberals came to power in Manitoba. After a resounding Liberal victory in August 1915 the success of woman's suffrage in the province was assured. The measure was introduced in January 1916 and received Royal Assent on January 28.

This success in Manitoba was paralleled by similar successful campaigns in the other two prairie provinces, both of which granted the suffrage to women in 1916. The history of the suffrage struggle in the rest of Canada need only be summarized here. Constitutionally, the struggle in Canada paralleled that in the United States rather than that in England, since the federal/provincial dichotomy is similar to the federal/state dichotomy. In both countries it was necessary to fight on two levels, although the problem was considerably less overwhelming in Canada because of the smaller number of units involved. The Dominion franchise was granted to military women and the wives of relatives in the service in 1917 (a political maneuver on the part of the Borden government). Full Dominion suffrage was granted on May 24, 1918. Women won the provincial franchise in British Columbia and Ontario in 1917, in Nova Scotia in 1918, in New Brunswick in 1919, in Prince Edward Island in 1922, and in Quebec in 1940. (In Newfoundland, the suffrage was granted to women over twenty-five in 1922. In 1948, when Newfoundland became part of Canada, women were granted the right to vote in provincial elections on an equal basis with men.) The right to hold office was granted at the federal level in 1919, but achieved provincially at various dates from 1916 in Manitoba (with the

[22] *Record of the Roblin Government, 1900-1914,* quoted in Cleverdon, p. 60.

suffrage) to 1934 in New Brunswick. The right of women to hold certain offices, and specifically to sit in the Canadian Senate was not of course clarified until the successful outcome of the Persons Case in 1929.

Feminism in Canada was characterized by non-hostility, by a spirit of reconciliation which was in striking contrast to the fortunes of the movement elsewhere, especially in Britain. In that country the last phases of the suffrage movement were dominated, in the years leading up to World War I, by the militant Women's Social and Political Union, led by the Pankhursts. The WSPU courted violence from the police, used violence itself, and its members were treated with great brutality by the authorities. From most points of view Canadian women can consider themselves fortunate to have avoided such violence and the harsh consequences that followed from it. The achievements of the Canadian suffragists were in their own way as hard-won as those of the English militant suffragettes; in Canada the task was the sober one of convincing an opposition whose argument was usually based on the notion that "women-are-too-good-to-vote". Yet the violence of the English militants and their milder followers in the United States did accomplish something. The most important effects of the militant movement were probably psychological. The spectacle of respectable middle-class ladies courting arrest, defying the law and undergoing the difficulties and harassment of imprisonment and forcible feeding did much to destroy the image of Victorian ladyhood, an achievement that was very liberating.

The women who were shoved around by angry crowds and hostile policemen were made to feel the bitterness of their opposition. And from the point of view of the opposition, the fact that the suffragettes risked not only their reputations but their lives for their beliefs was a convincing demonstration of their seriousness of commitment.

In contrast, the suffrage movement in Canada did not bring with it the intense emotional and intellectual development that it did in Britain and to a lesser extent in the United States. The issue was discussed and the lives of the suffragists themselves were deeply affected, but the suffrage struggle was not bitter enough to alter general social and psychological attitudes towards women. For this no one is to blame: it would surely have been wrong to have resorted to violent tactics where they were not necessary. It would also be wrong to think that the Canadian feminists lacked sympathy for their more militant English sisters. McClung, for instance, was most impressed with Emmeline Pankhurst, and there are indications that she herself would not have opposed the use of similar tactics in Canada had they been necessary. In her autobiography she says: "The visit of Mrs. Emmeline Pankhurst and of Miss Barbara Wiley, also one of the British Militant Suffragettes, created a profound impression." And she tells of a meeting with Roblin in which she said to him that if the government did not give in on the suffrage question, the women would "make a fight for it".[23] McClung was not alone or even unusual in her support for the English militants. Most Canadian equal rights women supported their actions—but at a distance. Their attitude was one of sympathy rather than empathy. They never really believed that they themselves would be involved in such activity.

Because the women didn't really have to "make a fight for it" but won the vote through rational persuasion, it was possible for many women to accept the Victorian clichés without question: that maternal feminism was the ultimate justification for equal rights feminism, and that self-sacrifice was central to woman's role and the key to her psyche. The experience of the militant suffragettes forced English and

[23]Nellie McClung, *The Stream Runs Fast*, pp. 101 & 108.

American women to question the whole idea of self-sacrifice because their experiences showed them that society's idolization of women veiled a determination to restrict them to a severely limited sphere of action, by violent means if necessary. It should be said that the militants themselves sometimes seemed to revel in self-sacrifice; at times militancy appears as Victorian feminine self-sacrifice carried to its ultimate limits. But it produced as a reaction a clear realization of masculine hostility. In some ways Canadian women might have benefited from the experience of being forced to confront the reality of this hostility.

In recent years, the history of the Canadian women's movement (along with the history of the women's movement in other parts of the world) has begun to enter a new phase. In the past historians of feminism have tended to view the movement in a fairly narrow context. At the same time historians as a group have tended to ignore the women's movement unless they were directly concerned with it. Although these weaknesses have not yet been overcome, the situation is improving.[24] Several new interpretations of the Canadian feminist movement have recently appeared. Since two of the most interesting interpretations[25] emphasize the role of "maternal feminism" in Canada, this chapter will conclude with an examination of some questions relating to the origins of nineteenth-century feminism, in a way that may shed some light on the difference in progress ex-

---

[24] Even "general" history is beginning to improve. The new general interpretation of the period by Ramsay Cook and R. Craig Brown, *Canada, 1896-1921: A Nation Transformed* (Toronto, 1974), does say quite a lot about women—although it could say much more. It is encouraging that the authors include what they have to say about women as an integral part of their text, rather than relegating everything concerning women to one separate chapter.

[25] V. Strong-Boag's introduction to the new edition of McClung's *In Times Like These,* and Ramsay Cook's introduction to the new edition of Cleverdon's *The Woman Suffrage Movement in Canada.*

perienced by the movement in the west as contrasted to the east and which may at the same time offer an explanation for the strength of maternal feminism.

One constantly recurring explanation put forward by historians to account for the greater success of feminism in both western Canada and the western United States, as contrasted to the eastern portions of both countries, is that the milieu of the frontier was more conducive to feminism than was the more settled society of the east. The importance of the pioneer tradition and its relationship to the development of the suffrage movement has in fact become a glib historical cliché, the sort that does answer a number of questions, but which is nonetheless unsatisfactory because of the questions it leaves unanswered.

The usual statements about the connections between the pioneer mentality and feminist ideas are very much of the same order as the statements made about the connection between the ultimate success of the suffrage movement in England, the United States and Canada, and the war work done by women during World War I. Women's participation in the work of pioneer society, it is argued, persuaded their men to stand behind them when they demanded their political rights.

Speaking of the Canadian movement, Cleverdon puts it this way: ". . . the theory generally prevailed that women as well as men had opened up the country, had shared the experiences of settling a new land and were, therefore, entitled to a voice in making the laws".[26] Ramsay Cook in his introduction to the new edition of Cleverdon's book says that the women of the west "had an advantage: since they had to play the role of equal partner in pioneering conditions, their husbands could hardly fall back on the argument of the different spheres".[27]

[26] Cleverdon, p. 46.

[27] Cook's introduction.

In writing of the American movement, Eleanor Flexner says essentially the same thing: ". . . by the demands it made on human beings for survival, frontier economy established concepts of propriety. Women were just as indispensable as men, since a household which lacked their homemaking skills, as well as nursing, sharpshooting and hunting when needed, was not to be envied."[28]

The undeniable fact that the suffrage was achieved earlier in the west than in the east, in both Canada and the United States, does seem to support the frontier-as-equalizer statements of Cleverdon, Cook, Flexner and others. Why, then, is the theory not completely satisfactory? Because it implies that in pioneer society, for the first time in human history, women made themselves indispensable, and this is obviously not true. The model that Cleverdon, Cook, Flexner and others have in mind as a contrast to the pioneer woman is the middle-class Victorian lady who did not perform economically valuable work, but whose function was rather to symbolize by her economic uselessness the economic success of her middle-class husband. The Victorian lady was, however, a new phenomenon, a product of industrialization and the rise of a new middle class, and this fact is generally overlooked by those who advocate the pioneer-as-equalizer explanation.

Women had performed indispensable work in European society (as they have in every society in history) before the nineteenth century, and nineteenth-century working-class women, along with their children, were performing indispensable work at lower rates of pay than working-class men. Exploitation served not to raise their status but to lower it. This is of course true of working-class men as a group as well as of working-class women and it is also true of blacks and of any other group which is exploited: indispensability can and does lower one's status

[28]E. Flexner, *Century of Struggle* (Cambridge, Mass., 1959), p. 9.

rather than raise it, and the tragic plight of the women and children workers of the industrial revolution is that they were exploited not only by their capitalist employers, but also by their own men, who, for the most part, systematically excluded them from unionization and radical political activity.

It is clear, then, that it could not have been their indispensability that persuaded the husbands of the pioneer women to give them their political rights. But was there no connection between the pioneer tradition and the improvement in the status of women in frontier society? I think that there was a connection, but that the usual statements about the way in which the connection functioned leave out an essential part of the picture.

I spoke earlier of the Victorian middle-class lady who was a product of urbanized industrial society; her grandmother, in many cases, might have been a yeoman's wife who performed many functions directly analogous to those of a frontier wife in the North American settlements.[29] Although such a woman was aware of her own usefulness, and was often valued for it, there is no question that institutionally and by custom she was subservient to her husband. Many social historians of the Victorian period have analyzed the metamorphosis that the middle-class woman underwent, as the new industrial middle class emerged. It was not that the Victorian lady served no function, but rather that her function had changed. From the bustling manager of the dairy, she became "the angel of the hearth". Her duty was to make of her home a refuge from the world, "a sacred place, a vestal temple",[30] and to maintain the moral standard. In his book *Victorian England: Portrait of an Age*,

---

[29] This analogy was first suggested to me in 1970 by Susan O'Connor, a student at St. Patrick's College, Carleton University.

[30] The phrase is Ruskin's; he uses it in his essay "Of Queen's Gardens". *Sesame and Lilies* (London: Everyman, 1925), p. 59.

G.M. Young characterized this moral function in a memorable phrase. "The most influential women of the nineteenth century," he says, "were reared in an atmosphere which made them instinctively Custodians of the Standard." [31]

It is this new moral role to which middle-class women were assigned that Kate Millett attacks in her discussion of Ruskin and Tennyson, and which she calls the "separate spheres" answer to the feminist demands which were beginning to emerge in mid-Victorian England.[32] The effectiveness of the "separate-spheres" propaganda was manifest in the fact that middle-class Victorian women, including most middle-class feminists, generally accepted this new stereotype. But this was true not only of the middle-class Victorian lady who remained at home in Britain, it was also true of those women who came to North America as pioneer wives. I would suggest that it was this new image of themselves as moral guardians and protectors of the hearth that was decisive in changing their status in the new society.

It proved especially effective because as well as maintaining the role of moral guardian and spiritual centre of the home, these women also had to resume their old roles and become once again economically productive. It seems plausible that it was a combination of the two roles which altered and improved the status of women. An analysis of frontier society and of pioneer family structure in Canada indicates that both men and women believed that women in that society performed an essential emotional function, and it would seem reasonable to suggest that it was because they did so that the men of the frontier were able to perceive women as human beings and not simply as work and sex objects.

In her study of the institution of the family as it devel-

[31] G.M. Young, *Victorian England: Portrait of an Age* (London, 1936), p. 3 (footnote).

[32] Kate Millett, *Sexual Politics* (New York, 1970), 88 ff.

oped during the period of settlement in Upper Canada, Jean Burnet offers considerable evidence that women were considered as an essential part of frontier society not merely because they were needed to perform useful work but because they provided an emotionally stabilizing influence. Burnet quotes from one commentator on Upper Canadian society who observed of unattached men that "removed from all social intercourse and all influence of opinion, many have become reckless and habitual drunkards. The only salvation of a man here is to have a wife and children." Although the wife and children may benefit the man economically, what is clearly implied is that their chief function is to be his moral salvation.[33]

A significant number of the early settler women in Upper Canada came from middle-class households in Britain. Indeed, such women frequently found that one of the most difficult features of adjustment to their new life was that they were forced to give up the culture and leisure to which they had been accustomed. For example, in *Roughing it in the Bush* Susanna Moodie writes: "It was long, very long before I could discipline my mind to learn and practise all the menial employments which are necessary to a good settler's wife." One can safely assume that middle-class women like Mrs. Moodie would have been influenced by Victorian ideas about the role of women as moral guardians and keepers of the hearth, and that she and others like her may have been sustained by the desire to fulfill this role, and may even have been strengthened by it if they were fortunate enough to have the inner capacity to conform to the pattern. It is possible that the North American frontier was one place where these Victorian ideas about the spiritual

[33]The quotation is from Anna Jameson's *Winter Studies and Summer Rambles* in *Upper Canada:* quoted by Burnet, J., *Ethnic Groups in Upper Canada* (Ontario Historical Society, 1972), p. 58.

function of women may well have served a genuinely useful function.

The women who adapted themselves to such a role did so, no doubt, because of cultural pressure; under different circumstances, the women rather than the men might have fallen to pieces. In most cases, it appears that they did not do so. It was the men who were overcome by the fear of the loneliness of the frontier, while the women were usually able to take hold of themselves and cope with the situation. (This was not universally true, of course, and there were a few women who could not face the difficulties, the hardships and the loneliness of the frontier.)

The sort of family that was held together by the successful pioneer wife is of special concern to us, because it was this family pattern which produced many Canadian feminists. It was certainly true of the family pattern in which Nellie McClung grew up. One of the major impressions that emerges from the first part of her autobiography, *Clearing in the West,* is the central role that her mother played in the family. Her mother's moral strength, her capacity for hard work, even her aesthetic sense were obviously central factors in Nellie McClung's upbringing. Here is a description of Nellie McClung's mother's house:

> The floors were pine boards and were scrubbed every week, using very little soap, for soap yellowed the wood. Elbow grease was the thing. . . . The floor had lengths of rag carpet in pale strips and there were red and brown mats, hooked in circles and triangles . . . the two front windows had hand knitted curtains done by mother, in a fern pattern and paper lace valentines were hung on them.

Those hand-knitted curtains and rag carpets meant something important. They were physical and also spiritual symbols of the fact that the mother in the pioneer family was determined to civilize the bush according to British middle-class standards and not merely to eke out a living from it.

McClung's mother was not a public figure. The task of widening out these virtues into the public sphere belonged to the next generation, but one might venture to suggest that the active creative spirit of the mother which had been used up in her generation by the task of keeping the family together, was in the daughter translated into a wider field. And indeed, as Strong-Boag points out in her introduction to *In Times Like These,* McClung did see women's involvement in politics as an extension of their guardianship and housekeeping role. McClung put it this way: "Women have cleaned out things since time began; and if women ever get into politics there will be a cleaning out of pigeon holes and forgotten corners, on which the dust of years has fallen, and the sound of the political carpet beater will be heard in the land."[34]

McClung's civic housekeeping and her mother's private housekeeping share a number of features in common. Some of the origins of McClung's maternal feminism were present in her mother's set of private values. Through these values the mother had ordered and strengthened her pioneer home and infused it with moral significance. McClung intended to perform similar functions in the wider society and she set to the task with the efficiency and dedication of a good pioneer wife.

The maternal feminism exemplified by McClung was a powerful force in Canada. But as has been indicated earlier the idea of maternal feminism does not provide a complete and totally satisfactory framework for understanding Canadian feminism. The most important new attempts at form-

[34] McClung, *In Times Like These,* p. 48.

ulating a conceptual framework (Cook's and Strong-Boag's) seem to assume that it does, and perhaps they both do so because this view accords well with current thinking about movements for social reform in Canada in the first decades of the twentieth century. But we do not in fact have enough information about Canadian feminism to support broad conceptual generalizations. There were other motivating forces very different from the disposition to engage in civic housekeeping, and until more is known about a greater number of the women involved, perhaps we should withhold judgement about the universality of this outlook. It would be unfortunate to enclose Canadian feminism in a new orthodoxy at this stage in the discovery of its history.

It is my hope that this brief account of the suffrage movement in Canada will lead some readers to explore women's history further. For women especially, history often seems meaningless and unrelated to the real concerns of life— and indeed for women it often is. Reading history can often make us feel that we never existed, or existed only as an unchanging part of the natural background. But women do have a history: the idea that we've always done the same things in the same way is merely a convenient fiction. Other disciplines (notably anthropology and sociology) are forcing historians to realize that even "natural" institutions like the family are in a constant state of change, and always have been. As women we have been intimately involved with institutions like the family; much of our history will be rediscovered through a re-examination of these institutions. Better interpretations of more traditional areas of historical enquiry—like the suffrage movement—will then be possible. The revival of feminism will, it is to be hoped, make it possible for this re-examination to take place in a way that recognizes the validity of female consciousness.

Further Reading:

Stephenson, M. (ed.), *Women in Canada* (Toronto, 1973). Contains two useful bibliographical articles: an historical bibliography, "Cousin Cinderella", by V. Strong-Boag, and a sociological bibliography by M. Eichler and L. Primrose.

I would especially recommend the following books:

Canadian Women's Educational Press, *Women at Work: Ontario, 1850-1930* (Toronto, 1974).

Cleverdon, C., *The Woman Suffrage Movement in Canada*, new edition in the *Social History of Canada* series, with introduction by Ramsay Cook. (Toronto, 1973: first published in 1950). This pioneer study of the suffrage movement in Canada is still indispensable.

McClung, Nellie, *In Times Like These*, new edition in *Social History of Canada* series, with introduction by V. Strong-Boag (Toronto, 1972).

The two volumes of Nellie McClung's autobiography, *Clearing in the West* and *The Stream Runs Fast*, reissued by Thomas Allen Ltd. in 1964 and 1965.

Zaremba, E., *Privilege of Sex* (Toronto, 1974). Some diaries of early Canadian women, with an interesting introduction.

The following non-Canadian books will prove especially helpful:

Kraditor, A., *Ideas of the Woman Suffrage Movement* (N.Y., 1965). Excellent analysis of the ideology of the suffrage movement in the States.

O'Neill, W., *Everyone was Brave* (N.Y., 1969). Although in my opinion this book takes a sexist point of view, it is an absorbing, provocative study, well worth reading.

Rowbotham, S., *Women Resistance and Revolution* (1972). A major study, by an English historian, of the development of the relationship between socialism and feminism.

Vicinus, M. (ed.), *Suffer and be Still: Women in the Victorian Age* (1972). Excellent collection of articles, including a bibliographical article.

Born in Britain in 1940, Caroline Pestieau is an associate economist at the C.D. Howe Research Institute, Montreal and vice-president of the Quebec Council on the Status of Women. She is also a member and former vice-president of La Fédération des femmes du Québec. She has taught economic history at the University of the West Indies, Trinidad and been assistant vice-dean for the Vocational Section, CEGEP de St. Laurent, Montreal. Her publications include Canada and Latin America: Potential for Partnership *(1971) and* A Balance of Payment Handbook *(1974).*

Women in Quebec

Caroline Pestieau

*"Evolution when blocked and suppressed be-
comes revolution."*

The status of women in Quebec is as ambiguous as in most
countries and perhaps more so. Simplifying a lot, one could
say that the role of Quebec women[1] has changed radically
twice: once gradually after 1760, and once again very
rapidly after 1960. The Quebec Civil Code was notoriously
illiberal to married women until its recent reform in 1964,
and they were, as one of their own representatives remarked,
"the laughing stock of the universe".[2] Yet in the 1960s the
younger generation not only of students but of wives and
mothers liberated themselves apparently wholeheartedly,
with a joie de vivre and an absence of inhibitions astonishing to anyone familiar with pre-1960 Quebec society.

It is the rapidity of the change in the last fifteen years
that distinguishes the Quebec experience from that of the
rest of Canada, or the United States or of France. The
1960s in Quebec were a time of social and political experi-
mentation in all fields. So many new structures were being

[1] "Quebec women" is taken here to mean French-Canadian Quebeckers. The
evolution of English-speaking Quebec women was different and more similar
to that of Ontario women, and their history would require another article.

[2] See Marie Gérin-Lajoie, "La communauté légale", *La Bonne Parole*, janvier-
mars, 1927.

created and so many institutions being reformed that women were able to jump in and make an equal contribution.
They had no less experience in the new environment than
many of the men. But now, although experiments in social
relationships are continuing, a lot of the euphoria has
evaporated and a large number of women are frustrated in
their aspirations.

The Traditions

It is necessary to look at the past to understand both the
absence of civil rights endured by Quebec women prior to
1960 and their sudden emancipation in the last decade.
Quebeckers have often looked back to the pre-Conquest
period as a Golden Age, and from the point of view of
women at least, this view seems to be largely justified. A
number of remarkable women played important public
roles in New France. In the mid-seventeenth century, women sat on the Montreal municipal council, in the early
eighteenth century they created local textile industries,
and of course, they organized the financing, construction,
and defence of what were for a long time some of the most
imposing buildings in Canada—the hospitals and charitable
institutions of Montreal and Quebec City.[3]

The modern generation of Quebec women are unlikely
to look on the great pioneers—Marguerite Bourgeoys,
Jeanne Mance and Marguerite d'Youville—as models. They
were "oversold" to their mothers and grandmothers with
undue insistence on the religious inspirations behind their
phenomenal energy. In fact, the whole history of North
American colonization in the seventeenth and eighteenth
centuries is permeated with very explicit religious motiva-

---

[3]The dates of the most important early foundations are: L'Hôtel-Dieu de Québec-
1639, L'Hôtel-Dieu de Montréal-1644, L'Hôpital Général de Québec-1692,
L'Hôpital Général de Montréal-1737.

tions, whether Protestant or Catholic. New France was, at this stage in its history, hardly different in this respect from Boston or Pennsylvania.

A more interesting point, recently put forward by Micheline D. Johnson,[4] is that there was less occupational sex-typing in New France than in contemporary Europe, or even than in contemporary New England, because the economy was based on agriculture, rather than on commerce or industry. In Europe, the legal status of women deteriorated in the transition from an agricultural society, based on customary law, to a commercial one, based on Roman Law which gradually took place from the fifteenth to the eighteenth centuries.[5]

New France's legal system was based on the *Coutume de Paris,* which to our eyes, was not very enlightened in its treatment of women. They only enjoyed full civil rights if they were over twenty-five years of age and unmarried. But the nature of pioneer life, when husbands were often absent, led to Canadian adaptations of the *Coutume* that made it considerably more liberal than the same customs practiced in contemporary France. French visitors to Quebec were struck by Quebec women's independent spirit and participation in public life, including protests.[6]

After the Conquest of New France in 1760, a change for the worse began with regard to the status of women in Quebec. As the options open to French-speaking Quebeck-

[4]See "Histoire de la condition de la femme dans la province de Québec", in *Tradition culturelle et histoire politique de la femme au Canada,* studies prepared for the Royal Commission on the Status of Women in Canada. I have used this source extensively.

[5]It is interesting to note that a teach-in at the Université du Québec à Montréal (December 2—3, 1972) carried this line of thought forward by linking exploitation of women to the predominant role played by movable property rights in capitalist society.

[6]See R.L. Sequin, "La Canadienne au XVIIe et au XVIIIe siècles" in R.H.A.F. vol. XIII, no. 4.

ers narrowed and they began to be cut off from alternative value systems, their institutions and codes of behaviour became more restrictive. While this change in Quebec society is too complex to be analyzed in this brief chapter, one can sum up the situation by saying that whereas the nineteenth century was a crucial stage in the emancipation of women in the Anglo-Saxon world, Quebec was almost completely cut off from important nineteenth-century currents, particularly those of industrialization and female emancipation.

The British Parliament decided in 1774 not to attempt to impose English Common Law on Quebec, and Quebec customary law was progressively codified, a process completed in the adoption of the Quebec Civil Code of 1866. The code marked a culmination of the gradual worsening of women's legal position in the province. Women who had been able to vote in provincial elections (because the law said nothing to the contrary) lost this right. Married women were reduced to a state of permanent minority—among other things they could not bring an action nor defend themselves before the law, they could not be their own children's guardians, they could not receive a legacy, they could not practice a profession different from that of their husbands. This very restrictive code was adopted just six years before the Ontario Married Women's Property Act was passed, and it remained in force, with some ad hoc modifications, for the next three generations.

Cultural, legal, and economic circumstances combined in the province to offer only two models or life-styles to Quebec girls in this period—motherhood or the religious life. The ideal French-Canadian mother of a numerous family was a myth that grew up in the second half of the nineteenth century,[7] just as the model bourgeois family,

[7] See Jacques Boucher, "L'histoire de la condition juridique et sociale de la femme au Canada français" (mimeo), Montreal, 1966; and Jean Lemoyne, "La femme dans la civilisation canadienne-français", *Convergences*, Montreal, HMH, 1961.

self-sufficient and responsible for the moral and political formation of its members, was a myth of Victorian England and North America. The trouble with the myth of the perfect mother was that the ecclesiastical establishment enthusiastically cultivated it right up to 1960. This image of the married woman is reflected in French-Canadian literature where the paragon was something of a matriarch, her husband dependent on her and often hen-pecked. Until recently, wives in rural areas typically had more schooling than their husbands, but this gave them little interest in participating in politics. In the 1920s, nearly 40,000 women signed a petition saying that they did not want the right to vote.[8]

Single women had no greater political rights than married women, but if they joined, or founded, religious orders they had ample scope for exercising all kinds of talents from business administration to nursing. Nuns travelled, they could sometimes go abroad for their education, and they were responsible for hospitals, orphanages, and all schools other than classical colleges and seminaries for boys. Quebec women founded twenty new orders in the nineteenth century and in large numbers joined sixteen already existing ones.

For a long time paid employment of women had no place in this scheme of things. There were, of course, schoolteachers and nurses who were not nuns, but the "vocational" nature of their work was stressed, justifying the ridiculously low salary levels. In 1936 the Legislative Assembly reduced the minimum salary for rural teachers from $300 to $250 per annum! After concerted action it was raised to $600 in 1943.

Although industrialization came slowly and there was little factory work outside a few urban centres, legislation to prevent the exploitation of female and child labour was conspicuously absent. Quebec had more female factory workers under sixteen years of age than any other province

[8]See Micheline D. Johnson, *op. cit.*

at the beginning of the century. A minimum wage—$11.50 a week—was established in 1937 but the law was not respected. Yvette Charpentier, a woman who had started work in the garment industry at the age of eleven, after one year's schooling, led a successful strike to obtain the minimum wage. But a tradition of exploitation had grown up unthreatened by government intervention or by public indignation, since women factory workers were regarded at best as marginal and at worst as outcasts. This tradition of exploitation continues in the scandalously low piece-work rates paid for work done at home in some areas of the province today.

The situation of Quebec women in the first part of the twentieth century was objectively one of alienation and inferiority, although, of course, many thousands of individuals did not experience it as such and managed to lead satisfying lives. Leaders of Quebec society were opposed to both industrialization and female emancipation. They saw no need for women to have access to higher education. The instruction of future mothers was taken care of by a network of Family Institutes which were, for a long time, the only type of public secondary schooling open to girls. The first classical college offering academic secondary education to girls was the Collège Marguerite Bourgeoys, founded in Montreal in 1908. By 1950, fifteen such colleges had been established for girls, but since they were dependent on students' fees only a very small minority of Quebec women attended them.

The question of university education for women was therefore a purely speculative one for the vast majority of them, and it was the English-speaking Quebec women who led the way in forcing the universities and the liberal professions to admit women. It was they also who initiated the demands for provincial suffrage, while the Quebec church forced the women's group, the *Fédération nationale Saint-Jean-Baptiste,* to stop all references to women's suffrage early in the century.[9] But this cause was taken up again with great tenacity by Thérèse Casgrain. In 1926, and in April 1940, women were once more allowed to vote in Quebec provincial elections, despite a solemn warning against the measure by Cardinal Villeneuve. It was not until 1962 that a woman, Claire Kirkland-Casgrain, was elected to the Legislative Assembly.

No further details are needed to show that in the first half of this century Quebec women were severely underprivileged compared to their sisters elsewhere in North America. Changes were incubating during the fifteen post-World-War-II years and they blossomed out into the accelerated evolution of the 1960s. These fifteen years witnessed the failure of the ruralist ideology that Quebec cultural leaders had tried to reimpose on French Canada.[10] Industrialization and urbanization were here to stay. Communications media were breaking down some of Quebec's isolation, and the notion that women can only find legitimate self-fulfillment as mothers of large families or as nuns was no longer tenable.

Change

Several phenomena catalyzed and accelerated change in the role of women, and the causal links between them cannot be discussed here. First of all, the Quiet Revolution following the Duplessis era led to a revival of nationalism and a flowering of self-confidence which created a new environment for women. The Lesage government, and its successors,

---

[9] See Micheline D. Johnson, *op. cit.*

[10] Pierre Elliot Trudeau's introduction to a collection of essays dealing with the postwar asbestos strike in Quebec throws a great deal of light on this question.

used the machinery of the state extensively to achieve their aims. The public service grew enormously. Sixty percent of the 260,000 public and para-public employees who struck in the winter of 1972 behind the Common Front demand for a minimum wage of $100 a week, were women. And they were naturally angered when one of the reasons the government gave for its refusal of their demands was that most of the claimants affected were women (and therefore did not need such a high minimum wage?).

Secularization of the service professions accompanied the expansion of the public service. The number of religious vocations in Quebec declined in the 1950s and then fell dramatically in the 1960s. The state assumed responsibility for health, welfare, and education for reasons of equity, finance, and efficiency, but also because voluntary personnel was no longer available. Nurses, teachers, and social workers became civil servants. Salaries had to be raised from the previous miserable levels to recruit sufficient numbers in a period of economic expansion. Women carrying out these functions abruptly stopped considering their work in purely vocational terms and became ardent union members. It is interesting to note that since salaries and working conditions have greatly improved in these occupations, quite a large number of men have been attracted to what were previously regarded as predominantly female careers.

A complete reform of the province's educational system followed the creation of a Department of Education by the Lesage government. The much-vaunted democratization of education partly fulfilled its promises with regard to women since free schooling up to university level, and including two or three years of community college, was established. Private classical colleges were no longer the exclusive or normal path to university. But the great expansion of continuing education has been even more important for the present generation of adult Quebec women. Courses leading to academic, vocational and artistic qualifications have been set up all over the province. The female enrollment has been enormous, to the edification of some foreign observers.[11] It is symptomatic of the change that in urban areas, at least, husbands consider it normal for their wives to go to evening classes while they deal with the children and the dishes, a situation that is still unthinkable in many parts of Europe, including France.

The negative side of the educational picture remains that of trades and preparation for the labour market. Quebec women have responded enthusiastically to openings in new professions requiring college training, such as paramedical jobs, but they have made no headway in the skilled trades. Canada Manpower centres in Montreal, for example, can offer little training to non-clerical female workers other than the courses for sewing machine operators. One experience in trying to place a girl trained as a small-appliance-repair worker was enough to convince them that it would be fruitless to offer the course to women. So those who do not get through community college programs or receive clerical training are likely to find themselves part of the unskilled labour pool for Quebec's traditional industries.

Reform of the Civil Code was finally achieved, also in the 1960s (1964), under the aegis of the Legislative Assembly's first woman member and minister. Certain modifications had already been made; for example, women were allowed to have their own bank accounts in 1934, and articles of the Code were tacitly ignored so that many women in fact practiced different professions than those of their husbands. But these ad hoc amendments were regarded as exceptions rather than as reforms. The 1964 re-

[11] See Pierrette Sartin in *Chatelaine* (French edition), juillet 1972.

form, although it was so long overdue, met with serious opposition from the Quebec Bar. The majority of women may not have experienced any change in their status, but Bill 16 gave Quebec women the title to rights that had long been enjoyed elsewhere, and led the way to further reforms including the possibility of obtaining a divorce in the province.

As well as leading to concrete improvements, the burst of national feeling that accompanied the Quiet Revolution was, and remains, important for the feminist cause for two less obvious reasons:

First, it has led to at least a minimal political awareness among a larger proportion of women in Quebec than is usually the case in Western countries. In Quebec there have been so many major changes since 1960 that it has been difficult to remain unconsciously part of the "silent majority". At the same time, the existence of the Separatist option and the experience of unequal opportunities for French-Canadians have obliged a large number of women, who would not otherwise do so, to think about politics and to be prepared to take a stand of one kind or another.

A second point is that more women in Quebec than elsewhere in North America (except of course in black and minority groups in the United States) are familiar with concepts such as "alienation", "cultural oppression", and "social violence". Despite their previous lack of interest in public affairs, they are now able to communicate with radical women's liberation and post women's liberation groups elsewhere, because they feel that they have a double experience of exploitation and alienation, as women and as French-Canadians. While these feelings are only expressed by a small minority, it is a vocal one, and can probably establish dialogue with radical groups outside Quebec more easily than the "moderate" French-speaking feminists can communicate with "moderate" feminists outside the province.

The Present

Emancipation or liberation seems to have come so rapidly that it is impossible to review the status quo. One result of the 1960s has been an almost unbridgeable generation gap within families, although perhaps the widest gulfs have been felt in the immediate past, and the gap may be diminishing. Typically, communication between different women's movements, and between officers and younger members of the same movement, is often laborious. Lay voluntary service groups do not have deep roots in Quebec society—there was no reason for their existence until recently. They are not so disturbed as are the English-speaking women's voluntary groups about the state's takeover of responsibility for all welfare services. Fragile transplants, they may disappear if younger women see no point in them.

As everywhere else in the Western world, young women are rethinking the notion of the family cell or unit in contemporary Quebec society. Their answers are largely "creative" since there are few precedents in Quebec tradition to guide urban professional couples who intend to have very small, or no families. (The astonishing fall in the Quebec birth rate in the last fifteen years, whether a cause or a result of the developments described above, must be taken into account in any discussion of changing roles for women.)[12] Quebec female graduates have the highest rate of labour force participation of any of the ten provinces. Most of them fully intend to pursue careers, not just take up occasional work, when they marry, either through com-

[12] In 1945, the Quebec birth rate was 29.3 per 1,000 and the Canadian average, 24.3. In 1972, the Quebec birth rate was 13.8 per 1,000 and the Canadian average, 15.9.

munal living or an equal sharing of "women's" chores between husband and wife.

Yet despite the joyous effervescence and sexual liberation, the position of women in Quebec remains basically
weak, particularly in the labour market. As numbers of
recent graduates are finding to their cost, the attitudes of
the work world change very slowly, particularly in a province with a very high rate of unemployment and an im-
mobile labour force.

Sexual discrimination in hiring, promotion, pay and
fringe benefits is rampant in Quebec as can be seen from
the fact that women while making up a third of the labour
force only take home one fifth of the total wage and salary
mass.

In the last ten years, several women's groups have tried
to get equality for women established on a firm legal foot-
ing. In particular, La Fédération des femmes du Québec
(which was founded in 1966 and now includes twenty-two
women's associations with a total membership of about
150,000) pressed successive Liberal and Conservative governments to legislate against discrimination in the labour
market.

Their efforts being of no avail on the labour front, members of the federation finally asked the Bourassa government to set up a Women's Council to be responsible for the
vast catching-up operation which was necessary if women's
rights and status were to be recognized and entrenched in
the province.

The Council on the Status of Women was established in
July 1973, as a result of the federation's initiative (and in
conformity with the recommendations of the Royal Commission on the Status of Women in Canada), and began
work at the end of that year. Its members were immediately
confronted with a host of problems, needs, and striking

abuses, among which it was very difficult to draw up a list of priorities.

One of the basic elements in the situation of women in contemporary Quebec, as in many other societies, is the fragility of their status. While all progressively-minded people may endorse their right to complete equality, sex-typing in education and in labour practices, anachronisms in the Civil Code, abusive media images and bureaucratic inertia, conspire to deprive many of them of their rights. The results show up in the over-representation of women among welfare recipients and the mentally ill. While women are better represented in Quebec than elsewhere among M.A. and Ph.D. students, there are also proportionately more of them who are heads of family with an income below the "poverty line" drawn up by the Senate Committee on Poverty in Canada.

The Quebec Council on the Status of Women's main thrust to date has been directed to the twin evils of sex discrimination in employment and sex-typing in education. It is to be hoped that the vacuum in the Quebec statute books in the area of civil rights and equal opportunity will soon be filled. (The Bourassa government introduced an umbrella-type civil rights bill in 1974 and the Council on the Status of Women brought out a complete set of detailed proposals for equal opportunity legislation.)

However it is obvious that women's rights cannot be established in Quebec, or elsewhere, by a series of fire-fighting actions. Long-term sustained strategies are needed to change fundamental attitudes. This truism bears repetition in the Quebec scene where the avant-garde, the centre, and the traditionalists frequently lose contact with one another and find it difficult to bring common pressure to bear on the forces of inertia.

Kay Macpherson has been president of Voice of Women and of the Association of Women Electors of Toronto. She is active in the National Action Committee on the Status of Women and in Women for Political Action and was a candidate in the 1972 federal election.

Meg Sears is a housewife with newspaper and political experience who does a variety of volunteer community work. She has been vice-president of Voice of Women.

The Voice of Women:
A History

Kay Macpherson and Meg Sears

"War is the antithesis of all our teaching."

Voice of Women was born on a tidal wave of emotions—
hope, fear and anger. The failure of the Paris Summit Conference had sent up its own mushroom cloud of terror, the
impression that nothing could prevent the drift to nuclear
war.

A Toronto *Star* columnist, Lotta Dempsey, wrote a
column on May 21, 1960, on this theme of helplessness,
and asked: "What can women do?"

The column triggered an enormous response. In subsequent issues of the paper Dempsey quoted letters from
readers and cited phone calls from women who declared
their own willingness and need to do something. "Can we
live with ourselves if any children suffer the effects of even
one atomic bomb?" . . . "Let us scream for the preservation
of children all over the world." . . . "Couldn't women can-
vass their communities, sending views to the heads of
governments?"

The feed-back ran parallel to the thinking of a small
group of Toronto women. Lotta Dempsey's desk became a
clearinghouse for the first organizing efforts to "unite
women in concern for the future of the world". A mass
meeting in Toronto's Massey Hall was the next step, and

71

Voice of Women was founded on July 28, 1960.

Dedicated to "crusading against the possibility of nuclear war", and appealing directly to women, VOW was not simply a Ban the Bomb group. From the outset it presented and sought a more "respectable" image than some of the earlier anti-war groups. Its leaders were usually described as "prominent" or as "wife of the well-known. . . . "

One of the first acts of the organizing committee had been to send a delegation of two to Ottawa. They received a warm welcome and congratulations, as Dempsey reported. "If I hadn't lived through practically every moment . . . I would find the story of their unprecedented venture almost too astonishing to credit," she said. The late Lester Pearson, then Leader of the Opposition, said, "I've never seen anything like it." Prime Minister Diefenbaker gave the delegates a hearing, and External Affairs Minister Howard Green kept another delegation waiting while he talked to the two women.

The press expressed worries about how VOW would preserve its virtue. "How," they asked, "do you intend to go ahead with this plan and keep clear of subversive infiltration, or free of ideologies and religious or political pressures?" Jo Davis, one of the founders, replied, "That is why we came to the government at this early stage."

The politicians' message to the delegation was, "Go home now and get solidly organized across Canada." VOW's Newsletter later reprinted the comment from an enthusiastic new member: "Apparently they are non-partisan—just a group of women interested in acquiring as many members as possible. . . . "

In September a national office was opened in Toronto, despite the fact that there were less than one hundred paid-up members. (Dues were $2.) Five months later there were 2,000 across Canada, with a mailing list of 10,000 for the

Newsletter. The activity and woman-hours of volunteer work were prodigious. Groups were formed, campaigns-of-the-week planned, plebiscites for peace collected, letters written to M.P.s, to Cabinet ministers, to mayors, to newspapers, to organizations, to women in other countries. Esperanto was studied, vigils held, delegations sent, press conferences arranged, radio and television shows produced, public meetings held. To finance it all, members gave theatre parties, coffee parties, teas, auctions; they donated baby bonus cheques, published cookbooks and greeting cards, held bazaars and canvassed their communities. In such an emotionally charged whirl of activity, hard sense and heart-felt sentiment were not always in perfect balance, the former sometimes losing out to the heaving bosom and quivering perorations that began, "As a Woman and Mother. . . . "

By the fall of 1961 membership had risen to 5,000. The members threw their new organization behind the national campaign of the Canadian Peace Research Institute of Norman Alcock. Action began on an international scale. Delegates were sent to meetings in Vienna, Geneva, India and the United Nations. In 1963 a "travel mission" of twenty-eight women, led by Helen Tucker, VOW's first president, went to ten European countries, including the Soviet Union. Other "Voices" went to Moscow as guests of the Soviet Women's Committee, to the United Nations with the American Women Strike for Peace, and to Italy for a meeting with the pope.

The preparing and presentation of briefs was an activity which members took up with special enthusiasm. One went to British Prime Minister Harold Macmillan, contending that nuclear testing was illegal. (He didn't agree.) Another brief on nuclear testing was presented to the Canadian government, with the plea that Canada stay out of the "nuclear club"; a second urged China's membership at the UN, and one to the UN itself called for an International Year of Peace.

In the beginning, then, VOW basked in the kind of acceptance and approval usually given to "motherhood" causes. What, after all, could be more pleasing than women raising their voices in hymns to peace, international understanding and goodwill towards most men?

The issue of biculturalism in Canada raised its head when a 400-member delegation led by Thérèse Casgrain, VOW's second president, went to Ottawa on a special Peace Train. The predominantly French-speaking delegation was met by a government representative who spoke no French, and when they forcefully expressed their indignation the press recorded the event as a scene of hysteria—obviously the type of behaviour to be expected from a group of women prepared to discuss foreign affairs.

Among the VOW members travelling on the Peace Train were writers Gwethalyn Graham and Solange Chaput-Rolland. They began their dialogue on French-English relations that grew into their book, *Dear Enemies*.

VOW's efforts to establish and maintain a bilingual organization, and the uniting of French- and English-speaking women on important issues, contributed in some measure to the growing demand for attention to be paid to Quebec's needs. The "Bi-Bi Commission"—the nickname was coined by one of VOW's French-speaking leaders—followed closely on publication of *Dear Enemies* and disclosure of experiences of French-speaking people as second-class citizens in English, and often even in French Canada.

An early controversy within Voice of Women over civil defence was a microcosm of the larger one to come, over Canadian nuclear weapons. On the issue of the Emergency Measures Organization in general, and fall-out shelters in particular, one side argued that it was possible to be in favour of a fall-out shelter in the back yard while being opposed to any and all nuclear arms. The other side contended that it would be a ludicrous inconsistency. The argument was finally resolved by the government's recognition of the uselessness of precautions against nuclear bombs. As Thérèse Casgrain said, "The only defence is peace."

There was no easy resolution for the internal battle that shook the organization in 1963, from its leadership of "prominent" women to the grassroots of its membership, when the Liberal Party, under Mr. Pearson, reversed its stand on nuclear weapons, and voted to place Bomarc missiles in Canada. This switch put the non-partisan, non-political VOW to an agonizing test. Could one swallow the Liberal decision and still campaign against nuclear weapons without its constituting an attack on the party?

The majority decided that such a swallow would gulp away VOW credibility. The organization attacked the policy, and its Liberal members were very unhappy. During the emotional upheaval that followed, Solange Chaput-Rolland wrote in the Newsletter: "VOW's policy has not changed. It has only condensed its thoughts on one precise, moral attitude toward nuclear armament or nuclear tests . . . ; one day, at one specific hour, one is called upon to choose one's truth and live by it."

Many members disagreed; some because they wished to support and vote for Liberals, some because they were convinced that the loss, apparent or real, of an apolitical posture would destroy VOW's effectiveness. Others argued that it was one thing to oppose policies in general, but quite a different and disturbing thing to oppose particular leaders on specific matters. To these latter, open disagreement with father-figures was a new and terrifying sensation.

In letters of resignation that followed VOW's action there were expressed feelings of pain and hurt so personal that they read more like epitaphs for a love affair than withdrawal from an organization.

Not surprisingly, Mrs. Pearson was one of those who felt obliged to resign, but not before CBC radio satirist Max Ferguson had done a skit on strife over the issue within the Pearson household. The skit had Mrs. Pearson, entertaining Peace women to tea, hurling the cups bought with Pearson's Nobel Peace Prize money at the head of her warmongering husband as he came home from the House of Commons.

After this and other episodes, Ottawa's approving smiles for the Voice of Women began to disappear.

Since the NDP and at first the Conservatives also shared VOW's policy on nuclear weapons and other foreign affairs issues, they rarely received the criticism which the "Voices" directed at the Liberals. Newspaper editorial writers gave avuncular warnings about fellow-travelling innocents and the perils of being led down garden paths. By others VOW was accused of being "soft on socialism" or "pinko" or just plain Communist.

VOW's reply to all such accusations was that it stood by its policies, including the refusal to query the political affiliations of its members, and wanted no part of the North American hobby of Red-baiting.

The slightly battle-scarred organization continued along its more activist path. VOW delegates went to the NATO Women's Meeting at The Hague in 1964. Dutch officials, not forewarned, saw a sinister threat in the arrival of 1,500 women from many different countries to talk peace at a NATO meeting, and stopped some of them at the border, including Kay Macpherson, president of VOW, and Ava Helen Pauling of Women Strike For Peace. However, after a flurry of protest and publicity, all were admitted.

Later that year VOW sent another delegation to Europe, this time to Paris, with the mission of opposing NATO's plans for a multilateral nuclear force. Within a few hours of their arrival Ms. Macpherson and Mme. Casgrain, along with other women delegates from NATO countries, found themselves in a Paris jail. They were picked up by the police as they sought, quite legitimately, to deliver a letter to the secretary-general of NATO. Once again their cause received maximum publicity. Eventually the idea of the MLF was dropped.

While some VOW members in Toronto were distressed by the cheerful (some called it shameless) behaviour of their representatives in Paris, Mme. Casgrain in contrast was publicly embraced by the Quebec premier as he welcomed back his "jailbird".

That same year the Soviet Women's Committee sent a delegation to Canada as guests of VOW. Led by a woman ambassador, the delegation toured the country with great success, arousing surprisingly little hostility of the "Red, go home" variety. The final hours of the tour were upset by the fall of Khruschev and the first Chinese nuclear blast, facts of which the visitors (who were in constant touch with their embassy) were aware before public announcements were made in the West. They were naturally rather preoccupied.

VOW proudly claimed credit for inspiring the United Nations designation of International Cooperation Year. The idea of a Peace Year had been proposed at VOW's 1962 International Women's Conference, and later India's Prime Minister Nehru brought it to the UN. "Voices" mounted hundreds of projects for ICY. There were children's international villages, student camps, book displays, art exhibits, essay and drawing contests. Information centres and booths were set up in appropriate places, "twinning" of cities was arranged—and the number of travel exchanges and conferences multiplied.

Even in the midst of all this national and international amicable activity, VOW was headed for more controversy. There was a vaudeville touch of low comedy to a run-in with the Department of Immigration. Manitoba VOW had invited a scholarly American, Mulford Q. Sibley, to address a meeting. Professor Sibley, a Quaker and a "peacenik", was not allowed to leave the airport when he arrived in Winnipeg. Dumbfounded VOW members were told by straight-faced immigration officials that the professor was deemed an unfit person to visit Canada on the grounds of his alleged views supporting free love. The federal Minister of Immigration upheld this remarkable ruling. A wave of incredulous delight at the fact that a minister could lead his government into such an absurd and politically vulnerable stance swept the country. It afforded much joy to editorial writers and also to cartoonists, who depicted the RCMP grilling sinister Mafia-like figures for their views on free love while ignoring their arsenal of sawed-off shotguns.

On a second attempt, Professor Sibley was allowed into the country, and soon afterward changes were made in the Immigration Act.

Across the border Women Strike for Peace leaders Dagmar Wilson and Donna Allen were facing contempt of Congress trials for their lack of cooperation with the House Un-American Activities Committee. The unorthodox behaviour of their supporters who thronged the courtroom bringing flowers and even their babies created an atmosphere of encouragement and humour which did much to hearten the courageous defendants. VOW sent messages of support, and backed the stand of the U.S. women's peace groups in opposing nuclear weapons for West Germany.

VOW had taken aim at the manufacture and sale of war

toys, seeing them as encouraging acceptance by children of violence and war. The campaign, intensified for Christmas, made VOW the target for some irrational responses. Members were said to be suffering, individually and collectively, from penis envy, and of attempting to emasculate red-blooded Canadian males, including male children. But some people did stop buying "GI Joe" dolls, baby sten guns and toy tanks that blew up toy jeeps. By the following year war toys had almost disappeared from the pages of the mail-order catalogues.

Another small victory—for which Quebec members were largely responsible—was the preparation of a *Mémoire* to the bishops attending the Vatican Council. This statement developed the pope's "Pacem in Terris" theme, and Cardinal Léger included parts of it in his address before the Vatican meeting.

As time passed the issue of Vietnam drew VOW, almost unwittingly, into the struggle that was to devour most of the time and energies of the organization for the next six years. VOW's protest began slowly in 1963 when it sought to verify reports of war conditions and brutality received from women in Vietnam. These were soon documented as being only too true. VOW called for a ceasefire in a statement presented to the Minister for External Affairs and to the Ottawa embassies of the six countries involved. (India and Poland were joined with Canada on the International Control Commission, Britain and the USSR jointly chaired it, and France and the United States were militarily involved in Indochina.)

VOW also embarked at this time on what was to become one of the central issues of the Vietnam struggle: the Americans' use of weapons such as nerve gas, defoliants, pellet bombs and napalm. Telegrams were dispatched to the International Red Cross, to the U.S. ambassador, the U.K.

foreign minister and to the Canadian government. The telegrams demanded that the United States stop using so-called "riot gases" in their warfare.

By 1966 the cover of the VOW Newsletter carried a picture of Vietnam refugees, a mother and child. VOW attacked Canada's role in the Control Commission, and called for an end to export of Canadian military supplies to the United States for use in Vietnam. The U.S. resumption of bombing of the North early in the year brought the strongest letters and statements VOW had ever delivered. Nuremberg, the Geneva Gas Protocol and the Geneva Agreements were cited. The theme was that Canada, rather than "honouring commitments", in the phrase of the External Affairs department, could do more to end the war. A newspaper campaign preceded the delegation of eighty members from across Canada who went to Ottawa to urge an independent, peacemaker role in Vietnam. The delegation also presented briefs on Canadian uranium sales and birth control laws.

VOW members no longer expected the red carpet treatment in Ottawa. They in their turn were casting critical eyes upon many individual M.P.s as well as the government and its policies. The Minister for External Affairs was judged "a master of double talk in two languages". The Newsletter observed acidly, "VOW's had their breath taken away by the depth and breadth of ignorance of some of our elected representatives," but took heart from being "pleasantly surprised by the willingness of others to listen, and delighted by the numerous requests to supply more information". The M.P. who didn't know where Vietnam was undoubtedly made one of the most vivid, lingering impressions.

As far back as 1964 VOW's Annual Meeting had voted to support a private member's bill coming up in the House of Commons to repeal the section of the Criminal Code which made it illegal to disseminate information about birth control. After a long debate, the Quebec delegation abstained from voting on the issue. The following year, however, Quebec members led the pressure for repeal on the basis of human rights and freedom of choice for women. And 1966 saw a Quebec vice-president of VOW explaining the fundamentals of birth control techniques to the House Committee on Health and Welfare, while she presented a brief. Finally the law was changed, but the section relating to abortion is still, in 1975, under the Criminal Code.

VOW was one of the national women's organizations whose members were active in calling for a Royal Commission on the Status of Women in Canada, since they recognized that a peaceful world would not be achieved in a society where women were oppressed and ignored.

Turning again to the international field, VOW members reasoned that if talks and negotiations were preferable to confrontation and conflict, it followed that the United Nations should be supported and given adequate powers for negotiating and peacemaking. It also followed that all nations must have a voice at the UN. One-fifth of the world's population should not be excluded. Since 1949 Canada had had no diplomatic relations with the People's Republic of China, and had not voted for its admission to the UN. In 1961 VOW had begun to urge the Canadian government to recognize China and vote for UN admission. Ten years later, in 1972, the campaign was successful. However, VOW was not blind to the fact that this was done with the blessing of the United States, whose president soon after visited Peking. And also that, as it happened, it was very much in Canada's economic interests to improve relations with China.

VOW has consistently argued that Canada's foreign policy should not be wholly determined by what is economically beneficial to Canadians (and to U.S.-owned Canadian subsidiaries) regardless of humanitarian or moral considerations. Sometimes increased pressure of public opinion has led to changes in Canadian policies. Vietnam, South Africa, NATO, and South America can all furnish examples of the changing climate of public opinion which eventually is reflected in government policy. In 1968 VOW prepared a brief entitled "The Effect of Defence Production and Trade and Commerce Agreements on Canada's Foreign Policy", in which the point was made that trade and economic considerations did in fact determine Canada's foreign policy. Later, VOW called for a moratorium on exploitation of the North until adequate research was done to determine whether in fact it should take place at all. These discussions are now widespread. A women's peace group talking about James Bay and the MacKenzie pipeline was not given much attention in 1970, but soon everyone was talking about pollution, ecology, and native rights and resources.

Similarly, a women's peace group submitting a brief to the Senate committee inquiring into Canada's science policy may seem incongruous. The point was made, however, that all citizens should be responsible through Parliament for the country's science policy which is, in fact, her social policy. This should not be the prerogative of the government, represented by the party in power, backed up with the exclusive right to expert opinion and research.

It is sometimes not easy to connect some of the many concerns mentioned with those of women working for peace and disarmament. The relation between the interests of the multi-national corporations—whose continuous expansion demands resources and markets regardless of cost— with weapon sales and war is more direct. So too is the connection between VOW's concern for peace and its campaign to collect children's baby teeth—bone tissue where Strontium 90 is deposited—and so to investigate the connection between atomic testing, nuclear fall-out, and the incidence of leukemia and other such diseases. It is undeniable that the actions of thousands of women, in the United States as well as in Canada, resulted in the partial Test Ban Treaty of 1963.

If radiation is dangerous when nuclear weapons are tested, it is equally true that radioactive waste or leakage from nuclear power plants is also dangerous, and potentially disastrous. VOW had for a number of years been trying to make these facts known and appreciated, as it had the dangers inherent in leakage from nerve gas and other lethal weapons being manufactured and tested.

That Vietnam and other Third World countries had been a testing ground for many horrifying weapons and police techniques had long been known to the women of the peace movement. The Vietnamese and the Americans had documented the facts in reports, films, pictures and eye-witness testimony. Yet few scientists, particularly those employed by government, would shoulder the responsibility for making decisions to test or manufacture atomic, biological and chemical weapons. VOW delegates were told several times, "These decisions are made by our political masters. The politicians are responsible to the voters."

Are they? This question was repeatedly asked by members of VOW. Asked so many times that some members decided that they themselves should try to get into the political decision-making areas, such as Parliament, the legislatures and municipal councils. The group "Women For Political Action" was a logical outcome of the decision.

With the resurgence of the women's movement and the emphasis on the liberation of women in the late sixties, the young intellectuals were effectively occupied in discovering themselves and the facts of their oppression. To raise one's consciousness as a woman became to them more urgent than peace, civil rights, foreign affairs or disarmament. Meanwhile the peace movement was totally involved in trying to bring an end to the slaughter in Vietnam, only to see it extended to Laos and Cambodia. VOW's members, under its new president, Muriel Duckworth, led many of these actions. Women from countries contributing to the war—including Canada—met with women from Indochina. They met in Vietnam, in Europe—Prague, Warsaw, Moscow, Paris—and VOW brought the Indochinese women to Canada to tell their story to Canadians and Americans. It is notable that this group of a few thousand Canadian women, who were certainly not wealthy (nor did they receive any govern-grants or funds) could raise enough money to take two groups of Indochinese women from coast to coast. On another occasion they raised $17,000 to organize an International Conference of Women for Peace, as a Centennial project.

This project involved bringing together 300 women from twenty-five countries to talk about what women can do to achieve peace. It was held during a time of tension—the Arab-Israeli Six Day War—with women present from the countries involved. Women came, too, from the Soviet Union and other socialist countries, as well as from Japan, South America, India, Africa, Europe and North America.

During the meetings vivid personal experiences were shared. One African woman described her attendance at a previous conference where everyone had to be on the floor to avoid the stray bullets which were coming through the windows. A Bolivian woman described police raiding her home. Another did not know whether she would get back into her country when she returned, since there was a civil war going on. Another national representative pleaded, "Don't send us arms to kill each other."

The conference report summed it up: "Strange concepts

took on familiar outlines as women discovered they had, individually and from disparate cultures, come to basically the same conclusions. These conclusions were sometimes couched in sophisticated terms, sometimes in simple emotion-laden words. The participants came to realize that their ideas of how these aspirations could be realized were strikingly similar. Women who had feared their concepts were idealistic and unworkable were given courage by this consensus."

Some of these women formed part of a delegation that went to Ottawa and spoke on Vietnam, arms sales and disarmament with the Secretary of State for External Affairs. Afterwards they took part in an informal and happy weekend of talk, singing and relaxation which took place at the Quaker Peace Centre on Grindstone Island in Ontario's Rideau Lakes. Great understanding and lasting friendships were built among women from countries "with differing ideological assumptions". And they have endured over the years.

The cause of women in Indochina was the uniting factor when Voice of Women was responsible on another significant occasion for bringing together "peace women" and the women's liberation and Third World representatives. That unity was not achieved until many hurdles and struggles had been surmounted.

Previously, in 1969, three Vietnamese women had come to Canada. It was a poignant moment when they gazed across the Niagara River at the United States, the symbol and cause of their suffering and the destruction of their cities and countryside.

In 1971 six women and their interpreters, from North and South Vietnam and (for the first time) from Laos, came to participate in women's conferences in Vancouver and in Toronto. The announcement of the conferences met with an overwhelming response, especially in the United States, with the result that many American women came to Canada unaware that the main objective was to express support for the Indochinese women and work to end the war. The different views, background, ages and life-styles of the hundreds of women who attended led to many confrontations and arguments. Canadian women, almost swamped by the avalanche of "American imperialism of the left" as it seemed, felt a new awareness of the need to establish their own national identity, while still acknowledging their bond with women everywhere.

Sometimes almost by chance and with a degree of naiveté, sometimes by well-executed design, VOW has initiated or contributed to the climate of opinion which has led to changes in national attitudes and policies during the past fourteen years. Often what began as a small local campaign developed into a full public debate which brought about subsequent policy changes. Some examples have been cited. Others include boycotting of certain food products (such as California grapes), attitudes to women and minorities, legal rights and civil liberties, prejudiced textbooks, radiation hazards, and the treatment of prisoners in Vietnam, Chile, Greece and Spain.

In addition to affecting the climate of opinion, Voice of Women activities taught the necessary techniques to those involved, so that when they moved on to other fields of endeavour they took with them their newly-acquired expertise.

Although VOW worked as a national organization, provincial and local groups have taken up many issues of concern to their particular area, and some of these issues have later developed into national campaigns. Nova Scotia VOW's concern with Africville and the black community pre-dated general community awareness. New Brunswick VOW's actions with regard to the chemical spraying of the U.S.-Canadian border drew attention to this and other pesticide hazards to public health. Quebec VOW was especially concerned with civil rights, French-English problems, James Bay; Ontario with education prejudice and women's rights. The prairie provinces focussed on native rights and resources, U.S. military violation of Canadian sovereignty, research at Suffield. British Columbia VOW's many continuing concerns pin-pointed radiation hazards (Amchitka and Pacific tests and nuclear power plants), threats to the ecology and resources, and U.S. naval and military installations in Canada. These are a few examples. Individual women mounted their own personal campaigns on many issues.

During the Vietnam war a great deal was done by VOW members to help American draft resisters, young men who preferred exile or imprisonment to being part of the military machine which was destroying Indochina. VOW membership was also enhanced by the tremendous contributions made by American women who, in protest against their country's policies, came with their families to live in Canada, or who, from the United States, contributed to VOW's extensive Knitting Project for Vietnamese Children, part of Canadian Aid for Vietnam Civilians.

It would be gratifying to be able to trace the family trees of the current women's groups back to Voice of Women; history, however, can seldom be tailored so neatly. Human activity is always so untidy; today's mainstream has an unfortunate way of turning into tomorrow's blind alley, and what looked at first glance to be a small by-path often becomes the new route of the march.

It could be argued that the activity of VOW had a greater effect on its own members than on the particular events towards which it was directed. VOW members made the discovery that they could sometimes be agents of change, and in doing so, they were themselves changed. After taking that first step forward from ladylike anonymity and finding themselves in the limelight, some women scuttled back into the familiar shadows. Others found it exhilarating, and never looked back.

The growing wave of female disaffection with much of the male-dominated world was naturally also reflected on the domestic and personal level. Many VOW "men's auxiliary" members, as husbands referred to themselves, were supportive and gave encouragement to their wives. Others objected to their wives' involvement and made an issue over whether a stint on the phone for peace should take precedence over the appearance of dinner on the table on time. Quite a few marriages disintegrated, but whether from VOW activity itself or from pressures that were thrown into sharper focus by VOW work it is of course impossible to say. The growth of VOW was part of the liberalization of a previously much more rigid society.

In addition to public action, VOW members used their influence on families, friends, colleagues and neighbours. Women who took a stand on birth control paved the way for public discussion about abortion; women who have debated foreign policy with political spokesmen have been made aware that gender and position is not a determinant of intelligence and ability; women who have argued the relative merits of political systems with Russian and Vietnamese counterparts are not likely to regard local editorial pronouncements as the ultimate in human wisdom.

Sometimes it was the media that propelled VOW members into a closer examination of themselves and the world around them. Despite the fact that most news editors relegated VOW news to the women's pages or programs, editors and reporters regularly used VOW spokeswomen for instant comment on a wide range of issues. Often the press and other media personnel relied on "Voices" to fill in their background information on matters before the public.

Having publicly expressed VOW's policies, members often went on to play active roles in the campaigns which grew up around these issues. Equal treatment for women in a factory strike, child care groups, "free" schools, anti-pollution actions, measures to solve housing problems—all got VOW's support.

This degree of involvement probably also explains the continuing decline of the women's peace groups, so that only a hard core remains in both the United States and Canada. The structure of the organizations has become much looser, often based on specific shorter-term issues. Members have become involved in other kinds of community work and have often taken jobs there. But the chain of concern forged over the years as a peace group remains. Across the country VOW members continue to communicate, knowing that their concern for peace unites them on many other issues.

The Present

Born in Toronto, Cecelia Wallace is presently pursuing a degree in history at Atkinson College, York University, with a view to writing Canadian social history. She founded the Canadian section of St. Joan's International Alliance in 1965 and is member of the Advisory Status of Women Commission to the Canadian Catholic Conference of Roman Catholic Bishops of Canada, Ottawa. She has published several articles on women and the church in various Catholic, interfaith and secular journals around the world such as National Catholic Reporter, Ferment, *and* Women Speaking.

Changes in the Churches

Cecelia Wallace

"The preaching of the church, having been done by men, has given us the strictly masculine viewpoint."

In June 1970 Ann Dea, as head of a group of Edmonton Roman Catholic women, sent a letter to Archbishop J.A. Plourde, then president of the Canadian Catholic Conference of Bishops. (The conference has headquarters in Ottawa.) Her letter commented on the numbers of Catholic women leaving the church "because of its ancient, discriminatory attitude to women".

The bishops of Canada should take steps to eliminate discrimination against women in the church, Mrs. Dea said, and declare unequivocally that women are full and equal members. They could begin by placing the question of the status of women on the agenda of the next national meeting of bishops to be held in Ottawa in April 1971.

Ann Dea's request was a tall one. The Roman church has never regarded discrimination against women as a priority concern. In his reply Archbishop Plourde suggested that Ann take up the matter first locally with her bishop, Bishop Anthony Jordan of Edmonton. She refused, saying that the problem was a national one for Canada, not a local one, and must be dealt with by the bishops at a national level. Besides, she pointed out, her archbishop was aware of her

93

concern and agreed that it was a national, rather than a local problem.

Finally, officials of the Canadian Catholic Conference agreed to invite representative women to Ottawa, to discuss their status in the church and state. Moreover these women were invited to participate *officially* in the bishops' synod to be held during the week of April 17, 1971. Never in the modern history of the Roman Catholic church had women been officially invited to participate in a bishops' synod. The event was watched with interest by Catholics throughout the world.

Prior to the Ottawa meeting a number of briefs had been submitted to the bishops on women in the church. One tabulated the results of a survey held in Edmonton, and among the questions asked was, "Do you think the celibacy of the Catholic priest has influenced the position of women in the church?" A majority of women replying said "Yes" and added pertinent comments:

"The church has been afraid of women. Celibate priests have been accustomed to view women as a danger to their vocation."

"We are thought of as 'temptation' and held at arm's length."

"How can a comfortable bachelor possibly conceive of the worries and problems of married life?"

Other replies indicated total dissatisfaction with the help (or rather lack of it) offered to women by priests:

"I no longer attend the parish in my area, where help is given in an artificial and stilted form."

"What we receive is not the Word of God, but dry theological ruminations at best and stupid financial exhortations at worst."

"I only remember one sermon in my life. It was a dialogue sermon in a small church with relaxation and perfect rapport between priest and people. And oh, the joy and discussion for days after!"

Many sermons were criticized as being "very poor, anachronistic, and levelled at an immature congregation".

Other criticisms were levelled at the priests' (and the church's view of the "ideal" woman. She is maternal, stays in the background, works hard for her family and parish. She is passive and subservient. One woman commented sardonically that Catholic women were expected by the official church to be "pallid, submissive, and prolific".

On April 19, 1971, a group of about sixty Canadian Catholic women, half English and half French, met with the Canadian bishops at Ottawa. For two days previous to this they had met together and had come to some conclusions about the role of women in four main areas: in the family, in the world of work, in society and in the church.

At the synod the bishops were told that women have a dignity and worth *other* than in marriage and childbearing, and must become more conscious of their own personal worth. Catholic education must be conducted so that women will learn to *choose freely* their role in life, without being coerced by religious teaching into marriage or the convent.

The bishops were asked bluntly if they were conscious of the discrimination in society against working women and were asked to support the awakening social consciousness of working women against that discrimination. They were requested to make church property available to working women for their needs, for example, day-care centres. Quebec women told the bishops they should visit factories and other places of work in their dioceses, and take a stand on the side of workers suffering from injustice, particularly women workers. They were asked to encourage women to take leadership roles in the working world.

Other recommendations asked the bishops to (1) Declare unequivocally that women in the church have the same rights, privileges and responsibilities as men; (2) Make representations to synods held in Rome (made up of bishops throughout the world) asking that discriminatory barriers against women in the church, such as those held tradition-ally in theology and appearing in church canon law, be removed; (3) Ordain qualified women to the ministry; (4) Encourage the presence of qualified women on all bodies in the church dealing with matters of concern to all church members; (5) Ensure that the attitudes of clergy to women respect their equality and inherent dignity.

After presenting their recommendations to the bishops the women went home to await further developments. And they found upon their return that many Catholic women did not know why they had gone to Ottawa in the first place and that many women were appalled at the very idea of women telling Catholic bishops what they should do.

The Second Vativan Council
This attitude is a result of the subservient role women have played in the Roman Catholic church. Told to occupy themselves either with domestic or convent chores they have been denied any insight into the inner workings of the church. Few women until recently have had any ac-quaintance with the great controversies in church history or theology. Even nuns have been given a watered-down "religious" education which was thought to be suitable for their rather childlike "woman's temperament". Until very recently (and probably still in Rome), the minds of women were thought to be incapable of mastering the "abstractions" of philosophy and theology which were reserved for the superiority of the male mind. Male theo-logians have regarded any theological speculations on such

frivolous subjects as the role of women in the church as beneath their interest. The role of women, most theologians thought, had been settled once and for all by St. Paul and the tradition of the church: it was to be found either at home or in the convent. Even when recent popes such as Pius XII agreed that women had a social role as well, the view hinged not on a woman's intrinsic value as an individual, but upon the so-called "maternal" benevolence she could bring to society. Even the role of woman as "wife", rather than mother, placing her at least in some confrontation with man, is foreign to the traditional Catholic theological mentality. She is primarily seen as tied to children rather than men, and confined to the family, headed by a patriarchal spouse, rather than as having anything to contribute to the larger world community.

Given this mentality it follows that when an important event occurred in the church, namely the calling of the Second Vatican Council (held in Rome from 1962 to 1965 in Vatican City), no women were initially invited to attend (except the wives of non-Catholic clergy). Representatives of all the major religious denominations, including the Jews, were invited to be present. Overtures were even made to non-Christians, atheists, and Communists. But no need was seen to have Catholic *women* represented at the council!

It wasn't long, of course, before some informed women in the church complained of being ignored. St. Joan's International Alliance, a sixty-year-old Catholic feminist organization, immediately requested Vatican officials to allow women to attend the council. Members of this organization and sympathizers began talking to the press about the unfair exclusion of women. The world press began to comment. The situation became alive with stories —about the bishop who, when asked why women had not been invited, looked blank and said, "We never thought of it"; about the woman journalist in Rome asked to leave a gathering "lest her presence defile the pope", who was expected at any time; about women forbidden to receive Communion at mass along with the men in Vatican City; about the wives of visiting journalists being asked to sit in the balcony at meetings addressed by bishops and cardinals, while their husbands remained on the main floor. (One American journalist refused to be separated from his wife by quoting the scriptural phrase: "What God hath joined together, let no man put asunder!")

The situation became even more ludicrous when it was learned that a number of bishops attending the early sessions of the council had accepted an idea sent to them by Barbara Ward, the internationally-known economist. She wanted the Vatican to do something *practical* about injustice and poverty in the world. The bishops responded by agreeing to erect a Vatican secretariat to deal with the problem. Miss Ward, however, was not allowed to speak to the bishops about her proposal from the council floor —because she was a woman! Instead, her ideas had to be formally presented to them by an American layman, J.L. Norris, who thought this situation incredible. Later Barbara Ward spoke on behalf of the underdeveloped nations of the world from the pulpits of Protestant churches but could not speak from the pulpit of a Catholic church, her own denomination. One wonders also whether the secretariat will make anything of the fact that much injustice and poverty in the world is inflicted on women. (It is noteworthy that the problems of women in the world did not merit a Vatican secretariat.)

Women were finally invited as "auditors" to the third session of the Vatican Council—to listen, but not to speak. Those invited represented nuns and lay Catholic women prominent in church-related women's organizations. But, typically, no member of St. Joan's Alliance, the organization which has fought for the equality of women for more than half a century, was invited to be present.

Meanwhile, in Canada, forty-two "position papers" highly critical of certain areas in the Canadian church, and urging reform, were written by a group of concerned lay Catholics, men and women. They were presented to the Canadian bishops as they left to attend the second session of the council (1963). Later these were published as a book entitled *Brief to the Bishops*[1]. Ironically this book, available in public libraries, is better known and better read in Protestant circles in Canada than it is among Catholics.

Three of the articles in *Brief to the Bishops* are about women. Sonja Nabieszko, of North Bay, Ontario, complained about the waste of female brain power in the church and excoriated the clinging-vine, passive, submissive, obedient, immature woman that church indoctrination has tended to produce. She also pointed out that as far as the church is concerned the single woman is non-existent. Janet Somerville in "Women and Christian Responsibility" reiterated this by commenting on the working woman who feels "mistrusted by the church". My own article in the book (entitled "Redefining the Meaning of the Sexes") criticized the failure of the Vatican to recognize women, and attacked attitudes to women in Catholic theology.

Traditional Catholic Theology on Women

Many Catholics are surprised to hear that Catholic theology regards women as inferior to men. Few have ever read Catholic theologians on the subject of women, or are acquainted with the biased views of women held by the

[1] Paul Harris, ed. (Longman, 1965).

early church fathers, from which much Catholic theology is derived. Many Catholics, too, are hazy about what the word "theology" means. There are a number of schools of theology in the church, many of them opposing each other. This, in itself, should be enough to indicate that theological opinion is not to be confused with faith and doctrine. Yet, because theologians are almost always priests, and because priests are surrounded by an aura of authority in the church with regard to her teaching, many lay Catholics have unsuspectingly been led to swallow as doctrine whatever theological *opinion* the local pastor happens to subscribe to. Doctrinal teachings in the Roman Catholic church come from the bishops and the pope, not the theologians. There are very few such doctrinal teachings, for even the majority of the statements of popes and bishops are not necessarily hard and fast doctrine. Basically *doctrinal* statements, to be accepted as such, must be made according to rigidly defined rules. The average lay Catholic understands little about all of this.

The theological arguments on the inferiority of women in Catholicism are largely based on the views of St. Thomas Aquinas, regarded as the leading theologian of the church since the Middle Ages. Aquinas, in turn, based his views on the thinking of the Greek philosopher-scientist Aristotle. Thomas Aquinas was a thirteenth-century theologian and philosophical scholar at the University of Paris who quickly absorbed the Aristotelian thought brought to Europe by the Arabs in the twelfth century. (Aristotle himself lived in the sixth century B.C.)

The Greek philosophers used natural reason to arrive at the idea of a transcendant God. For this reason Catholic theologians have, for centuries, used them, particularly Aristotle and Plato, to substantiate Catholic religious claims. It should be remembered that Greek philosophical thought almost certainly influenced St. Paul and in fact, the whole culture of the Middle East, including that of the Arabs and Jews. *All* were influenced by Greek views of the inferiority of women.

How the Greeks arrived at their views on the inferiority of women is an historical study of itself that cannot be gone into here. But basically they thought that the male sperm or seed contained the perfect human form, also male. The woman merely acted as an incubator for the seed until the child was born, which should, if perfect, be male. If the child were female, this was a sign of a defect in the seed. Aristotle reasoned that an external defect, perhaps something harmful brought by a moist south wind, accounted for the fact that a girl rather than a boy was born. The Greeks also believed that the intelligence of the male mind was breathed into the male directly by God. But the woman's intelligence was indirect, coming to her in a defective way, via man. The woman was not only *physically* inferior to man, but also morally, intellectually and spiritually inferior. Now we have the philosophical and religious basis in Western society for the belief that the woman is inferior and these ideas can be traced back through all of the Western educational system, particularly in those theological and university schools where Greek thought has been highly revered.

Aquinas thought he saw Aristotle confirmed by Holy Scripture and St. Paul. He was once asked whether the father of a child or the mother should be loved more. His "reasoned" reply was that, since the father is the more perfect human, and greater love should be given to that which is more perfect, the father should be loved more than the mother.

The question of whether or not women can be ordained was raised to Thomas. He argued that a priest ought to be drawn only from the more perfect specimens of the human race: the males. Besides, he argued further, a priest must exercise authority and a woman cannot exercise authority because, according to Genesis, she is in a state of subjection to man. Aquinas conveniently ignores the fact that the Old Testament is superseded by the New Testament, the record of the coming of Christ, who is to fulfill and perfect the Old Law. And in the New Testament, even according to St. Paul (whose statements on women are contradictory), women are equal.

When it was pointed out to Thomas that in Scripture women are sometimes prophets (and the office of prophet is superior to that of priest); and that authority is given to women even in the Old Testament (e.g., Deborah); and that mediaeval abbesses in the church exercised quasi-episcopal jurisdiction—he merely reiterated his position, undeterred by these arguments. The woman was in subjection to man and could not be a priest. Like most male theologians on women he chose to argue from Greek philosophical "authority" rather than scriptural reality; and, like the devil, Thomas could quote Scripture to his own purpose.

Aquinas's views on the superiority of male over female is extended even to animals: "In perfect animals, generated by coition, the active force is in the semen of the male, as the Philosopher (i.e., Aristotle) says, but the foetal matter is provided by the female."

Aquinas has been regarded as the leading and most eminent theologian of the Catholic church up until the time of the Second Vatican Council. His influence has been all the more pervasive because he is a canonized saint. Almost all theology taught in seminaries in the Catholic church throughout the world has leaned heavily upon him.

In 1962 Dr. Gertrud Heinzelmann, an attorney-at-law of Zurich, Switzerland, presented a paper to the Preparatory Commission of the council taking issue with Aquinas's views of women. She pointed out that the upholding by the church "to this day" of his biologically and theologically inaccurate teachings on women have prevented them from reaching their full stature in the church. She also criticized the inconsistency of Thomistic teaching; for, having said what he did about woman's inferiority, Thomas also had to admit that man, in the act of generation, could not create the human soul: it had to be created by God. The woman's soul therefore had to be created by God, or else she had no soul. (No doubt because they also noticed this, Catholic theologians of Aquinas's time were involved in arguments about whether women had souls!)

Dr. Heinzelmann further argued that the conferring of ordination on a priestly candidate is a spiritual matter affecting the soul, and since there is no difference between male and female souls women should be admitted to the priesthood.

Such arguments are continually ignored by the Vatican. Two or three years later Vatican theologians were still using Thomistic arguments in the pages of *L'Osservatore Romano,* the Vatican newspaper, to deny that women may be ordained. Even the pope remains a Thomist on this question.

The Attitude of the Canadian Bishops

A major question discussed at the Second Vatican Council was that of the authority of bishops in the Roman Catholic church vis-à-vis the authority of the pope. Traditionally Catholics have been brought up to emphasize the authority of the pope as if the bishops had no local authority of their own. The bishops are now pointing out that their authority was handed down to them from the first twelve apostles and does not depend on the authority of the pope. The pope must act in collegiality with his bishops and *they* must act in a way that involves discussion with clergy and lay people on concerns in the church.

This question of collegiality may have a profound effect on the status of women in the church, but only if local and national groups of bishops take firm stands with Rome.

In October 1964, Bishop Gerard Coderre of Saint-Jean, Quebec, spoke in the name of forty Canadian bishops and asked the church, at the Second Vatican Council, to acknowledge the modern women's movement by proclaiming and promoting the dignity and equality of women within the church itself and in the entire human community, "until it reaches its completion". Similar sentiments were expressed the following day by Augustin Frotz, auxiliary bishop of Cologne, Germany. Paul-Emile Cardinal Léger, then bishop of Montreal, criticized the view that Thomas Aquinas's philosophy should still be revered as the "perennial philosophy" of the church, and retained as the basis of seminary education.

In October 1971, Cardinal Flahiff of Winnipeg called for an in-depth study of women in the church. He was addressing an international synod of bishops in Rome. He rejected previous theologies limiting the role of women in the church, saying there was no dogmatic objection to women being ordained (a position also taken by Archbishop Pocock of Toronto).

The pope agreed, in response, to set up a commission to study the status of women. But it was also announced that the commission's job would be *temporary* (other commissions are permanent, but women evidently don't rate a permanent commission; their problems appear to be seen as fleeting). Terms of reference were also given for the commission and it was unequivocally stated that "from the very outset the possibility of conferring sacred orders on women must be excluded". This continues to be the Vatican position.

The members of the Vatican commission include fifteen women, but the professional qualifications listed belong mainly to the male members. There are only two women for whom professional qualifications are given: a doctor and an obstetrician. All women are listed according to their nationality and marital status. But the male list includes a sociologist, a liturgist, a canonist, a lawyer, three theologians, a biblical scholar and a journalist. There are women Catholic professionals in all of these fields but it seems that on questions relating to all of them we are to continue to have only male points of view expressed. We can probably expect little new light, really, to come from such a commission. Another problem arose when women auditors were initially invited to the Vatican Council. Those invited were not trained theologians and were therefore at a disadvantage in assessing the significance of the theological debates going on at the council.

So, the Vatican commission was set up at the instigation of the Canadian bishops. In October 1972, it was announced that the Canadian bishops had set up their own sixteen-member committee to carry out a national study on the role of women in the church and society. (This was two years before the setting up of the Vatican committee.) Members of the committee represented clergy, nuns and laity.[2] No stipulations were made as to what the committee would discuss. In fact the members were asked to sub-

---

[2]Members of the committee were: George Cardinal Flahiff, Winnipeg; Bishop Gaston Hains, Amos, Quebec; Mrs. Ann Dea, Edmonton; Sister Catherine Wallace, Halifax; Sister Joan Halmo, Bruno, Saskatchewan; Mrs. Mary Matthews, Toronto; Miss Cecelia Wallace, Toronto; Mrs. A. Howlett, Montreal; Sister Jeanne Dussault, Edmonton; Sister Corrine Gallant, Moncton, N.B.; Mrs. Simone Chartrand, Montreal; Mrs. Lucie Leboeuf, Hull, Quebec; Mrs. H. Pelletier-Baillargeon, Montreal; Miss Renée Brisson, Ottawa; Mrs. Suzanne Blais Mauviel, Hull, Quebec; Sister Ella Zink, Ottawa.

mit their areas of concern to the bishops and the committee is still in the process of doing so. It recommended
that lower down, at the level of the archdiocese or diocese
and the parish, an attempt should be made to assess through
discussions with Catholic women what they think of their
role in the church. How much of this will actually be done
depends too often on the personal attitudes of the women
themselves and their pastors. (In the past women who have
had the temerity to raise questions about women in the
church have been promptly silenced by the ridicule or
hostility generated by other members of the parish councils.)

Catholic Lay Reaction

How do the eight million people in Canada who call themselves Roman Catholics react to changes in women's
status? Unfortunately many of them are confused and
resentful about *any* change in the church, let alone changes
that would benefit women. Most Catholics (and this includes many nuns) have never been adequately informed on
church history and theology or the reasons behind the
need for reformation in the church; neither are they deeply
conversant with the meaning of the issues discussed at
the Second Vatican Council. By and large the Catholic
press in Canada (with one or two exceptions) produces
only very superficial comment. In contrast British, European and American Catholic newspapers are backed by
well-informed Catholic magazines, thoroughly conversant
with the current religious issues. Many Canadian Catholics
do not bother to read the Canadian Catholic press at all
(perhaps because they are tired of its paternalism and tendency to gear itself to an adolescent level).

At the very moment, then, when widespread and deep
discussion is needed to bring about reform in the church,

the media for doing it is largely non-existent in Canada. Uneasily aware of this, women of the Catholic Education Club of Montreal complained, in a brief submitted to the Canadian bishops, about the lack of communication in the Canadian church. The brief stated that "the stages between layman, priest, bishop, national conference, and Rome, are not providing an adequate flow of information or feedback. Many attempts to produce suitable Catholic newspapers in Canada have foundered on economic rocks."

The newspapers have also foundered, more often than not, on the irreconcilable differences that arise when good journalists are faced with a choice between adequately providing information, however unpalatable, and heavy-handed opposition from conservative opinion in the church—either in the higher echelons of the editorial board, or elsewhere among clergy, laity or hierarchy. Faced with this, many competent Catholic editors have simply given up and resigned their positions to men of lesser quality. Now there is a conservative backlash becoming predominant in the church. An example of it is an article published in *Saturday Night* (April 1974) by Anne Roche. Entitled "When the Convent was a Magic, Timeless World", the article is part of a book on the contemporary church called (significantly) *The Gates of Hell.*[3] The reference is to a well-known traditional belief often quoted among Catholics, that even the gates of hell cannot prevail against the church. We can see from this where any liberalizing trends are placed, in the opinion of the author. Her article shows a childish romanticism and lack of awareness of the real need for change in many convents. The author herself found that she had to leave the convent, but she does not say why. Apparently (like Monica Baldwin, the British author of *I Leapt Over the Wall*), Anne Roche blames *herself* for her lack of ability to stay

[3]McClelland and Stewart, 1975.

rather than telling us about the conditions she may not have been able to tolerate there. The conditioning of women to blame themselves rather than the conditions under which they are expected to live has, of course, been amply documented time and again by the women's movement.

In marked contrast to Anne Roche's eulogy of traditional convent life is the dissatisfaction expressed by many nuns today regarding the convent's archaic view of women. Unreasonable restrictions on how they should dress and live have resulted in a decline in numbers of some eighty percent in several convents. Many nuns are becoming extremely critical not only of convent life but every aspect of the church. A group of nuns in the United States, for example, criticized in these terms a report circulated by their bishops which rejected the ordination of women:

> Who has determined the major questions? What chance has woman when man has been the "sacred scribe" who monopolized the opportunities for scholarship, composing the Scriptures in ancient times, interpreting them in later days, canonizing them as man's record of revelation for man? NCAN (National Coalition of America Nuns) affirms that this masculine view of the major questions is myopic . . . as Poulain de la Barre wrote in the 17th century, "All that has been written about women should be suspect, for the men are at once judge and party to the lawsuit."

Some things written by women are suspect, too. Anne Roche believes that she is defending the orthodox, traditional view of the church and that the one she was taught is the only correct one. Yet her book *The Gates of Hell* is totally bereft of any real historical and theological knowledge of the church, for much of what she regards as "traditional" dates only from the Middle Ages, not from the early Christian church, in which priests were married and women were given a higher status (even by St. Paul).

Questions relating directly to women—birth control, abortion, clerical marriage, the ordination of women—are the most severe stumbling blocks to reform in the Catholic church. The male church can't cope with any of them, it seems, and its dog-in-the-manger policy of allowing only male clerics to do the authoritative thinking prevents women from having a try.

This is true in all Christian churches and in Judaism; the application varies but the underlying assumption of woman's fundamental inferiority remains the same. As I have pointed out, Christian and Jewish (and Arabic) thought concerning women has a common root: Greek philosophy (particularly Aristotelian). The continued acceptance and development of this Greek-based theology down through the centuries by Christian theologians and rabbinical teachers has given it the stamp of "authority" and "tradition"—although it may not even be authentically Christian (or Jewish) and certainly need not be accepted as *doctrine.* Yet that is exactly what has happened. The exclusion of women from the centre of religion, which is lodged in the clergy, and their relegation to the sidelines is largely a result of this historical chain of assumptions.

This article is a discussion of the ramifications of these assumptions for women in the churches today, taking the situation of women in the Catholic church as my prime example. But I will also outline briefly the (very similar) situation of women in other Christian churches and in Judaism.

The Anglicans

The year 1968 was a year of "crisis" for women in the Canadian Anglican church. Bishop Scott, convener of the church's Commission on Women, used that word to sum up the state of affairs existing between the church and its professional female workers. These were deaconesses, members of religious orders, and lay women church workers.

Many Anglican women were leaving church work for secular jobs. They said it was "impossible for them to discover what it was the church wanted them to do" and that they had no security within the life and work of the church. They could not expect promotion because there was no place for them to go. Failure of the church to attract new women workers was based on its refusal to recognize and take seriously their professional status.

One woman with training, experience and seniority in church work discovered that the salary of the curate in her parish, just out of theological school, was hundreds of dollars more than hers. This was accounted for by the fact that he was married and his family had to be provided for. Yet in such cases the wife often works too, providing the family with a two-salary income, while the single woman is penalized for being single, although she too may be caring for dependents.

The Anglican women asked for full acceptance of their work and sufficient numbers of women represented in synods and commissions in the church to make their requests effective.

The Ordination of Women in the Anglican Church

The lack of status for women is directly related to the fact that what women do in the church is seen as trivial compared to the work and status of the male clergy and women in the Canadian Anglican church are not yet being ordained (although eleven women in the United States have been). As is the case in Roman Catholicism Canadian Anglican women operate only as marginal members of the church, barred from the important theological and pastoral concerns going on at its male clerical and hierarchical centre. For confirmation of this in both Anglicanism and Roman Catholicism, all one has to do is check the vast quantity of Church literature, past and present. Very little of it concerns the needs of women, or takes cognizance of their contribution, although women, of course, are asked to financially support and subsidize the churches and the publication of the literature which fails to take them seriously.

The Anglicans, at least, have been one step ahead of the Catholics. They have granted Anglican women the role of deaconess, although there has always been controversy over what a deaconess really is.[4] "Ordination" of women deaconesses was accepted in the Anglican church for a long time, but it was carefully distinguished from ordination to the priesthood. The Anglican church recognizes the deaconess as performing a ministry, in which she exercises most clerical functions except distributing Communion, granting absolution, or benediction, these begin reserved for males. Deaconesses are employed at the parish level, work hard and for long hours for small pay, like the lay women workers.

Thinking on the question of ordaining women as priests had progressed far enough in the Anglican communion by 1966 for the church office in London, England to produce a report on it, entitled the *Report of the Archbishops'*

[4]This clerical order for women was abolished in the Roman Catholic church in about the eleventh century, amid denials that it was a clerical order. No one, however, has yet provided satisfactory evidence that the roles of male and female deacons are essentially different—except that in the early Christian church each tended to minister to his or her own sex. The deaconess was replaced by the nun. Before total replacement some nuns were also deaconesses. The nun regards herself as a "religious", but this title means nothing. She is *officially* classed as a "lay" person in the church but can really identify with neither laity nor clergy. She is the female counterpart of the monk—not the priest, as many seem to think—although the monk can aspire to ordination and be ordained, while the nun cannot.

Recently the Roman Catholic church has decided to revive the order of deacon for males, especially married males—who were appointed and allowed to officiate at Catholic altars almost overnight—but we hear little or nothing of any serious effort to revive the order for women. The married male deacon is now another hurdle to be faced by Catholic women who want to be ordained.

Commission on Women and Holy Orders. Commissioned by the archbishops of Canterbury and York, the report influenced Anglicans around the world. It came to no conclusions on the matter of ordaining women, however, but simply presented arguments pro and con. Some of them were based on the Aristotelian views of St. Thomas Aquinas. One paper, submitted by Robert F. Hobson, presented once again the old ludicrous argument (based on a male interpretation of a text in Ecclesiastes) that "in public worship men are less likely to distract and stimulate the congregation sexually . . . because men are more quickly aroused than women and respond to a wider variety of symbolic stimuli".

Catherine Beaton (a Roman Catholic) of Aurora, Ontario, responded to a similar argument in her own church in an article in *The Critic*.[5] She asked why *women* had to be penalized because men are so easily aroused to lust. One is left also to wonder why women take part in mixed church services at all if such is the case, or why a mixed group of men and women courted sexual temptation by meeting together in the deliberations of the Anglican commission!

In November 1972 the *Canadian Churchman,* national newspaper for the Canadian Anglican church, commented on another report written by Christine Howard, a leading English churchwoman, urging the ordination of women. She dismissed the arguments against this as "anomalous and absurd". Her book noted that the Anglican bishop of Hong Kong had already gone ahead and ordained two women and three men to the priesthood in 1971, as a result of which the Hong Kong diocese stood in doubtful status with the rest of the Anglican church. Yet it was felt that the men would be recognized as priests throughout the Anglican communion, but the "same certainty does not apply to the women's ordination".

[5] Chicago, June-July 1966.

In December 1971 the *Canadian Churchman* announced that the year 1973 might at last prove to be a year of decision on the question of women priests. "Suddenly the question has become serious." This was because in October a majority in the House of Bishops of the United States had voted for the right of women to be ordained priests and even bishops. Now it remained to see what the American General Convention of the Anglican church (known as Episcopalian in the United States) would do in September 1973. For a measure to pass it must be approved by the House of Deputies. Constitutional changes (required on the woman priests issue) require approval by two successive triennial general conventions. The September convention did not accept the proposal to ordain women.

In 1968 the *Canadian Churchman* polled thirty-eight active Anglican bishops in Canada on the issue. Of twenty-three who replied thirteen said they would support ordination, six said they would not, and twelve were undecided or declined to answer. Objections centred on the difficulty of such a vocation for women, viewed women as less acceptable pastors than men, or maintained that neither the Anglican laity nor Anglican women wanted female priests. The last argument, often put forward, is an avoidance of the issue, for the ordaining of women is a *theological* question relating to whether or not women have full membership in the church and equality under God, not a question to be decided solely on the basis of how one *feels* about it. However in May 1973 the General Synod of the Anglican Church of Canada did in fact accept the *principle* of ordaining women as priests. But it recommended that the reality of ordination not take place "until the House of Bishops in Canada has worked out a pattern for the Canadian church that would include an educational process for the church".

The "educational process" in love of neighbour and

common Christian charity appeared to be badly needed. The General Synod decision aroused anger in many quarters. People at lower levels felt they had not been sufficiently consulted and pitched battles were fought in the local diocesan synods. One diocese passed what amounted to a motion of censure of the General Synod. Bishop J.B. Creeggan of Kingston told delegates to an Ontario diocesan synod that he will *never* ordain women to the priesthood. He said he had heard from four of his priests that they would have to consider leaving the church if women were ordained.

"It appears to me quite open to question as to whether, after two hours of debate, General Synod has the right by resolution to change a tradition of the church, which has been in existence for nearly 2,000 years," the bishop said. (Considering the vast changes that came about after the Reformation, when the Anglican church introduced an untraditional married clergy, this was an odd and unhistorical remark for any Anglican bishop to make.)

The Huron, Fredericton, and Toronto diocesan synods either reversed the approval given to ordaining women or placed strict limitations on it. They claimed to have had no time to study the question. An editorial writer in the *Canadian Churchman* commented:

> No time? Ordination of women has been a top priority for the Canadian Church since 1968, when the Lambeth conference directed it for study by national churches . . .
>
> Dioceses have had five years in which to set up their own committees to study the ordination of women. They have had five years in which to seek opinion throughout their membership and convey those opinions to General Synod. But very few have chosen to do so. . . .

Letters poured into the paper over the controversy. Joyce Walker of West Hill, Ontario, wrote: "It is time the church took its place in the 20th century; if it does not it will become a prehistoric fossil, extinct, because like the dinosaur it was unable to adjust to its environment."

William J. Anderson of Montreal said: "I was disappointed to hear of the acceptance of the principle of ordination of women to the priesthood by General Synod . . . for those in the Church who cannot accept the idea of women priests there is no choice but to move elsewhere. One can only hope that the nine bishops who opposed the motion will continue to fight against it until the issue may be settled by the Church Catholic, not simply the Anglican Church."

(He meant by this the need to consult with Roman Catholics and the Orthodox churches. It is an old ploy on the question of ordaining women to use the excuse that in the current ecumenical climate the other churches might not like it. This ignores the fact that it may be the women in all the churches who eventually decide they cannot accept their second-class status and leave the church altogether to prejudiced males.)

Anglican bishop Hugh Stiff of Keewatin begged the Anglicans to wait and consult with the Roman Catholics. Roman theologians opposed say they do not want to offend the Orthodox churches. The Orthodox churches have a closed mind on the subject, refusing to entertain the idea of women priests, although they admit there are no theological reasons for doing so.

In January 1974 the *Canadian Churchman* reported that when the matter was finally brought up to the House of Bishops of the Anglican Church in Canada they "squeezed discussion of the ordination of women into an already overcrowded agenda, and decided to do nothing on the matter for the foreseeable future".

The cause of ordained women, however, was progressing faster in the United States. On July 29, 1974, eleven women were actually ordained priests of the Episcopal church in Philadelphia.[6] The furor surrounding this event made it the top religious news story of the year.

The bishops who performed the ordination were threatened with suspension but, since they were near the retirement age anyway, had not much to lose. They went ahead despite an outcry in the press and sacristy pro and con the ordaining of women. Speculation was raised as to whether the ordination could possibly be valid. At least one voice in favour came from a Roman Catholic theologian who maintained that doctrinally there was no reason to doubt the basic validity of the ordinations. The fact that women were involved simply classed them as "irregular", and such irregularities could be resolved. Initial hostility to the women seems to have lessened for some of them have received pastoral posts.

In January 1975, the Toronto *Star* reported that the General Synod of the Anglican Church of Canada gave "overwhelming" approval to a resolution allowing the ordination of women priests "at the discretion of diocesan bishops . . . in consultation with the House of Bishops". But the synod was warned that the issue would cause a split in the Canadian Anglican church, with members resigning from the church if women were ordained. Votes of some bishops agreed with ordination "in principle" but were against implementing the principle at that time. So the situation here appeared to be similar to that of the Anglican church in Britain which the Kansas City *National Catholic Reporter* commented on laconically with the headline: "Britain's Anglicans say yes, no, yes yes no, to ordaining women".[7]

[6]The women were Merrill Bittner, Emily Hewitt, Carter Heyward, Marie Moorefield, Betty Schiess, Nancy Wittig, Alison Cheek, All Bozarth-Campbell, Jeanette Piscard, Suzanne Hiatt, and Katrina Swanson. They were ordained by Bishops Robert DeWitt, Daniel Carrigan, and Edward Wells, assisted by Bishop Romos, at the Church of the Advocate in Philadelphia.

[7]August 1, 1975.

On October 31, 1975, in Winnipeg, the Canadian Anglican bishops voted by a large margin to ordain women as priests, as of November 1, 1976, "provided that there be no overwhelmingly negative reaction in the meantime from Anglican churches in other countries". Significantly, this decision was reached after consultation with the Orthodox and Roman Catholic churches in Canada.

In spite of this 350 priests in the Anglican church have signed a manifesto calling for a total boycott of any women who may be ordained, thus indicating their intention of disobeying their bishops. Using outdated arguments to bolster their views they maintain that "it is an impossibility in the divine economy for a woman to be a priest". This is another way of saying that they will decide what is possible for God. A group of lay Anglicans calling themselves the "Council for the Faith" have also set themselves up against the ordination of women, calling this "schismatic" or "heretical". Both groups cling to theological reasoning that has been debated in the churches for years and found wanting in the light of authentic Christian doctrine, leaving them with a position based on little else but prejudice.

The Protestants

In an article in the *Christian Century* Sheila D. Collins comments on the attitude of men to women in the churches of the Reformation.[8] She says of Martin Luther that he held to the old patriarchal view.

> . . . his "priesthood of all believers" doctrine challenged the hierarchy of the Roman Church, but did nothing to reform the hierarchical relationship between men and women. Indeed he declared: "women are on earth to bear children. They die in child-bearing, it matters not: that is all they are here to do."

Even in our own day a theologian of the stature of

[8]"Towards a Feminist Theology", August 2, 1972.

Karl Barth holds to the same revelatory religion which has always excluded the existential experience of women. "Women," he wrote, "are ontologically inferior to men."

Ms. Collins points out that Barth chooses not Christ's but St. Paul's view of women, when he says, "Why should not woman be the second in sequence, but only in sequence? What other choice has she, seeing she can be nothing at all apart from this sequence and her place in it?"

Commenting on the sequence argument in Roman Catholic theology (it maintains that women are subordinate to men because God created Adam before Eve), Catherine Beaton in her article in *The Critic* comments drily, "If it's a matter of orderly progression then men ought to be subject to monkeys!"

Peggy Billings, a member of the United Methodist church, feels that women's liberation is not about to sweep the congregational life of American Protestantism. Claire Randall, of Church Women United, thinks that women themselves are "a stumbling block to other women in fulfilling decision-making roles in the church. Many women do not believe in other women because they do not believe in themselves or in their own ability to fulfill this kind of responsibility."

Both women agree that the Christian churches—even those which seem on the surface to be quite liberated—are considered by the women's movement to be among the worst perpetrators of sexism. Dr. Nelle Morton, a consultant on women's liberation for Church Women United and a theologian, says:

The Church has supported commercialization of motherhood as the norm for the true existence of all women. Through its sentimental madonnas, bland advent sermons, insipid "baby Jesus" stories it has made Christmas not incarnation—God with us—but alienation—

God separated from common life. Thus it has put woman on a pedestal to be adored—the goddess of heaven —or in a kitchen to be used.

The Protestant churches are no less guilty of exploiting women economically than is the secular world, a study of seventeen denominations by the National Council of Churches revealed. Forty-three percent of the women but only sixteen percent of the men employed by the churches earned less than ten thousand dollars a year. Only two churches reported recruitment programs for women executives. American Baptist women complained in a pamphlet that women do not have equal opportunity with men to sit on the church's major boards and committees, opportunities for women pastors are limited, and that fifty-three men but only four women have acted as presidents of the American Baptist Convention.

Many Canadian Protestant women complain of the rareness of women ministers in the major churches of Canada. The Lutheran church does not ordain women. The United Church has only sixty-four women ministers out of a total of about 1,950. A few groups such as the Quakers and the Salvation Army treat women as equals. There are a number of women elders and deaconesses, yet compared with the men they exercise little real power and their role in decision making is non-existent or minimal.

Commenting on the general Protestant attitude, Dr. Helmut Begemann of Lubeck, Germany (Evangelical Church of Westphalia) outlined notions about women common to all the churches for the Lutheran World Federation in Berlin (1966). He said they were derived from biblical thought, and from notions of Aristotelian natural law as developed by Thomas Aquinas:

There is the patriarchal notion according to which the father alone "rules" the family, while the wife, as the mother, with her children and with the servants and maids, is wholly subject to him. To the patriarchal superiority of the husband with regard to both legal and social positions corresponds the woman's inferiority. She has become his "chattel." Her virginity is considered to be the condition for an honorable marriage and for her marriageability. Woman is also inferior in a spiritual sense. A woman cannot take on any public responsibility in the Church, the more so as in the beginnings of Western tradition the problem was still being mooted whether woman had a soul at all. Concepts like "head" and "heart" for husband and wife, which have become familliar to us, are typical for patriarchal thinking and for the practical consequences derived from it, namely that man's place is in public life while a woman's is in the home and the kitchen. There are not only Roman Catholic but also Protestant ethical theologians of world fame who stand in this almost unbroken tradition. According to Emil Brunner the triad father-mother-child determines the structure of human existence. Accordingly the order of the family is a patriarchal hierarchy, and with this structure "unspoilt natural feeling" is said to agree. Furthermore, for Emil Brunner the family in its original hierarchical-patriarchal structure is the source and type of all social order. (Regarding Brunner's book, *Justice and the Social Order,* John A.T. Robinson, an Anglican bishop, makes the remark that as an Englishman he could not "help seeing peeking out from time to time the presuppositions of a conservative, somewhat complacent petit-bourgeois society".)

So the Protestant churches, too, are infected with Aristotelian notions of woman's inferiority—passed on to them down through the centuries through Catholicism and Anglicanism. We need to remember that John Knox and Martin Luther were once seminary-trained Roman Catholic priests.

Yet some Protestant churches do ordain women, posing a substantial problem for ecumenical theologians in all the

Christian churches who hope one day to be joined again in one Christian union. The very dividing point may be the question of women's ordination, which is almost sure to sever relations between some churches externally, just as it is dividing them internally. The efforts of the churches to respect one another in their efforts toward reunion can result in some ironic situations.

In Toronto, at an ecumenical service held at St. Michael's Roman Catholic Cathedral a few years ago (when ecumenical fervour was at its height) the late Dr. Harriet Christie, a woman minister of the United Church, sat up at the front of the church along with male ministers of various denominations and the Catholic clergy. No Catholic woman has ever been accorded such a privilege, because none has ever been ordained. Several Catholic women and nuns remarked on this wondering aloud when the time would come when they would be recognized in their own church? Catholic clergy accept ordained women in the other churches but will not accept them in their own. And it could be questioned as to how seriously ecumensim is really being taken, in view of the fact that all recent statements from the pope show him to be inflexible in his attitude to the question of ordained women. We can surmise that the ecumenical intentions of the United Church are not taken seriously in Rome, where the Vatican is more interested in cementing relations with the Orthodox churches—which are opposed to ordaining women. (Nevertheless, taking heart from ecumenism Roman Catholics have called for a conference on the ordination of women in Roman Catholicism, planned by representatives of twenty-six national organizations, seminaries and religious communities. The Ordination Task Force Committee is based in Detroit, Michigan, and the conference is to be held there in November 1975.)

Women in Judaism

In May 1972 a third-year rabbinical student, Sandy Sasso, shocked the American Jewish Committee when she spoke to them on male chauvinism in the Jewish tradition. She took them first on a scholarly tour of the book of Ruth, in the Bible, and after they had accepted her credentials as a scholar, she turned to the actual position of women.

In the Old Testament, she said, a wife is a possession of her husband. She gains status in the community only by bearing sons. A man can get a divorce if his wife is insane or barren, a woman cannot. Daughters cannot inherit unless there are no male heirs.

Ms. Sasso contended that present day ceremonies in Jewish life perpetuate the inferiority of women. The birth of a boy is still received with more joy than that of a girl. In Jewish art "the pious man is portrayed in ecstatic rapture, singing, dancing, praying or poring over pages of the Talmud. Women are eternally lighting the Sabbath candles or cradling a small child. With regard to them there's nothing else for the artist to paint."

When Sasso had finished her talk a man in the audience, with an edge in his voice, said to her: "I don't understand why women should be looking for equality when you've always had superiority!" A matron commented: "She's pretty enough—but she has a lot to learn."

Others wondered what would happen to the Jewish home if women became liberated from their traditional roles. Ms. Sasso said she wished she could predict what would happen to Jewish women in a new life-style. She added drily that "Maimonedes said that woman doesn't have the power to prophesy".

Maimonedes is a much-admired Spanish-born Jewish philosopher (1135-1204), who was a devotee of Aristotle. St. Thomas Aquinas, born twenty-one years after Maimonedes's death, was greatly influenced by the teachings of the Jewish philosopher which wedded Greek philosophy to religious thought. This influence is apparent in Aquinas's *Summa Theologiae* which has remained the definitive work of Roman Catholic theology down to the present day.

Unlike Aquinas, however, who was fond of quoting Aristotle on almost everything, Maimonedes differed at times with the Greek. But he never questioned Aristotle's low view of women, although he himself was married.

Maimonedes had an unprecedented impact on Jewish thought. His works were an entire reinterpretation of Judaism dealing with every question relating to its religious, ritualistic, ethical and social life. He was eulogized everywhere even in his own time, but some critics were afraid that his work would become the one permanent authority on Judaism and said that Maimonedes had set himself up as a Jewish pope. They even accused him of pretended infallibility. In much of his writing Maimonedes is arrogant and elitest. There is no doubt that he has a higher opinion of some men than of others. He thought that men of learning, like himself, should not mix with common people, not even in religious ceremonies. He acknowledged that common people and even slaves were human beings who should never be cruelly treated, but he had contempt for their ignorance.

Maimonedes is one of a long line of scholars so enamoured of their own thinking processes and the life of the mind that their thoughts revolve almost exclusively on those abstract processes. Poetry and literature do not appeal to to them. They have little time for play, ordinary social intercourse or the pleasures of the senses. Anything sensual is considered inferior, decadent, and effeminate.

The association of intellectual activity only with men left the woman entrapped solely within her body—her mind was not taken seriously. In 1963, Rabbi Abraham Feinberg (then of Holy Blossom Temple, Toronto) showed his uncritical acceptance of this view: "For women, childbearing will always remain the central reality of life . . . equality of sexes is nonsense when the most vital and necessary task of life, to reproduce itself, is the *primal responsibility of one sex,* and an auxiliary function for the other."[9] Such an extreme dichotomy in sex roles means that the male is oriented to public life, where he can dominate and control (ignoring the needs of women) while he is also free to disclaim responsibility for fathering his children. On the other hand women are oriented only to the family and can use the excuse that God (and Rabbi Feinberg, the spokesman for God) insists that they be there. This leaves them free to refuse to accept any social responsibility for public order, even when that affects their families and children. If they do accept such social responsibility and attempt to make the world they live in more humane they are accused of wanting to be like men, of wishing to take over the prerogatives of men. The view of women solely as child-bearers, of course, leaves unanswered the question of what to do with single women. (St. Paul himself stated that he did not know what to do about single women—virgins—since on that he had no command from God.)

Some Jews have not agreed with Rabbi Feinberg's dictum. In 1837, Abraham Geiger, a Jewish reformist rabbi in Germany, pleaded for woman's religious equality with men. This meant revisions of marriage laws and marriage services in which women were regarded as inferior, and taking down the partition in the synagogues segregating women from the male congregation.

Reformed Jews have made steps towards acknowledging the equality of women, including accepting them as rabbis,

[9]*Globe and Mail,* February 16, 1973.

but Orthodox Jews (like traditional-minded Catholics and Protestants) refuse to change any of their long-outmoded attitudes, and even reformed Jewish congregations retain, consciously or unconsciously, many of their prejudices.

Conclusion

Religious discrimination against women, as we have seen, is a long-standing tradition. The patriarchal legacy of Judaeo-Christianity, and Greek philosophical notions of woman's inferiority, have been passed down for centuries in universities and theological schools. The result has been the persistent and pervasive erosion of the esteem and self-esteem of women.

In contrast to the philosophical schools of Athens, Homeric Greece did not see the woman as inferior. And in very early Judaism the woman also had a high role. It is evident that the Greek philosophers and the Judaeo-Christian theologians are reinterpreters of a much older tradition and reacters against it. So-called "pagan" antiquity which preceded them saw the female's ability to give birth as awe-inspiring and powerful. Ancient man saw sex as sacred (as primitive men do today) and ritualized it in the temple to ensure fertility of both man and the land. He saw his gods as both male and female and was unable to visualize the creative power of God without these two forces. The Book of Genesis itself, which writes the first chapter of the ensuing demise of women, admits that male-female humanity is a reflection of God. The ancient male archetype of nature religion (from which all other religions have evolved) was the Sky-God, the father-husband figure who lay upon the earth and through the phallic rays of the sun penetrated her and made her fertile. The female archtype was the earth herself, giving birth to burgeoning life in all its forms, animal, plant and human.

In antiquity man's generative powers were highly re-garded, but Greek philosophy instead revered the *mind* of man. The male archetype went through an evolution—from Sky-God to Sun King, to the idea of the mind of man as the bearer of enlightenment, reason, as ruler of the world.

In the images of the earth-fertility goddess the attributes accented are breast and buttocks. The features are not delineated, the face is vacant. The "new thought" of the philosophers and the theologians left her that way. Ob-viously this vacant-faced mindless woman could not be trusted with anything except child-bearing, said St. Paul, influenced by the Greeks. In the Middle Ages St. Thomas Aquinas agreed with Paul and regarded the woman as "matter". The female presence was barred from the univer-sities and the theological schools where the male mind held sway. If she was given any education at all it was mainly to fit her to deal with children.

The male castrates himself with his own ideas of his men-tal superiority over the woman and then blames her for his castration. His mind, he feels, is able to transcend the body and wing its way directly to its creator, God. In con-trast the woman must remain forever fettered by her bio-logical, material and sensual nature, reaching God only indirectly through man—ever the object, consciously or unconsciously, of his contempt.

The rape of the earth and woman that has persisted for centuries is related to the view that both are under the domination of the mind of man, and that this has been decreed by God. And the same view is responsible for the abuse and cruel treatment of animals—regarded as inferior beings without souls and the reasoning power of the human male. Any race of people who retained close contact with nature (such as the "barbarian" hordes from the north who swept over Greece and Rome) were regarded as inferior.

When the New World was discovered and new races of people had to be assessed, they were weighed and measured according to Aristotle and found wanting (thus North American Indians were regarded as inferior and suitable to be enslaved).[10]

The further men have raised themselves to the heights in their contemplation of God, the greater their contempt for women. There are hundreds of examples of this: St. Augustine, St. Paul, St. Bonaventure, Thomas Aquinas, Maimonides, Tertullian, Luther, Calvin, John Knox—a vast array of popes, clergy, theologians, philosophers and scholars down through the centuries. And not only in the Western tradition. The contemplators of God who reject women are also in evidence in the Oriental tradition: Buddha, who leaves his wife and his marriage bed to embrace a life of solitary contemplation and divine enlightenment; Confucius, the sage of China whose contempt was so great that he was horrified if male and female garments were hung on the same peg; Manu, the religious law-giver of India who placed women always under some man's protection—her father's, her husband's or her son's (although in earlier times Indian women were equal and taught in the philosophical and theological schools). The list is endless.

Ultimately all discrimination against women can be said to have its roots in the male interpretation of religion. The feminist revolution now in evidence everywhere in the world often fails to grasp that fact because today we have managed to divorce religion from everyday life in a manner which was never possible even fifty years ago.

If women are really to destroy the *basic* prejudice against them they must deal analyticially with this long religious tradition and eliminate it by producing women scholars in

[10] Lewis Hanke's *Aristotle and the American Indian* (Bloomington: Indiana University Press, 1970).

every religious field who can effectively argue against the male-oriented view of religion. Little of this is being done. Until it is discrimination will continue, both in religion and in secular society, which retains in many subtle ways the prejudicial religious attitudes to women.

Ana Alberro was born in Spain and moved with her family to Colombia, South America after the Spanish Civil War. She attended university there, travelled throughout Latin America and later came to Canada where she received a degree in sociology at York University. With Gloria Montero and a group of Spanish-speaking women she founded the Centre for Spanish Speaking Peoples in Toronto. She is currently working on a study of the women's movement in various Latin American countries.

Barbara Adams

Gloria Montero is of Spanish ancestry and is a freelance writer, critic, broadcaster and filmmaker. She has worked on films in Canada, France and Spain and has recently completed with her husband, writer-director David Fulton, a film on the Canadian printmaker Leonard Hutchinson. She was one of the co-founders (with Ana Alberro) of the Centre for Spanish Speaking Peoples in Toronto. Her current project is a book on immigrant women.

The Immigrant Woman

Ana Alberro and Gloria Montero

"My association with the girls from Europe gave me a chance to know something of the minds of their employers and some of this knowledge was painful, but revealing."

There is no doubt the oppression of any woman in a minority group is always overshadowed by the common oppression suffered by both males and females of the group. However, information available on the immigrant woman in Canada is especially meagre. She is sometimes viewed in terms of her ethnicity, her cultural background probed through studies of racial-religious differences. But usually she is seen simply as an appendage to her man. Her own values and concerns have been largely ignored.

In 1971, 121,900 immigrants entered Canada. Of these, 61,455 (slightly more than half) were female. Of this figure, 17,429 were single women over sixteen years of age. Add to these the 4,529 widowed, divorced and separated women and we have in this one year alone, 21,958 immigrant women—one in three of every woman entering the country—financially responsible for themselves and, in many cases, for their families, too.[1] This in itself belies the standard image of the small, self-effacing figure dressed in black who has little concern beyond what she puts on the table for

[1]Immigration Statistics, 1971. Canadian Immigration Division, Department of Manpower and Immigration.

131

her husband to eat for supper. Yet for a great many Canadians this continues to be the stereotype of the immigrant woman.

Our own experience with immigrant women proved so many of the common assumptions about them to be false that early in 1974 we undertook a study of women in the Latin American community of Toronto in order to provide a basis for a more accurate assessment of the woman who comes to find her "second chance" in Canada.

Latin Americans form one of the biggest migratory waves to Canada in recent years. In 1963 there were few Latin Americans in Toronto. By 1973 the number had grown considerably. Most of them do not yet appear in official statistics. The majority entered Canada as visitors before the November 30, 1972 change in immigration ruling and then applied for landed status from within the country. Most of those who have arrived since the November 1972 cut-off date have remained with tourist visas and work permits which allow them to take jobs Canadians refuse to do.

We chose two of the largest sub-groups in the Latin American community for our study: Ecuadorian women of peasant or working-class background,[2] and as a contrast the urban, middle- or lower-middle-class, more professional women from Uruguay.

Fifty women from each group were interviewed. All of them had arrived in Canada between 1969 and 1973, were landed immigrants and ranged in age from twenty to thirty-six years. The Ecuadorian women had an average of grade six education plus training in a vocational skill, such as sewing, dressmaking, or hairdressing. The Uruguayans were primary and secondary school teachers, guidance teachers,

---

[2]Differentiation must be made between the small-holding peasant and the labourer peasant whose economic and social conditions are such that she cannot dream of emigrating.

infant care specialists, social workers, nurses, music teachers, and so on, with an average of five years post-secondary education.

All the Uruguayans had European ancestors. Uruguay is a country whose population is almost entirely white. Native Indians were exterminated during colonization and discrimination has kept the small black population from mixing racially.

The Ecuadorians were a racial mixture of either Indian-white or Indian-black-white. Unlike Uruguay, Ecuador has a large population of Indian or Mestizo stock. Along the coast the presence of the black slaves is still carried over in the racial make-up of the population though few pure black Ecuadorians are to be found today.

We learned that the respondents were forced to emigrate to Canada by the economic situation in their countries. This follows a classic pattern. While war and political oppression always have forced millions of people to abandon their countries and seek new lands and an opportunity to start again elsewhere, history shows us that the major migratory waves to North America have consistently coincided with economic pressures in the country of origin, that immigrants have had to look for new means of subsistence outside their regional boundaries.

Ecuador and Uruguay are the smallest Spanish-speaking countries in South America, though both are rich in natural resources. Ecuador's oil is exploited by United States interests and Uruguay is a classic model of a pseudo-British colony whose economy is now dependent on the large American monopolies. Inflation is at an all-time high in both countries. Inflationary conditions, the high rate of unemployment, and the repressive political policies of the military dictatorships endured by both countries have been the main reasons for the recent migratory waves.

Interestingly, among the working class women we found a general consensus that if it had been possible, they would have preferred to go to the United States. In a world divided into what economists have called the centre and the periphery, it is understandable that the peoples from the periphery turn to the centre in the hope of improving their lot. But with the hardening of United States immigration policy with respect to Latin Americans, they chose Canada as the "second-best" land of opportunity. This opinion was not shared by the more educated, middle-class Uruguayans, who chose Canada for reasons of international policy and because of an anti-American bias prevalent among many middle-class Latin Americans.

It might be pointed out that contrary to a popularly-held view of immigrants, none of the women involved in the sample (or their husbands) had ever collected unemployment insurance or been on welfare.

Canada has provided the Ecuadorian women with their very first adequate medical and dental care, the chance to save a few cents, and their first real entry into a tantalizing consumer's market.

They are not interested in owning a home of their own here. At least 70 percent of them claim that in a few years, when they have saved enough to start a small business of their own, they would like to go back to Ecuador. In the meantime, they buy everything they can—small electro-domestic appliances, clothing, jewellery—planning to take it with them when they return.

The Ecuadorian woman concedes that her relationship with her man revolves around maintaining intact his sense of manhood. However, she is well aware of her own strengths and maintains a certain independence. In almost all cases she has her own bank account separate from that of the man, makes most of the decisions regarding purchases, and considers herself financially responsible for her children.

Though all of the Ecuadorians were living with men, only 50 percent of them had entered into a legal marriage contract. Instead, they enjoy more or less stable relationships and very often have children fathered by a man other than the one they are living with at the moment. If it should be necessary for them to be formally married in order to legalize their immigrant status in Canada, they are presented with a real dilemma. One woman in this situation who had been living with a man for eighteen years, who had borne three of his children and who had a well-paid job compared with most other immigrant women, told us that she was not prepared to lose her freedom and chose instead to leave the country.

This reluctance by the Ecuadorian woman to legalize her marital status does not indicate a lack of loyalty to her man. She expects, too, that he be loyal to her. But different standards apply for married men and women. There is a tacit understanding that an occasional adventure on the part of the man will not have a destructive effect on the marital relationship. But the woman is well aware that he will not accept the same type of adventure from her.

However, we found that the Ecuadorian women approached the problem of companionship in a practical and straightforward manner. If a woman has come to Canada without her husband she may arrange to live with another man under the clear understanding that this situation will be temporary. A twenty-six-year-old woman told us that she felt this kind of arrangement was absolutely necessary to her since living by herself in a strange culture had proved to be a lonely and distressing experience. As a woman living alone here, far from her family, she also felt very vulnerable.

The feeling among all of these women is that they have

come to Canada to work, to save a few cents and eventually to go back to Ecuador. This is not a time for distractions. Their lives revolve around other immigrants, not necessarily Spanish-speaking. They have no contact with Canadian men. Any fair-complexioned male is considered a *gringo*—handsome enough, perhaps, but definitely remote from their lives.

Strong family ties prevail among Ecuadorian immigrants. Many of these women first became mothers while still in their teen-age years. And even now, faced with all the problems of migrancy, their lives revolve around their children.

Many of the women who entered Canada without an immigrant visa and who then applied for landed immigrant status from within the country—a lengthy process of deportation and appeal that may take up to two years—left their children in Ecuador in the care of a grandmother or aunt, intending to send for them once they became established. But after being here for a short time a mother begins to realize that the lack of adequate subsidized day-care facilities and Spanish-speaking babysitters presents serious problems. If she sends for her children she wonders how she will take care of them. Sometimes the husband and wife work different shifts so that one of them is always at home with the children. But even this solution, when possible, is far from ideal as it means the man and woman are rarely together.

One young woman, mother of three small children, only agreed to leave her relatives and her country and come to Canada when it was arranged that her children would accompany her and her husband in their move. The journey was financed by the sale of their small house in Ecuador, plus money they borrowed on the understanding they would pay it back soon. Both the woman and her husband knew it was imperative that they begin work as soon as they arrived here. The first shock came when the children were handed a deportation order while the parents were given work permits. They started to fight the children's deportation while looking for work and for an acceptable way of solving the problem of the children's care. Eventually, the woman was given a deadline to start work by a prospective employer and feeling desperate, opted for leaving the two smaller children alone in the care of their older brother, five years old. The children were to be alone from 6:30 a.m. to 3:30 p.m. when the father returned from work. The parents fought the deportation with all their resources but eventually had to give up and send the children back to Ecuador to be with their grandmother.

Because of all these pressures many women prefer to leave their children in Ecuador and work long, hard hours here to send back what money they can for their support and education. Their main concern is that their children get an education. It is a concern not always shared by the man who sometimes feels that children do not learn much of practical value at school and that, in any case, there is little chance for a member of the "poor", as they call themselves, to make it in a professional life.

These women have tremendous endurance; they know that only through their courage and will can their children survive. This knowledge provides them with a great source of strength from which to draw in the dozens of oppressive situations they face every day in their homes, their work places and in the community at large.

Very few of the Ecuadorians in the study were churchgoers, although almost all had strong religious beliefs. Most of them wore religious medals around their necks along with amulets that they believed would bring them health and good fortune. The explanation for this lies, perhaps, in the fact that Christianity was introduced to Spanish America with the sword. Acceptance of the Cross thus became a form of self-preservation. The native peoples accepted it, but without surrendering their traditional rites and symbols.

Asked how many Canadian friends they had, the Ecuadorians all came to the realization that not only did they have no Canadian friends but that, in fact, they had almost no contact at all with Canadians. The immediate person supervising their work at the factory was usually a non-Canadian, non-Spanish-speaking immigrant. Neighbours showed little curiosity about them. None of them had ever been invited to share a cup of coffee with a Canadian neighbour.

Of course it is hard to talk to someone if you have no common language. The Ecuadorian woman usually enrolls in an evening English language course. It is a difficult learning experience. Her lack of formal education in her own country is an almost impossible barrier to learning English now as an adult. What is more, by the time the class begins she has been up since 5:30 or 6:00 a.m., has worked hard all day at the factory, has come home, made dinner and cleaned the house. Perhaps her husband's work hours are different from hers and the children have to be taken care of. She soon decides that those hours in the evening are too precious to be spent in English classes. Besides, the teacher talks about verbs and prepositions but not how to ask for a raise or how to buy a pair of stockings.

Most of the women work in labour-intensive industries with a low level of automatization where wages are consistently minimal. Even in the more automated industries, a division of labour keeps them in the low-paid, labour-intensive jobs as assemblers and packagers. Many of them work as cleaners for maintenance firms, in hotels or restaurant kitchens. But whatever the work, they rarely are paid more than $2 an hour.

None of the women interviewed belongs to a union. In fact they are sceptical of any talk of unions. Even after becoming landed immigrants they fear that being a union member might somehow affect their right to stay in Canada. There is a general feeling that union activity is considered anti-government. The sensation of being in a precarious situation is never lost. The women have almost no knowledge of their rights as immigrants or workers in Canada. Canadian unions, infamous in the past for their lack of recognition of women workers, today almost totally ignore the special problems of the immigrant woman. Only one of the women had ever been approached by a Canadian union organizer; her reaction had been one of fear and mistrust.

The Ecuadorian has been brought up in a society where political activity at any level is denied women. Suffrage was granted to the women of Ecuador in the 1950s. But not one woman at the present time is in a position of political authority. With rare exceptions, only middle-class women hold university degrees. Indeed, until 1968 blacks and Indians, both women and men, were banned from the universities.

There is a deep feeling among the Ecuadorian women that something in this society is not right. The desperation they suffer when after leaving their own country, their families, and in some cases their husbands and children to come here they must work hard simply to exist; the immense, largely unattainable market forever in front of their eyes; the cramped attic rooms that must serve as bedroom, kitchen and bathroom all in one; the worry about leaving tiny pre-schoolers alone all day because they are unable to find day care for them; the display of wealth seen from a distance; the patronizing they must endure; the hostile, unsympathetic attitude of many official agencies—all this mounts steadily into a silent rage of frustration, indignation and rancour.

The situation among the more middle-class immigrant from Uruguay differs in a number of aspects. The married Uruguayan comes to Canada with her husband. He may even have preceded her by a few months in order to establish himself and find a place for them to live. Children arrive with the mother. In almost all cases marriages have been performed in the traditional legal manner.

The family may begin by renting a flat in an Italian or a Portuguese district of the city. As soon as they can afford it they will move to an apartment and start saving for the down-payment on a house. In most cases buying a house is the first economic goal set by the Uruguayan couple. They have come to stay.

The question of English is an important priority for the newly arrived Uruguayan. She enrolls immediately in an English language class leaving the children in her husband's care or paying an English-speaking babysitter. She does well in the course (after all, she already knew what verbs and prepositions were), and after two or three months ventures out to the nearest Manpower office where she is reassured that "people like you are what Canada needs". Two weeks later she may be called by Manpower for a job making sandwiches in a cafeteria and barely paying the minimum wage.

A certain disenchantment begins to grow. But she realizes that it is not possible to go back to Uruguay. The economic situation in that country continues to deteriorate, the political outlook is unstable. Anyway, they sold all their possessions before coming to Canada and spent what had taken years to save to pay their passage here.

She starts a long pilgrimage to government offices in an attempt to validate school diplomas. Usually she finds that though it took her five years after high school to become a teacher she cannot teach in Ontario. The six years of specialized training to become a day-care centre supervisor does not qualify her to work here in a day nursery. Though she was head nurse in a well-known Montevideo hospital she is not allowed to work as a nurse in Canada.

At the same time she feels herself cut off from most of the cultural activities to which she was accustomed in Uruguay. People here read different authors from the ones she knows; Canadian theatre-goers know almost nothing of the Hispanic theatre tradition; the French cultural influence so strong in her own country finds little echo here. In short, she is culturally isolated.

But life goes on. Somehow from the $2.00 or $2.20 per hour she earns in the factory or restaurant she manages to pay the babysitter and finds at the end of the month that by careful planning she and her husband have even saved a little money. Among the Uruguayans we find a strong resistance to entering the consumer market. Their goal is to save for a house and, in contrast to the Ecuadorians in our study, the Uruguayan immigrant will not buy the appliances shown on TV commercials until she first has a home in which to put them.

She continues to attend English language classes until she passes the Michigan Test of Proficiency in English or until she realizes that there is not much more to be learned at school. Her problem now is to find people with whom to speak English. She still speaks Spanish at home—it is important if the children are to remain bilingual. Her friends are all Spanish-speaking, often Uruguayan or Argentinian. However, she does go to P.T.A. meetings, has periodic talks with her children's teachers and feels free to let her feelings be known if she disagrees with what she sees happening at school. Eventually she may even meet non-Spanish-speaking people who share her values and her personal circle will expand. Yet very often she still does not have a Canadian friend.

Asked their motives for coming to Canada the Uruguayan women generally replied that they thought Canada could offer a better future for their children. University education is free in Uruguay but getting a job after graduation is difficult. There is a firm belief that despite the hardships incurred in the process of immigration there is always hope for the future. In a few years they may own a home, diplomas and certificates may be validated, and an acceptable job will be possible at last. Above all, there is always the hope that the children will form part of a Canadian middle-class society without language or ethnic barriers.

Family life among the Uruguayans differs little from that of any middle-class Canadian family. Motherhood is generally regarded as the ideal state for a woman. She may take a paid job, but if her family demands her presence at home there is no argument: her first obligation is to them.

Most of the Uruguayan women we interviewed attend church regularly. Going to church seems part of a social routine that enables a woman to meet both old and new friends. It also provides a base for the children's adjustment to the new culture. Generally the children of these Uruguayan families have little difficulty adjusting to life in Canada. Both parents place a great deal of emphasis on the importance of education and the children seem to integrate quickly into the total school environment.

The sexual relationship between the Uruguayan woman and her man follows traditional middle-class patterns found almost everywhere in the western world. The Canadian man does not seem as remote for her as for the working-class Ecuadorian woman, a fact usually demonstrated in a more vigilant attitude on the part of her husband.

Half a century ago, in the 1920s, the then President of Uruguay Jose Battle y Ordonez, a radical in his time, introduced some of the most progressive legislation of the age: schools and hospitals were secularized; the word *God* was deleted from the presidential oath; the eight-hour working day was introduced, along with the pension plan and other social benefits; and suffrage was granted to women.

However, fifty years later, though Uruguayan women play a more active political role than their sisters in Ecuador, only one woman has ever succeeded in being elected to the Legislature.[3] In Canada, the idea of becoming an integral part of politics on any level is generally disregarded as impossible by the Uruguayan immigrant. Elections in France or Britain are often given more attention than a provincial election in Ontario.

However much the Uruguayan might be considered the prototype of the "ideal" immigrant to Canada, she too suffers always a deep sense of alienation from the country and its people.

There is a strong suggestion throughout this study that the ability to integrate into Canadian life cuts right across national boundaries to the class structure of the community. It does not matter much if a woman speaks Spanish, Chinese, Greek or Italian. There may be minor discrepancies because of cultural or religious customs. But if her background is middle-class she will have values and habits that make it easier to manoeuvre the brash, every-woman-for-herself con-

---

[3]Early in 1973 all democratic procedures were suspended in Uruguay and the country is now ruled by a military junta.

sumer society she finds here. And however successful the process of integration, it is only relative. The sense of isolation remains, compounded by the fact of being a woman in a society still geared in its laws and attitudes to the dominance of the male.

Canadian women are now seeking ways to work together to meet the problems of a new age. They pushed for a Royal Commission on the Status of Women. Why shouldn't all the recommendations of that report, not only those affecting immigration, be applied to immigrant women as to all the others?

In 1967, 57 percent of all postwar immigrants to Canada were living in the province of Ontario. In 1968, 52 percent of the landed immigrants arriving in Canada planned to settle in Ontario and half of these (47,736) were women. Over 75 percent of the women were between fifteen and sixty-four years old, thus falling into what is commonly regarded as the working-age group. In the Ontario population at large only 61 percent was of working age in the same year.[4] Thus in Ontario there are proportionately more women of working age among immigrants than in the population at large.

Forty-six percent of the women immigrants to Ontario in 1968 intended to work.[5] In fact proportionately more immigrants, both women and men, form part of the labour force than do native-born Canadians. A study done in 1967 showed that 40 percent of postwar immigrant women were in the labour force compared to 33⅓ percent of the Canadian-born.[6]

[4] *Working Women in Ontario,* Ontario Deparment of Labour, Women's Bureau.

[5] *Ibid.*

[6] N.H.W. Davis and M.L. Gupta, *Labour Force Characteristics of Post-War Immigrants and Native-Born Canadians 1956-1967* (D.B.S., Special Labour Force Studies No. 6).

The same study indicated that the higher proportion of immigrant women workers derives from the fact that more of them had always worked, whether married or not, and this pattern was continued in Canada. This is no doubt because a very high percentage of immigrant women have working-class backgrounds and (unlike their middle-class sisters who often stop working when their first child is born) continue to work throughout their lives, taking only a few weeks off to have their children. Since economic need is accentuated when a family emigrates to a new country, the traditional work pattern is reinforced upon arrival in Canada.

Another factor in higher work-force participation among immigrant women is education. Surprisingly, for it violates another stereotype, when the educational level of the immigrant woman is compared to that of her Canadian sister we find that although many immigrants have only an elementary education or some high school training, more female immigrants than native-born Canadian women have completed secondary school or university.[7]

Once she has obtained work the immigrant woman experiences many difficulties, some of which she shares with all working women, some specific to her as an immigrant. One of these, of course, is low wages. Most immigrant women, like women in the population at large, work to supplement a low family income of less than $4,000.[8] It is incongruous that the attitude persists that women need (or deserve) less money for their work than men.

Barriers exist to women's financial independence although statistics and changing life-styles indicate women ought to be independent regardless of marital status. A wife

[7]*Ibid.*

[8]Zuker and Callwood, *Canadian Women and the Law* (Copp Clark, 1971).

who goes to work must consider the expenses of employment, especially child care, the additional taxes her husband will have to pay, all of which cut greatly into the total family earnings.

Some otherwise good provincial legislation on labour matters leaves many immigrants open to exploitation. Ontario's Equal Opportunity Act of 1970, which prohibits discrimination because of sex or marital status, is applicable only to those businesses with six or more employees. This leaves unprotected the thousands of women, a great many of them immigrant women, who work in some 3,500 small manufacturing establishments.[9]

In many instances women are denied the same fringe benefits as men. Some 90 percent of Canada's one-parent families are headed by women, yet the whole area of health and pension plans, where legislation is inadequate, contains many factors which are discriminatory toward women. Many pension plans provide for earlier retirement for women than for men despite the fact women have a longer life expectancy. Other plans provide fewer benefits for the survivors of married women employees and even fewer for single women. In some cases the benefits for all women, with or without dependents, are less than those for men.[10]

Immigrant women workers continually ask why it is not possible to take their maternity leave in a more flexible manner. Why does it always have to be eight weeks before and six weeks after the birth? Many immigrants feel that if they could work up to two weeks before the birth when they are well and have ten weeks to nurse the baby afterward, the whole process would be more natural and easier to deal with emotionally.

[9] *Canadian Women and the Law.*

[10] *The Status of Women in CUPE 1971,* pp. 18, 19.

Despite all the figures showing that most immigrant women—single or married—work and will work throughout most of their lives, almost all of the programs for immigrant women across the country take place during the day, usually with day care provided. They are programs for women with pre-school children. Many of the programs are excellent, providing contact and friendship for the immigrant on a personal, one-to-one level. But they are directed at only a small part of the total female immigrant group.

What of the women who are here alone, living in a small room with little opportunity outside work to meet anyone at all? Or the women who work all day, come home to cook dinner for their families, take care of their children, then fall exhausted into bed? For many of these women, sheer survival is the only issue. The old, warm, extended family relationships are not there anymore to soften the stress of living in a new country. On top of this, a husband struggling with the extra problems of working in a strange land very often places heavy demands for emotional support on his wife.

The questions that the immigrant woman asks of the society are exactly the same questions for which native-born Canadian women are seeking answers. Yet Canadian women and their immigrant sisters continue to view each other warily, if at all, through a haze of stereotypes. This despite the fact that as women, mothers, daughters, sisters and lovers they have much in common and could provide each other with significant mutual support.

Canadian women, now so determinedly seeking new ways to bring down the old barriers, cannot afford to ignore any longer the enormous potential of this group of their sisters.

Family planning, day care for children, job discrimination, union organizing, the law, the status of women, are all topics which touch, affect and concern every one of the 10,772,942 women living in Canada, whether she was born here or chose to come here to live. They are the logical starting points toward bringing immigrant women and native-born women closer together.

But the onus is on the Canadian, more or less secure in her own culture. She must find ways to involve the immigrant in smashing the stereotypes. She must invite her to explore new strategy to organize around the problems of living as complete, caring human beings in a society whose values are increasingly material.

The Canadian woman has a great deal to share with her immigrant sisters. If she can keep an open mind and look beyond the surface she might even find she has something important to learn from their different values and lifestyles and, above all, from their experience.

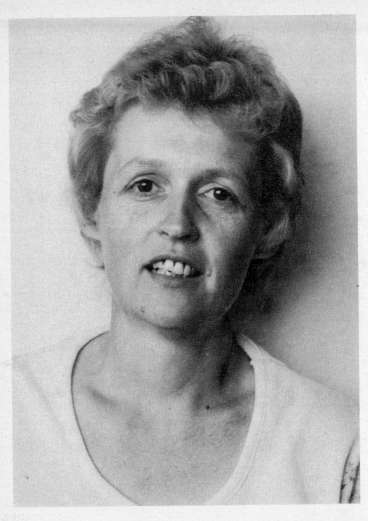

Norma Taylor lives with her husband and three of their five children on their sheep and grain farm near Biggar, Saskatchewan. She is an active member of the National Farmers Union and of the Saskatchewan Environmental Advisory Council. Of major importance to her is the redevelopment of rural Saskatchewan and especially the formation of labour intensive cooperative farms in which women and men would work as equal partners.

"All This for Three and a Half a Day": The Farm Wife

Norma Taylor

"There is no class of people who have suffered so much from wrong thinking as the farmer. Perhaps the women on the farm felt it more than the men, for women are more sensitive about such things. . . ."

In 1972 I spoke to a group of New Democratic Party women in Saskatoon on the role of women in politics. Also on the speakers' list was Mary Carter, a Saskatoon judge. Mary said something I'll never forget when referring to women on welfare and women who are poor: "You see, the trouble with the poor is that they just haven't enough money."

I have had the opportunity to travel through much of rural Saskatchewan these past few years working with the National Farmers Union and the former Saskatchewan Farmers Union. I have watched a slow, sick deterioration of farm homes—still no running water, still no improvements, still no paint on buildings. You see, the trouble with the poor farm wife is that she just doesn't have enough money.

Yet economic necessity has made the farm wife an integral part of the entire farming operation. It has always been difficult to afford hired help, and she is the cheapest possible source of labour. She is cook, baker, gardener, accountant, part-time butcher, seamstress, hired man and mother. And all this for three-and-a-half per day. (No, not dollars—three meals and half the bed.)

The work that farm wives have performed over the years

151

has in fact been largely responsible for maintaining the position of agriculture in the Canadian economy. Forty-two percent of Canada's Gross National Product is derived from farming and its related industries. In Saskatchewan the figure is closer to 80 percent.

The farm wife's work begins, as it does for other women, at home. Lack of adequate water supplies on farms is still a reality for most farm women. I can think of no other convenience that is so necessary for the well-being of the whole family. Water is taken for granted in towns and cities, but many farm wives still catch it in rain barrels to heat for washing. I waited twenty years to have the flush toilet installed. It had to be done finally on borrowed money.

Being the gardener and the cook/baker is a full-time job in itself. Processed foods appeal less to the farm family because they are used to home-grown, home-cooked meals. Huge gardens are planted, cared for with the help of the whole family, and prepared for winter. It is not unusual to spend three hours a day in strawberry or raspberry patches. I have frozen as much as 300 cobs of corn for winter. Most farm women bake their own bread; the quality of commercially-baked bread leaves a great deal to be desired. Chickens, ducks, geese, and turkeys make up a large part of the winter's meat supply. Most farm wives kill, pluck, draw, and prepare these fowl for the freezer.

In harvest time meals are very often packed and served in the fields. If the cook is lucky the fields are close and she will have plenty of time to start the next meal. Huge amounts of food are cooked during some harvests. A typical list might include a half of beef, one whole turkey, one whole lamb (approximately 250 pounds of meat), and all the related vegetables, desserts, and side dishes. We have often had twelve people to feed.

And of course being the mother means that family demands are ever-present—school lunch preparation, clothing maintenance, homework supervision, housekeeping.

But what makes the farm wife different from her urban sisters is that she is also the "hired man". This makes all the other jobs much more difficult to keep up with. Despite their heavy workload, however, I believe that most farm wives are happy to stay on their farms. What they find frustrating is that their labour is neither recognized nor adequately rewarded.

As a farm wife I am totally dependent on my husband's income. He can claim me as a tax exemption, of course, but if I earn more than $250 he is placed in a higher tax bracket and can no longer claim me as a dependent. Nor can he deduct my salary as a business expense: the federal Income Tax Act prohibits it. A farm wife may save her husband hundreds of dollars by hauling the grain herself, but the Income Tax Act discourages him from paying her. It is cleverly designed: my husband is allowed to deduct as an expense the wages paid to any other person, including our children.

> In 1973 a child could have received income up to $1,700 and still be claimed as a dependent child. No individual tax return will have to be filed, unless the income was over that amount.[1]

The farm woman is thus placed in a double bind: she's either just a deduction or her salary jeopardizes her family's income by increasing her husband's taxes. I have been told by an income tax consultant that if a farm wife is hired by her neighbour as a truck driver, cook or other worker, the wages can be deducted by her employer as an expense. Her husband could then hire his neighbour's wife and claim her wages as an expense, and a great round robin of farm wives set in motion. What a foolish, unnecessary arrangement! Certainly it is one that is seldom used.

[1]*Free Press Weekly,* January 12, 1974. Department of National Revenue and C.F. MacGregor, an Ontario economist.

It seems obvious that salaries paid to farm women who assist in the farm operation in the capacity of employees should also be deductible as business expenses. Such an improvement would not be enough in itself, however.

The recent publication *Saskatchewan Women and the Law* includes one small paragraph on farming operations:

> In Saskatchewan, the law appears to be well settled, that where a crop is grown on the land owned by a married woman, and she and her husband reside on that land, the crop belongs to her, but [and herein lies the crunch] it can be held to be her husband's only when it can be shown that he carried on the farming operations as "head of the family" or as tenant of the land.

Of course he is *always* considered head of the family, and of course she does not have her own set of equipment, which she would need in order to prove she did the work. Even though she may work very hard for it the crop is his—and the income as well. In 1973 a newspaper report stated:

> It is commonly assumed under the law that the husband is always the owner of farm property. If a woman is widowed or divorced, she is *not* automatically entitled to half the assets, even though she may have worked side by side with her husband on that farm for 20 or 30 years. When the marriage ends by death she could be disinherited by the terms of her husband's will. When the marriage ends by divorce, she is entitled only to maintenance. [2]

The Murdock case in Alberta was a notorious demonstration of the law in action. Although she had worked on the ranch for years in every capacity and operated it alone almost half the time, Irene Murdock was denied any share in the business and her contribution judged "only normal" by the

[2] *The Western Producer*, November 15, 1973. Pat Abramson, professor of Continuing Education, University of Saskatchewan.

Supreme Court of Canada. Recent proposals for reform of
matrimonial property laws, however, offer hope that such
injustices will eventually be a thing of the past.[3] The Saskatchewan Law Reform Commission has recommended that
there be an equal sharing of most matrimonial property but
would extend the scheme only to those married after legislation was adopted. This has been strongly opposed by the
Saskatchewan Action Committee on the Status of Women
who want participation to be made retroactive so that all
farm women would benefit. As of January 1975 the Canada
Pension Plan gives equal status to male and female contributors, a change which had been strongly urged by
women's groups across Canada.

Of course the wife's economic situation is locked into
that of her family. Whereas most people in the work force
can count on rising incomes the farm family cannot. Farmers have no bargaining power in determining the price they
receive for their produce. Thus the farm family's economic
situation is always precarious. Budgeting on farms is nearly
impossible. Income is sporadic and is tied very closely to
the needs of the farm operation. Vaccines, weed sprays,
fuels, fertilizers, taxes, new machinery—all must be bought
before any improvements can be made. Making repairs is
the culprit that really plays hell with the budget. Machines
are built to break down. It is incredible that in this day of
man on the moon and advanced technology a baler or combine can't be built to last one harvest. But then huge profits
are made from repairs so why would they? A handful of repairs could cost $100. The list price in 1974 for a combine
drive belt, three inches wide by five feet long, was $85.65.

Farmers must often resort to borrowing money. But
credit is not what the farmer needs. All credit does is keep

[3] The public outrage unleashed by the Murdock case seems already to have had
its effects on some more recent, and happier, judgements.

him on the wheel running faster and faster in order to stay in the same place. Farmers need an adequate, stable income tied to the cost of production. And so do their wives. If the farmer's wife must continue to perform the same role in the future, appliances such as deep freezers, dishwashers, automatic washing machines and dryers are not luxuries, they are absolute necessities.

I resent the attitude held by some women who say to us: "Isn't it too bad that you haven't adjusted to being a farmer's wife? Isn't it too bad that you want a nice house and running water, and a clothes dryer? Isn't it too bad...."

And I also object to the way children are conditioned by school books to place such little value on rural life. These books imply that a farm is not a place where a family earns a decent living producing healthful food. Nobody ever goes to the farm to live but just to visit Grandpa. Everybody comes from the farm to the city. Positive attitudes about rural life must be encouraged in schools if the tidal rush to the cities is to be slowed.

My young son was told recently by a teacher in school that farmers are lazy. Try to tell a young lad whose father spends fourteen hours a day working, in the spring, summer and fall, that farmers are lazy!—a young boy who with his brother helps with the chores and with cultivating, swathing, hauling grain, and baling. It would make just about as much sense to say that the farm wife is lazy too.

The fact is that farm children must also be used as slave labour. There is seldom enough money to pay them anything. All of our five children started steering the grain truck around the fields when they were about five years old. Older chidlren on farms must babysit at a very early age. Farm mothers spend many an anxious moment in a truck in a field while a small baby is in the house being cared for by an almost equally small older sister or brother. This situation means that mothers must hurry into the house between loads of grain, and in the daytime must take small children with them for many hours while they haul the grain.

Many farm women suffer from isolation. Neighbours are so few in places that we are glad to see a rabbit run across the yard. First and foremost we need more farm families on the land. The total number of farms in Saskatchewan is rapidly decreasing. According to a report from The Saskatchewan Department of Agriculture:[4]

> Total number of farms in 1966 — 85,686
> Total number of farms in 1971 — 76,970
>
> Net migration of farms each year between 1966 and 1971 in the province is calculated to be 1,743 (766 are estimated to have started every year).
>
> Total number who left farming each year for *age* and *other* reasons is calculated to be 2,529.
>
> Total number of farmers retiring each year for the next *ten* years because of age alone is estimated to be 2,836.

Nothing is mentioned in this table about the number who leave for *economic* reasons. I suspect that these may be included in the "other" reasons. If this trend continues, as current opinion tends to accept as inevitable, the family farm may disappear completely. The farm woman of the future may find her function absorbed by the incorporated farm. It is to be hoped that such a lamentable development can be avoided.

Rural women's centres would help to alleviate our present

[4]*The Farm Reconnaissance Survey,* Report no. 1. Planning and Research Secretariat, Saskatchewan Department of Agriculture, p. 4.

isolation. We need places where women can trade information about such things as birth control, abortion, medical and emotional problems, and where we can discuss our situation as farm women and possible solutions. We need other women to talk to.

If a farm woman decides that a solution to her economic situation lies in taking a job away from the farm, what can she do to receive training? My own experience and that of one other woman may serve as examples, although whether or not they are typical is uncertain. I refer specifically to our experience with Canada Manpower. The following account was written by a close friend describing her three-year contact with Manpower offices in North Battleford and Saskatoon. She farms with her husband nearby and found at one point in her life that she had to find a job:

> I began going to Manpower three years ago. It sounds like an excellent program. Manpower will up-grade you, paying your living allowance and tuition. You can then go on to a training program, and again your living allowance and tuition will be paid. You are eligible for a moving allowance and to receive help in the purchase of a house. It seems to be a good program but with a poor record of performance. It is difficult to find out who is at fault.
> You are assigned a counsellor and on each succeeding visit her role seems to be that of finding some further block to make you ineligible. Since my counsellor was the only one who knew the rules it put me at a decided disadvantage.
> I said I was becoming desperate because of lack of finances. They asked me to produce financial records, and I brought income tax records which showed a five year loss. They seemed duly impressed but reminded me that I was not considered "head of the household" and that I made out no separate income tax, etc., etc. This again disqualified me. Another requirement I

couldn't meet was that you must have worked for the past three years. I had not done this since being the "hired man" on the farm is not considered work. Also there are simply no jobs available in rural areas. I was forced to make repeated trips to the city to consult with them, a round trip of 200 miles. All telephone calls made were long distance. When you're already in serious financial difficulties these added costs are a terrible burden.

Never once did I receive word of a job opportunity.

With the financial situation at a breaking point, I had to pin my counsellor down to a decision. She became abusive and angry, informing me that since she had to pay her own way she saw no reason why I shouldn't.

Manpower has you over a barrel and they know it. Tests were repeatedly scheduled and cancelled with no reasons given. The system appeared to be deliberately designed to force you to give up. I asked to see the manager of Manpower. He heard me out but informed me that he had no jurisdiction and that the counsellor had to decide. He was the manager, but he could do nothing! I wrote a university entrance examination for the course I chose and underwent batteries of tests and countless interviews. All because I wanted to work.

I was finally able to get a job on my own seventy miles away. It was not doing what I wanted to do but there was no job training offered for farm women for that. It was the "up" of hope to the "down" of despair.

In my own case, I decided to apply to Manpower for a grant to take a straight administration course. Farm management courses like these are available with pay for farmers who qualify. But does the farm wife qualify? The course I had in mind could be a considerable help for farm women who want to learn how to do the accounts properly. The courses are sponsored jointly by the Department of Education, the Department of Agriculture, and Manpower.

Agriculture Representatives make the recommendations but Manpower pays the expenses and therefore has the final say. I phoned our "Ag. Rep." and he assured me that though no "girls" had applied so far he saw no reason why one shouldn't. One qualification is that the applicant must be between the ages of twenty-one and forty-five. I still qualified in that department.

I phoned the Manpower office in Saskatoon and was told it had not yet been established whether or not women qualified. It depended on whether she could establish that she was in fact a partner and whether she already did the books. In other words you might not get a grant to learn how unless you already knew how.

Manpower grants should, in my opinion, be available to any deserving farmer regardless of sex. The courses they subsidize could, in fact, be specially geared toward the needs of farm women, with child care provided as an integral part of the program. They should not be designed to force women to leave their farms if they don't want to but rather to help them become more efficient and productive in the work of the farm. For instance, appliance repairs are a serious problem for the farm wife who may live a hundred mile from the nearest repairman. When breakdowns occur, she may be without her washer or dryer (if she has these) for many weeks. Manpower grants should be available for farm women to take courses in repairing appliances. Why not? Any woman who runs a $17,000 tractor, a three-ton truck, or a $20,000 combine can surely repair a washing machine.

Even if she has or can get job training, working away from the farm involves other problems. If she has pre-school children the farm woman must find someone to come in to help since there are as yet no child care centres in rural areas. Hired help in this respect is very expensive so her job must pay well. She must travel to her work and therefore she removes the car, a much needed vehicle, from the farm. Her husband cannot stay with small children in spring during seeding, nor in summer during summer fallowing or haying, nor during harvest time. She cannot leave in harvest time anyway because she may be the hired man or the cook (or more likely the hired man *and* the cook). Even if her children are old enough to be left alone, she is still the hired man. For these reasons she must take winter employment, usually on a part-time basis. And part-time winter employment is not well-paid.

Oh yes, the farm woman can become the Avon Lady. She can do the ordering, advertising, delivering, and maybe she could even make a profit if she didn't have to travel so far. The Avon and Tupper companies are the most magnificent "rip-offs" I know of. Not only do they exploit their "ladies" but these ladies in turn are forced to exploit their neighbours.

I also have a neighbour who has chosen a somewhat different task. She cleans ducks for American hunters, sometimes forty per day. She gets fifty cents a piece. It is well earned. She must keep one of the children home from school to help her sometimes.

After much soul-searching, the farm wife may decide it is just not worth it. She may continue to provide slave labour and be totally dependent on her husband's income. Mothers' allowances should be provided to mothers in these cases. Some dignity of income should be afforded the mother who must or wants to stay home.

In Saskatchewan we have a great many so-called "farm organizations". There are grain growers associations, cattle producers associations, hog and sheep producers associations. They are not, in fact, "farm organizations" but rather "commodity groups" dealing only with the production and sale of one farm product.

Women in these groups are there only if they own land and produce the product, otherwise they make the sandwiches for meetings. In the elevator companies, such as United Grain Growers and the Saskatchewan Wheat Pool, women are members only if they have a permit book to own the land and produce the product. Otherwise they are tolerated at meetings usually because of their aforesaid sandwich-making abilities and their willingness to cook for banquets.

Women may rise in the Saskatchewan Wheat Pool to the "committee" level. Beyond that, where the real decisions are made, they cannot go. Delegates and other officials make the real decisions, and unless a farm wife has a permit book she cannot become a delegate. There are very few farm women who are delegates, needless to say. At a recent meeting in Regina National Farmers Union women were told by a Saskatchewan Wheat Pool public relations officer, "Yes, we do have women. Why, recently one woman received a twenty-five-year pin for being a secretary."

To be really meaningful to women farm organizations must recognize them as capable of taking part in the policy-making that affects them as much as their families. The only organization that does this so far is the National Farmers Union. The NFU encompasses the production, sale, and marketing of all farm products. It is an organization made up of, financed by, and led by farmers. Women can be full members, as well as children of fourteen years and over. The membership is based on the farm family as a total unit. The NFU is different from the Saskatchewan Federation of Agriculture, another so-called farm organization, because it is made up only of farmers. The Federation has among its members the elevator companies and the fertilizer companies that make their money off the sweat of the farmer's brow. The two organizations are incompatible for that reason.

The NFU has a comparatively advanced attitude towards women. For example, for every position that is available in the organization for men there is a position available to women and young people in a parallel structure. Women and youths are "policy-making members". They are also, unfortunately, "automatically" members. When the canvassers call on potential members, they are supposed to talk to the woman and the children over the age of fourteen as well. This is not done often enough. The membership fee is the same for the whole family unit whether or not the farm woman or the farm youth have consented to join.

The picture I have painted of the farm woman looks something like this:

She values her way of life.
Her way of life is subject to constant political engineering.

She is essential to the economy.
She is cheap labour.

She is the backbone of her community.
Her community is disintegrating.

She is indispensable to the farming operation.
She is just a deduction.

She has no income of her own.
She has needs of her own.

She has little if any earning power.
She may also be the "hired man".

She needs training.
She is rural and may not get it.

Is her future any brighter? In some ways it looks grim. But there are also hopeful signs that farm women may be beginning to take action toward changing their situation.

Early in 1975 I attended a conference in Saskatoon composed of women active in various farm organizations and women's institutes across the country. It was probably the first time farm women had gathered together to discuss their common problems. The major concerns, of course, were in the area of farm economics. The channelling of government grants to producers rather than farm industries, orderly pricing, and improved services and training programs in rural areas were measures proposed to fight rural depopulation. The delegates also recommended that a research action program be set up to identify and meet the needs of women in rural communities. Each community would set up its own program according to its particular needs, with day-care centres a priority. Of course assured government funding would be essential in implementing such a program.

I hope this is the beginning of substantial changes for farm women. We love the clean air, the good wholesome food, the family unity, the peace and quiet of beautiful rural Saskatchewan. But without those changes it's not enough.

Fiona Nelson is a past chairman of the Toronto Board of Education and former member of the Metropolitan Toronto School Board. Before her election to these boards in 1969 she taught kindergarten and junior high school science. She is now a student at the University of Toronto Law School, a writer, broadcaster and gardening enthusiast.

Sex Stereotyping
in Canadian Schools

Fiona Nelson

"Sex contempt . . . began in the nursery but was fostered on the street, and nourished in the school. . . ."

I am part of a teaching clan. My mother, my sister, my husband and I are all teachers; and the teaching profession is the one I have had most to do with both in and out of the classroom.

From my job as kindergarten teacher to my 1974 position as chairman of the Toronto Board of Education, nothing could be farther from my experience than the shrinking violet or helpless female role. My mother, a Scottish immigrant, was left to fend for herself in this country with two small children and a lot of debts. At the beginning of the war, she took a job in a gun factory and studied shop trigonometry at night so that she could become a foreman. She worked day and night for several years, cleared up all the debts, and finally was able to buy a house.

I think the main liberating factor in my upbringing was that in our family there were jobs to be done, and the person who was able to, did them. I was sent off to do all the banking at about the age of six. I used to like fixing things, too—lamps, plugs, washers. There was no "man of the house"; just my sister and I were there to do these jobs, hence no sex role division ever cropped up.

167

Teaching is one of the few professions in which women have predominated, especially in the primary grades. It has been accepted as one of the traditional female occupations, in the same way that nursing has. I suppose in the public mind they are both extensions of mothering.

So closely identified was elementary school teaching with women that men entering the field used to suffer from the same sort of stigma that might still attach to a male nurse or secretary. However, now that many more men have entered elementary school teaching, the stigma has begun to give way. But very often men still feel they have to justify a preference for the primary grades to other men by saying that they are in it for the experience they need for promotion. They will not admit that they like little children. But even that is changing to some extent, especially since we have been establishing day-care centres in some of the schools, and boys as well as girls are working in them. Also some of the Local Initiative Project (LIP) grants have often involved boys working with little children in day-care programs and similar activities. Thus, at least among the young, this type of discrimination against males who like working with younger children is declining. But in the over-thirty age group a fair amount of discrimination against a gentler or more "mothering" sort of male teacher/pupil relationship is still present in the primary grades.

The schools are still shot through with sex role stereotyping at every level from early education to staff allocations and promotional practices. The big problem for women in the school system is achieving par with men in promotion to positions of responsibility. There has traditionally been a huge discrepancy between the number of men and women who are pushed for promotion. Women themselves until recently have assumed that their prime role was teaching and they neither put themselves forward for promotion nor were considered by anyone else.

No such lassitude is to be found in the promotion of men. Up-and-coming, ambitious young men are encouraged by more senior men. For instance, in elementary schools where there is no vice principal, there has always been a "key man", usually the teacher of the senior grade. He is the stand-in principal when the principal is out of the school. It is the sort of position that will eventually lead to promotion. It is still widely assumed that men are the only ones to be considered for such posts of responsibility. Progress towards equality has so far been slow, but there are some signs of change. While it is still held that administrative positions are male prerogatives, and that women in such positions are anomalies, the Toronto Board has been making strides in correcting the imbalance. This is one area in which I feel that my being fairly vocal on the board has been effective.

By the time I became chairman of the board in 1974, in the second year of my second term as trustee, the board had broken almost completely with its bureaucratic past.[1] We were neither the upholders of simplistic nonsense about the need to retain the hickory stick and go back to the "three R's", nor were we taken in by the futuristic audio-visual toys being installed by the provincial technocrats who would have loved to computerize everything, including, and probably especially, the teachers. I look back with a certain amount of satisfaction at having initiated issues which to some may have appeared not specifically educational in the narrow sense, but which were clear evidence of the board's new understanding that the school is an integral part of the community. At the board this new awareness has been demonstrated in decisions relating to expressways, preservation of ravines, retention of housing stock, public

---

[1] For a glimpse of the Eocene period in board evolution, see *Centennial Story*, a self-congratulatory blurb written by the board, published in 1954 and dedicated to "our friends, the Chartered Banks".

health matters such as lead pollution and nutrition, and of course the central issues of sex role stereotyping.

As board chairman,[2] I was very active in breaking a lot of this new ground, and people have been asking me what it was like being a woman in this position. The basic duty was of course to chair the board meetings. I was also the chief signing officer, which meant I signed official documents on behalf of the board. I was spokesman (spokeswoman, if anyone really insists) for the board on public issues, and I was usually the one called by the press for information. I was often asked to speak at Federation and at Home and School meetings, both inside and outside my own ward. And I tried to use the chairmanship as a platform for getting action on some of the broader municipal and social issues which were having their impact on the schools.

Another area of special concern to me has been the Women's Committee. This committee was formed about three years ago when there were a number of openings at the senior administrative level. Several people had retired at the same time, and one of the trustees on the board—a man—suggested that we set up a committee to investigate ways of promoting women to these higher positions. I amended the motion to say that we should at the same time be looking at how we socialize female children. That's something that needs to be kept visible. How can it affect the little girl in elementary school, for instance, who has a secret ambition to be an engineer or an architect or a doctor, yet is subtly made to feel somewhat frightened

[2] I don't see the need for all the soul-searching that goes on about such terms as "chairman", and I dislike the awkwardness that results from the attempt to force a perfectly good generic suffix into feminist ideology. I doubt if either "chairwoman" or "chairperson" does much to serve the cause. And just as I am convinced that what a seamstress displays in making a beautiful garment is not "workwomanship", I am perfectly content that "mankind" should include (if not embrace) "womankind" in its reference. "Man" is a far more variable term than many suppose, and some of its connotations are not sexist. Of course, I realize that there are those who would disagree with me.

about mentioning it to her playmates or parents?

The Women's Committee is an advisory committee to the board, and it is also a very handy monitoring device. It studies the employment practices of both the teaching and the non-teaching staff.[3] There are two sub-committees—one for teachers, one for non-teachers. It looks at how we treat our women employees, how we prepare them for promotion, and related matters. It functions as a kind of collective "ombudsman" with respect to female teachers. For example, a woman concerned about maternity leave and its application might solicit the committee's help. It's a clearing house for women's concerns, and as such it has two very important functions—it gives the women a feeling that there's an appeal procedure for them specifically, and it keeps the woman issue visible at all times.

The Women's Committee once sponsored a one-day workshop to which two people from every school in the city came just to talk about the place of women and the socialization of children in the educational system. It opened a lot of eyes.

The Affirmative Action program was discussed at that meeting. This is a project in which a subcommittee of the Women's Committee has been involved for the last few years. Its chief purpose is actively to seek out women for training as principals, reversing the old unquestioned policy of automatically passing them over for such a position.

It seems to have been effective to some extent. We now have three women superintendents—more than the rest of the province put together—and a handful of women high school principals. These are very recent developments and signal the emergence of a new policy on women in senior positions.

[3]An inequity recently uncovered in our schools, for example, concerned the appointment of assistant physical education heads. The boys' physical education departments are entitled to proportionately more assistant heads than the girls' physical education departments.

The Toronto Board is probably more receptive to such change than any other board in the province. Many members are still resistant to the idea of women in the higher jobs, of course, but the fact that Toronto does have some very successful women in supervisory positions has meant that these women are encountering less and less overt prejudice in dealing with their male colleagues. Our three women superintendents, for example, are very competent women who cannot be faulted on their performance, credentials or experience, and hence are respected by their colleagues.

These three women are no doubt exceptional, but we must be just as concerned about improving the position of the average woman teacher. As matters stand now, an incompetent man could achieve a position of responsibility much more readily than a competent woman. The elimination of sex stereotyping in this field is a matter of eliminating sex as a criterion. If the "superwomen" keep up the fight, eventually they might be a factor in helping the less gifted women to make gains too. This has been called tokenism by some but is one of the patterns that has been followed by many groups trying to achieve equality.

Another of the sub-committees is monitoring books and teaching aids. For sexism at its most blatant one would have to turn to the readers, the text books, and the films purporting to be teaching health or social studies. They also have plenty of pernicious class bias thrown in for good measure. Many changes have been made already. One of them was an addendum to the film catalogue on women's studies and concerns. After viewing some of the films we inserted warning evaluations against those with class and sexist bias.

I remember one film in particular called "Big People, Little People"—quite an incredible little eight-minute production intended for primary social studies, made in 1971.

It was very careful to reflect a racial mix, showing a lot of children playing adult roles with a black boy playing the mayor. But apparently the idea of female roles had never occurred to the filmmakers. Throughout the entire eight minutes, females appeared twice; the total time they were on screen was thirty-eight seconds; and each time they were carrying mops. The committee viewing this film dissolved into hysterics. If it had been prepared deliberately as a satire on sex stereotyping it couldn't have been better done.

Our inner city schools, of course, need more appropriate materials. We are trying to get inner city readers that portray the children in apartments and tenements rather than always in a suburban garden with a huge lawn, a dog and cat, mother in her apron, and father driving his car into the driveway. We are also looking at reading material that talks about single-parent families, that recognizes the fact that there is occasionally divorce, that there is occasionally death, and that there are occasional mixed marriages.

The change is perhaps slow in coming. One reason for the delay is the natural resistance to such changes by people who don't believe in them yet. The other reason is the expense. Completely replacing sets of readers in the schools involves an enormous amount of money which the province isn't prepared to provide. When I went to school, the readers were seven cents each. Now they cost several dollars. Part of the problem is purely economic. But I think not being able to afford the replacement is very often used as an excuse. To that I say, fine, don't replace them. The sexism and racism, I believe, can be very useful if the books are taken off the primary list and used as specimens of social pathology in the secondary schools. This is superb material for sociology classes, for women's studies courses, for family life courses—provided the teacher clearly understands the implied (and unconscious) message of the book or film. If she or he is sensitized to the biased message of this "recycled" material, then in many cases it could be used to generate discussion. This would be a marvellous way of drawing children's attention to the problem. The person in charge of the children, incidentally, has a far more pervasive influence on them than any of the teaching materials.

The guidance counsellors could do much to counteract some of the sex stereotyping in the high schools. Occasionally there are counsellors who demonstrate a new consciousness of the need to promote equal opportunity between the sexes. But in quite a few schools it is found that the girl interested in medicine is channelled into nursing, and the boy into doctoring.

The new courses in women's studies which are becoming popular in the universities are also being introduced in the high schools, and these may have some effect on consciousness-raising in the actual teaching situation. Several of the schools have approved courses. Some of them are sociological, and some are about women in history. The sociology courses tend to look at the role of women both in an historical and contemporary perspective. The purpose is to encourage students to think about women's roles and what they should be. These courses also tie in to many family life programs which deal with such issues as changing roles and life-styles. In some of the family life courses a great deal of discussion takes place about such new concepts as the single-parent family, and the widespread rejection of the idea of marriage. In the process, all the old assumptions about woman's role and the function of the family are being challenged. They are not being completely rejected, but there is much discussion going on about the new options that may be available.

Oddly, perhaps, it's women themselves who seem most in

need of re-education. Men do not have to work very hard to keep women down because in many cases women do the job beautifully. Young mothers and women teachers in the primary grades particularly need a great deal of re-education to become aware of their own unconscious sexist bias. It is when children are very young, after all, that their sexual identity is established. Conditioned as children, women are just as prone as men to encourage the old notions that boys don't cry and girls must be demure. The patriarchal system with its rigid division of sex roles thus manages to perpetuate itself through a chain of conditioning.

When the secondary school teachers recently held an election, they sent me a letter telling me who'd been elected, once again designating the women as "Mrs." or "Miss". I wrote them a little note saying, "Thank you for your letter, and I'm sure congratulations are in order, and would you let me know the marital status of the men as well." They obviously thought I was slightly mad, but all I was trying to point out to them was that they are constantly introducing an additional criterion for women that is not used for men. This is unnecessary. I don't evaluate women on whether or not they're married, and I don't evaluate men that way. It's simply irrelevant.

There is no doubt that important changes are coming about and that this process could be speeded up by legislation. The fact that sex can no longer legally be considered a factor in employment is just as important as the elimination of age or religion or any of the other factors which are outlawed under the Human Rights Code. Of course until the attitude changes take place, an employer who is determined not to hire or promote a woman can find legal excuses to support his bias. The change in point of view will be a long, slow process.

Before we reach a stage of genuine attitudinal change, we

will pass through an intermediate stage of "embarrassed silence": people who cling to the old attitude will believe they are right, but know it isn't popular, and won't pursue it. This is the same stage that has been fostered to eliminate much overt racism. I think perhaps at the Toronto Board we're now at the "embarrassed" stage; there have been many people who might have very much wanted to say something funny about the woman chairman. Perhaps in an all-male group they might have attempted it with impunity, but not in most mixed audiences, and certainly not within my earshot. They knew they would be treated with some fairly withering scorn if they displayed their bias.

The transition from the embarrassed stage to the positive one is going to take time, but attitudes will change towards sex discrimination just as they have toward racial bias. There are some people who for years were accustomed to making jokes about blacks who would not dream of doing it now, and we are getting to the stage where jokes at the expense of women are no longer considered acceptable.

Recently an out-of-town speaker who attended one of our workshops let drop the "jocular" remark that he lets his wife (poor idiot!) win an argument once a year. Instead of the usual titter that kind of clergyman joke used to get, there was a stony silence, verging on hostility. Some of the people there might have sympathized with the man's disparaging view of his wife, but they knew better than to admit it publicly. The transition from the embarrassed stage to the positive stage will take much longer for some people than for others, just as it will be some time before the competent woman has the same chance as the "super-woman". But it will come.

I am often asked whether my being a woman has been in any way an advantage or a disadvantage in my job with the board. The fact is, I have not noticed any particular obstacles arising from my being a woman. That may have been due partly to the new service orientation of the board, and partly to my own background. Since my upbringing was not the typical one experienced by most girls in our culture, I have escaped some of the problems attached to it. People are thrown off guard when my behaviour doesn't meet with their expectations, and they often hesitate to use the same tricks to which I've seen other women subjected. Instead of becoming weepy and defensive, I tend to become aggressive in situations like that. Thus, my working relationships with colleagues and senior officials have been very much on an equal basis.

One distinct advantage I did have as chairman was the fact that I was a married woman. I could make all the part-time jobs—trustee on both Toronto and Metro boards and chairman of the Toronto board—full-time jobs, even though they all paid abysmally ($1,200 for chairman of the board). If I had had to assume these positions on top of another full-time job, I would not have been able to devote as much time as I did to board business.

In some ways a non-working married woman is in a position of power. (This applies to middle-class women only, of course. The situation for working-class women is quite different.) There are a great many middle-class married women who have tremendous resources at their disposal. They are free to engage their time and abilities usefully in society, and I think we have a positive obligation to do so. The problem is that many women who are supported financially develop a "kept" mentality. Nellie McClung said something about the "fatty degeneration of the conscience" that sets into the lives of some "comfortable" married women.

Many married women claim family responsibility as the barrier to any kind of serious work outside the home. If her husband keeps her on a leash, of course, the woman is imprisoned in her marriage. But I believe, perhaps rather uncharitably, that many women use their husband's disapproval as an excuse. They can say, "I have to ask my husband," or "My husband would kill me," and thus avoid taking responsibilities their conditioning has not prepared them for. Being relieved of the economic burden is rather like having a medieval lord as patron. If more married women had the courage to take advantage of that situation, they could accomplish much.

Equality, to some, means that men and women should be equal in their earning responsibilities. This is a narrow definition. The sex roles imposed by our culture are unfair to men as well as to women. It is absurd that a man should feel constrained to work all his life to support his family if in fact he would be a better home manager than his wife. In such a case, equality would mean the freedom to reverse roles. (There are also those who advocate wages for the homemaker, whether female or male.) The real change in consciousness about sex roles will come about when couples have the freedom to choose whatever life-style, whatever division of labour, suits them, without running into social pressure to conform to obsolete norms.

We should be preparing children to be productive, useful, and loving adults. And that has nothing to do with gender. I don't think, for instance, that I have "masculine" responses. I have simply never been conditioned to inhibit my *human* responses. When we train girls to be passive and quiet and subordinate we are conditioning them to repress their human responses, just as discouraging emotion in boys and always encouraging roughness and aggression is conditioning them to repress their human responses. If you can allow a girl to be active and adventuresome and a boy to cry or be affectionate, that's a means of fighting the stereotypes.

Of course, even if we succeed in bringing about new attitudes among administration, teachers, and students, we will still be in conflict with many parents who are shaping their children's attitudes in quite different directions. We encounter this problem constantly in Toronto which has an enormous ethnic population, especially people of Mediterranean background. The Toronto Board, for example, operates a science boarding school which is attended by grade six students for one full week. It's a great opportunity for children to become really immersed in natural science. But we have an extremely difficult time persuading some fathers that their children—their daughters—aren't going to be ruined for marriage by going into a residential situation with boys. They do not feel they're being properly chaperoned. We, of course, disagree and have never had an incident, but we still cannot convince some parents. I don't know if we'll ever change that. I suspect that girls from these homes will experience severe conflicts. Perhaps all we can do is help them to understand their fathers' motives in imposing such restrictions.

We also have to be very sensitive to the effects on these families of our work with the children. I sometimes feel a real sense of sorrow about the way we isolate the mothers in many of these families. The children are going to school, they're learning English, they're learning how to cope in a new culture. The fathers are out in society too. But the mothers, who are the strength of those families in Europe, are completely isolated in many ways. The children are gaining a kind of supremacy over the adults because they become more competent in the language.

We have to be extremely careful that in trying to encourage in these children values we believe are very important for their welfare, we aren't at the same time breaking down some special strengths. The close family structure is an important psychological support for these people which we must try to preserve—without also preserving the bonds that would cripple them. The whole thing is a delicate balancing act.

The ethnic groups have something to offer us as well, even with regard to sex roles. In my experience as a kindergarten teacher in west Toronto where many of the children were Italian, I found that the Italian grandmothers have a pre-eminent place in the family life and structure. There's a great deal of wisdom and strength in some of those women, and we must not isolate them from the people they have been conditioned all their lives to support. Our treatment of the elderly in Canada leaves much to be desired, but in many immigrant communities they are valued people. These extended families are not competitive, but cooperative, and we who value competition and material success so much that our children often become extensions of our competitive drive, could learn much from them.

The idea of community is what we should be working towards. That is the way to incorporate all the best values which every diverse group has to offer. In the same way we must strive to develop the full potential of each individual regardless of sex.

Frances Wilson was born in Edmonton. She went to Toronto in the forties to attend the University of Toronto where she graduated in 1951 with a bachelor's degree in philosophy and history. After fifteen years as a suburban housewife she returned to the U of T graduate school and received a Phil.M. in 1969 and an M.Ed. in 1975. Since 1967 she has taught at Glendon College, York University, and Sheridan College of Applied Arts and Technology where she is presently teaching and working on a doctorate in adult education.

The New Subject: Women's Studies

Frances Wilson

"Women have been deceived . . . into believing that they are the controlling factor in the world. . . .now women everywhere realize that a bad old lie has been put over on them for years."

The store-front campus of Sheridan College of Applied Arts and Technology in Burlington, Ontario was buzzing with activity. On that cold winter's morning coats, hats, and boots were piled on a table as about twenty-four women milled around, getting coffee, chatting together and finally settling into the discussion circle for the morning's class. Another session of "Discovery" was in progress: designed for women to explore and understand their feelings of boredom, frustration, emptiness, lack of confidence and fear, and to direct them towards changes designed to alleviate those same uncomfortable feelings.

The guest speaker of the morning was introduced. She was a woman close to fifty, who had begun her working life as a stenographer, gone on to university and then spent fifteen years as a suburban housewife—a pattern most of the women in the group understood only too well. Then, with her children half grown, she had plunged back into the university world, completing a graduate degree and becoming a university lecturer. This second return to education had been accomplished after she was forty and with the same kind of fear, lack of confidence, and misgivings experienced by the members of the group. The talk had been quiet, for

183

she had simply focussed on her own story, stressing her feelings, the discouragements, the reactions of friends.

Discussion began, questions arose, then one woman, fully the age of the speaker herself, asked wistfully, "Do you really mean that women *can* go back to school and become something other than a homebody? I want *so* much to do that. I just don't believe it's possible."

"I did it," was the guest speaker's quiet reply.

"Then I'll try," said the class member. She had been given the courage and support she needed to try to discover and to realize more of her own potential.

This "Search of Self" or "Discovery" kind of class in the Continuing Education Division at Sheridan College is reaching women who need what it has to offer, and women are responding. The examination of one's own needs, feelings, aspirations and possibilities is just one of the many forms that women's studies can take. At Sheridan, Search of Self was the first kind of course developed by people interested in women's studies. It was designed, according to its promotional brochure, "to help women discover themselves and their places in today's society, and to help women gain the confidence and knowledge necessary to deal with life today". The course was designed in response to the realization that large numbers of adult women were beginning to move out of the traditional role of housewife and were suffering from lack of confidence and disorientation in relation to the world of work and education.

Courses of this kind were begun in 1970 and by January 1974, when these statistics were compiled, Search of Self and Discovery had served 216 women in the community.

Many of these women who have begun their re-entry into the world of work and education through S.O.S. have returned for further part-time study through the Continuing Education division, and some are already completing full-time study at Sheridan or at a university. Others have found work of very real satisfaction.

By 1972 the Continuing Education division had added courses for evening students entitled Women in Contemporary Society and Women in Literature. Thirty-four women were enrolled. In 1974 a survey course was attempted, titled Women Here, Women Now, which covered the entire field of women's contemporary interests. The format involved guest speakers who were experts in their particular field, and discussion groups following each speaker. Forty-eight women registered for this course. It provided much data regarding the areas in which women wanted more information, thus suggesting other course titles to be developed in future years.

Like other Continuing Education courses, Women Here, Women Now had its victories and defeats. One of the victories concerned a bright, articulate and artistic woman who found herself at the end of the sessions ready and courageous enough to apply to the School of Design for full-time study. With real enthusiasm the facilitator of her discussion group wrote a letter of recommendation for admission.

Daytime courses in women's studies, incorporated in the regular program of the college, began in 1972 in both the Division of English and Media Studies, and in the Division of Applied and Liberal Studies. These courses were designed by women teaching college electives in the Liberal Studies division, and English and media electives in the English and Media Studies division. These courses are far more academic in content, following a traditional academic format of reading or film lists, research projects, reports, essays, and even occasionally an examination. They are aimed at researching the realities of Canadian society, or literature, or film. Some are historical studies, some are concerned with the contem-

porary scene. At Sheridan in 1974, the courses in these
two divisions included the following: Images of Women in
Film; Changing Role of Women in Canada; Politics of Sex;
Historical Writings on Women's Rights; and Liberation for
the Unliberated. Statistics from the two divisions indicate
that more than two hundred students in each division have
been involved in these studies and that there is a continuing
interest in the field.

In neither of these divisions was there any resistance to
the courses planned. Deans have been interested, helpful,
accepting. Each of us began teaching women's studies by
suggesting one course we'd like to teach in the subject area;
each of us got the backing to do more than one. Other
teachers heard about the courses, questioned, teased, and
even xeroxed off material they found in their reading. One
sociologist handed me his *American Journal of Sociology*
the month it was devoted to studies on women. "You'll be
able to use this," he said with a grin.

One of the exciting aspects of teaching this kind of class
in a community college in Canada is that you do not face
the converted. When one meets a class at the beginning of a
semester, it is unusual to find a committed feminist in the
group. The students are there for many reasons, often as
trivial as the fact that it was the only course that fitted into
their time-table. What this situation requires is a willingness
to examine the students' attitudes with regard to the traditional stereotyped male and female roles, and to lead them
into investigations which will uncover the ramifications of
these roles as played out in Canadian society. Sometimes
one succeeds. Sometimes one doesn't.

One such failure comes to mind. After a full semester
studying traditional sex roles and the effects on both sexes
of our present societal structure, we began a summing-up
discussion. Could the students identify those aspects of our

society that caused damage to some of its members? Yes, they could. They listed economic discrimination, socialization procedures, and then one member said, "It's those damn traditional sex roles that cause the trouble." "No, no, no," rejoined another. "Those have been with us since the beginning of time. They are natural. They *can't* be changed," she insisted loudly. After fifteen weeks of documenting the inequalities and injustices in our society, she wouldn't admit that the old male-female patterns were the sources of much of the problem.

It became obvious that these students knew very little about women's history. We worked our way through the major documents of the feminist movement, from Mary Wollstonecraft to the present. All of the writers were unknown to the students. Even Margaret Sanger was a stranger to them and I was asked to give a little background information about each writer so they would know what kind of people they were trying to understand. This means that those of us who teach women's studies within the colleges of applied arts and technology are spending much of our time presenting very basic material. Teaching at the university level can become more theoretical because the students tend to begin with some previous knowledge of the subject area.

It is also obvious that in the mid-'70s we are teaching the children of the '50s. Students of this generation are characterized by a seriousness and a conservatism that was totally absent in the late '60s, a conservatism which strongly rejects anything suggestive of radicalism or rapid change. A teacher in touch with the mood of the students moves slowly to avoid being shut out. It is to be hoped that this is a passing phase.

One of the questions raised by the college administration was the place of *men* in such classes. This question is often taken out of the hands of the teacher. Some administrations insist on open admission. Although I have noticed no strong opposition to an all-women's class, there have been subtle pressures to keep the classes mixed. In my classes I teach the basics: the realities of discrimination or the history of feminist literature, and I find no problem with mixed classes. In fact, some of the men have been among the better students. My experience, however, is uncommon and I am convinced that much of the difficulty experienced by some women's studies teachers is connected to the specific subject matter presented. Some courses obviously work better when men are excluded, i.e., courses such as Sexual Politics, Women in Literature, or Women and Health. Certainly all Discovery classes are for women only. Perhaps rather than setting all-inclusive rules we should consider very carefully each class on its own terms. Only then are we in a position to make a reasonable judgment.

In one class the students were discussing how men and women might feel when traditional rules are broken, for instance if a woman offered to pay the lunch bill. The women heard the men saying, "But I'd be embarrassed" . . . "I wouldn't be comfortable with that at all." When the men heard themselves they realized, perhaps for the first time, how caught up they were in their traditional role. In this way insight may occur which leads to changed attitudes. Continued experiments are needed to keep communication open between men and women as these changes in outlook progress; and to suggest that women's studies is not for men, or black studies must exclude whites, is perhaps to limit the possibility that education will do its basic work, that of creating change.

These experiments can, of course, take many forms. One might be separate men's classes dealing with the same material. I have not yet tried this plan but may experiment with it soon. Another is to invite the men to join the women's class occasionally when certain specific films, discussions, or special speakers are planned. A third possibility is to design courses in the field of women's studies especially for men, as we design some courses especially for women. Warren Farrell, author of *Beyond Masculinity,* teaches such a course at Washington University.

In my own teaching experience I have seen men undergo remarkable transformations. An interesting piece of primary research was done by a male student in one of my classes recently. He didn't believe any of the statistics about salary differentials or few promotions which had been presented by the group who researched women in the work force, and had made many comments to that effect in class. We believed we had a tough case on our hands. Nevertheless he agreed to work on his own research topic: "Women and Poverty". His approach was to go to the local welfare officer in the county where he lived and talk to him about the welfare allotments to women, their support from their husbands, and additional funds received from government sources. When he came back to the class to make his report he was a very different person. His report on the lack of support from absent husbands, the low level of welfare payments, and on other government policies regarding women on welfare was both an eye-opener for the class and for the investigator himself. "And my friend the welfare officer was very angry about this whole state of affairs, too," he commented.

Another young man came out of class mumbling to himself one day. I asked what was bothering him. His reply was, "I've been researching the laws on marriage and divorce. If I were a woman, I wouldn't ever marry; not under *those* property laws."

The development of women's studies courses at Sheridan

has been slow and steady, each course taught experimentally at first so that we could understand where the pitfalls lay and what sections needed revision or omission. To produce a total program without this careful testing procedure might possibly destroy the whole subject area in a school.

Generally, however, growth in the field of women's studies has not been slow. The *Women's Studies Newsletter,* published by the Feminist Press in the United States, reports in its Winter 1974 edition that "in 1971, when *Female Studies III* (the last volume in this series with similar content) was published, there were about 600 courses and about twenty programs. There are now well over 2,000 courses, and over eighty programs. Geographically they range in the United States from Orono, Maine, to Honolulu, Hawaii, and there is a small but growing number of courses in the United Kingdom and Canada." This edition of the *Newsletter* also reports that of the subject matter within these 2,000 courses, the largest categories are still history, sociology and literature, along with a consistently large number of interdisciplinary courses, and that education, psychology, political science, anthropology and law are making gains. In addition there is an increase of courses in the area of health sciences, human sexuality and alternate life-styles.

Resources for women's studies courses in Canada ought to be drawn largely from the history, literature, traditions and social structure of Canada. Much information is available in lists and bibliographies published in the United States, but there is the ever-present danger in Canada of completely adopting the pattern of study and materials used by our larger neighbour to the south. This would be most undesirable. Women's studies in Canada require in-depth looks at Canadian statistics and information, as well as those from the rest of the world. Canadian statistics on mental health, for instance, do not agree with American figures that the highest rate of mental illness is found among married women who stay at home. In this country the largest number of hospitalized mental patients are men.[1] Neither do American bibliographies and anthologies include the writings of Nellie McClung, one of the foremost Canadian feminists. Nor do researchers in the United States document carefully the cultural differences and background found in Quebec, nor in the Canadian prairies with its large Eastern European immigrant population.[2]

Recently I evaluated a term course in women's studies which I taught in three separate classes, at the same time trying to justify their value to the college administration. As I did this, basic questions came to mind. *Why* women's studies? *What* forms their special content? What do I expect my students to learn? *How* do I present the material? How do I evaluate?

Why?

Women constitute a class whose human experience differs in many ways from male experience. This experience has never been adequately recorded. Women as a group have in

---

[1]Dr. Linda Fisher, University of Waterloo, in an address delivered at Sheridan College, Mississauga, October 1973.

[2]Some Canadian materials which will be invaluable to women's studies scholars are the following:

a) the *Canadian Newsletter,* a journal edited jointly by Margrit Eichler and Marylee Stephenson;

b) two important bibliographies—one by Veronica Strong-Boag and published in Stephenson's book *Women in Canada,* and the other, a compilation of bibliographies on women's studies, by Margrit Eichler of Waterloo University available from the Canadian Association of University Teachers—both indispensible tools;

c) the Ontario Institute for Studies in Education's exciting multi-media kit of women's studies resources called *The Women's Kit,* which includes records, slides, film strips and printed matter aimed at stimulating the researcher and the high school or college class.

fact been almost invisible in the records of our culture and the cultures we have inherited. Our knowledge of ourselves as human beings has thus been painfully distorted. This imbalance is mirrored in every cultural institution, one of the most striking examples of which is education. No student of literature can gain an adequate experience of the human condition by concentrating solely on such authors as Dickens, Thackeray, Hardy, Shaw and Lawrence. We need the balance of Austen, Brontë and Woolf, and even more we need the emergence of new writers with a feminist consciousness.

Historians present us with battles and political decisions from which women are excluded, although they are profoundly affected by them. Nellie McClung, in a chapter of her book *In Times Like These* entitled "What do Women Think of War (Not That it Matters)?", suggests an alternative view of the concept of "military glory".

What? and How?

Some knowledge of women's experience may be discovered through many disciplines—in little-known works of literature (such as the writing of Aphra Behn), in archeology, art, and in the records of history—if we will but perceive, analyze and assess. For example, changes in the position of women may be traced through the madonna and child theme dominant for centuries in the art of many cultures, from the stiff, stylized ninth-century Romanesque figure, looking straight ahead, to the Renaissance portrayal of a delightfully alive young woman playing with a real child.

Sociology and psychology also provide tools and techniques which can be used to study the contemporary situation of women throughout the world. The findings of the research must be coordinated and synthesized in such a way as to give a cross-disciplinary picture of the life, activities, attitudes and difficulties of this one-half of the population that has, until now, been very much neglected by the usual specialized academic approaches.

It is not surprising therefore, that the University of Toronto lists its women's studies courses under its Department of Interdisciplinary Studies, and under that department teaches such courses as Women in Canada: An Historical Perspective; Woman: Object and Subject in North American Literature; Women and the Family; Women in Revolt; The Struggle for Suffrage; Women's Work: Economic Growth; and Ideology and Structure. It is also not surprising that the major women's studies courses at York University are taught under the General Education pattern, and are found in the divisions of Humanities and Social Sciences.

Interdisciplinary and cross-disciplinary study immediately raises major questions of a philosophical and methodological order, and these matters need careful scrutiny. Can one teacher, for instance a teacher trained in English literature, handle an interdisciplinary course on the history of women? Unless she has some training in the methods of historiography or the help of a partner from another discipline, it is unlikely that she will produce anything but an English course. On the other hand, there is a great need for the literature specialist who will do a detailed study of images of women in literature, or for the media specialist who can draw our attention to the images of women in film and television.

Within Sheridan's English and Media Studies division a specialist in film teaches a course on Images of Women in Film. In the Continuing Education evening courses, two English specialists teach a course titled Women in English Literature. Women's studies thus becomes a *content* area of study rather than a methodological discipline.

The teachers of women's courses at Sheridan have made an important discovery: they have never worked so hard. Teaching in an area where primary research is important, where the sources of material are magazines, newspapers, journals, television, and the give-and-take of daily conversation, one finds that the subject matter is not the easiest kind to control. Nor is it possible to be always up-to-date. The reading load alone is enormous. There is always something one hasn't seen or hasn't read, that someone else brings to the class's attention.

Are women's studies coming to the forefront of study now because certain ideological positions held by the teachers are presented to students in the hope that they will be converted to the teacher's point of view? I believe that there is a real danger here. Teachers and researchers who become involved in women's studies are usually convinced feminists: they believe that women have been ignored, misunderstood, pictured inaccurately, and discriminated against—in short, wronged—by the academic world. Otherwise there would be no reason for the study. This situation presents an ever-present danger that the teacher or researcher will become too much the propagandist. I have discovered that a method which seems to keep this tendency under control is to set the students to work on research, letting them report their own findings from the statistics, the stories, the magazines and the books. The students themselves make discoveries.

One woman had this kind of experience when she undertook a research assignment on lesbianism in Canada: its nature, extent, causes, and legal and social sanctions. Her report was meticulous, historical, sociological, psychological, and required an hour of class time to present. At the end of the report she led the class in a discussion about their own attitudes and finally said, "When I started this research I thought lesbians were just a bunch of sick people who need psychiatry. But now I have really changed my mind. That just isn't so. I discovered how many women *choose* a life-style devoid of men, simply in preference to the violent or unhappy experiences they have had earlier. I also discovered the phenomenon of bisexualism which, until I did the study, I was hardly aware of. I met and talked to lesbians and found them sensitive, pleasant and attractive people."

There are groups within the women's movement who have used women's studies classes as a forum for the propagation of political ideologies based on male political analysis. One needs to be aware of where the understanding and changing of women's position does, or does not, fit into presently formulated revolutionary political ideologies; and where and how necessary it is for women who research and teach in the field to be aware that our political theory has not, and cannot yet be completely formulated until all the information is in. Women engaged in bona-fide women's studies courses must keep an open mind on political ideology. The proper in-depth study of the female experience may point to completely new forms of social and political organization. Commitment to a political position at this stage is often the sign of the propagandist.

Educators have always been convinced that to learn means to change human behaviour. Therefore, education is usually conceived of as an agent for change, often in the direction of adjustment to present conditions. *Changed behaviour* is also the goal of women's studies courses, but not necessarily toward adjustment. *Change* can mean many things.

Change means women raising their vocational sights and developing a conviction that all occupations are, or ought to be, open to them. As the list of students changing their programs in the college crossed my desk I noted with satisfaction: "Jane P. transferring from Secretarial Science to Business Administration". Jane had just completed a study of the changing role of women in Canada.

Change also means new awareness about the media and its presentations, and change in individuals as awareness increases about themselves, others around them, and finally the civilization of which they are a part. "Something is happening to me," said one young woman after class. "I used to love to watch 'All in the Family', but last night, when I had the first chance in several weeks to see it, I found I couldn't stand to watch 'poor Edith'. That stupid, sad, unfortunate woman, I kept thinking. And I turned off the TV."

These are just two instances of what can happen within the framework of women's studies classes. One *expects* changes in *attitude* when one teaches in this field. One expects students to absorb new, factual information. Frequently, entire lives are changed. It is also true, of course, that one anticipates angry explosions when certain "sacred cows" are proved damaging to human beings. But the rewards are those moments of glorious enlightenment when learning has created a meaningful synthesis of formerly confused and unintelligible experience.

We must be careful, in the teaching and development of these courses, that we do not relegate the study of the experience of women to the academic periphery. If we are to come to grips with the experience of the "unstudied half" of humanity, long-term research and in-depth study will be necessary. These kinds of studies require an academic commitment of a permanent kind. Universities and colleges need and must begin to take this into account if human studies are, in fact, to become the study of all human beings.

Jill Vickers is an associate professor in political science and assistant chairman in the Department of Political Science at Carleton University. She is vice-president of the Canadian Association of University Teachers and past-president and chief negotiator of the Carleton University Academic Staff Association, the first faculty union in Ontario. She has a doctorate in political theory from the London School of Economics.

Women in the Universities

Jill Vickers

"Should women think?"

One would like to believe that an article dealing with female participation in higher education could suitably borrow McClung's phrase, "Should women think?". In Canada, however, as in most nations, universities are less and less institutions dedicated to intellectual progress. Universities serve as barrier mechanisms in what John Porter has called "the system of privilege"[1] in Canadian society with the prime function of certifying that a select group of persons in each generation should be permitted the status and remuneration accorded to "professionals" in our society. It is within this context that we will examine the problems of Canadian women in higher education.

North American societies are dedicated to the principle of equal opportunity. In theory at least, no class or race or sex or ethnic group enjoys a monopoly on positions of status and power. Since these societies are supposed to be achievement oriented, and since achievement or success clearly depends to a considerable degree on obtaining higher education and training, access to higher education has

[1] Porter states, "A system of privilege exists where higher occupational levels are preserved or tend to be preserved for particular social groups." *The Vertical Mosaic* (Toronto, 1965), p. xi.

commonly been seen as the key to the upward mobility and economic advancement of disadvantaged groups. It is not surprising, therefore, that the authors of the *Report of the Royal Commission on the Status of Women* shared this belief:

> Equal opportunity for education is fundamental. Education opens the door to almost every life goal. Wherever women are denied equal access to education they cannot be said to have equality.[2]

Clearly, equal access to education at all levels is a *necessary condition* for equal status for women. It is not, however, a *sufficient condition*. Canadian society is littered with evidence that women who do obtain the credentials for full participation in societal activities cannot or are not permitted to use those credentials.[3] In short, blind faith that equal access to education at all levels will ensure equal status for Canadian women is bound to result in disappointment since it is clear that the system of privilege in Canada operates differently in the case of women. More than equal access to education is required but certainly it is an important first step as yet unachieved in Canada.

The purpose of this article is to provide a preliminary analysis of the participation of women in Canadian universities. Because a strictly descriptive analysis of data could not begin to transmit the kinds of experiences women encounter as students and as working academics, a number of subjective and frankly impressionistic views will be presented to supplement the analysis of data which is documented primarily in the tables. In general, we begin with the

---

[2] Canada, *Report of the Royal Commission on the Status of Women in Canada* (Ottawa, 1970), p. 161.

[3] The experience of women in the legal profession is a good example. Although explicit quotas governing admission to law schools have been eliminated, young women who complete their law programs often find it difficult to obtain articling positions.

premise that legally sanctioned policies which discriminate against women have largely disappeared from Canadian universities but that societal attitudes and prejudices, the application of apparently non-discriminatory policies and the prejudices of academics and administrators continue to have the effect of depriving Canadian women of equal access to higher education and to the academic profession.

Women in Canadian Universities: The Undergraduate Years

Despite the "common wisdom" that universities are hot-beds of radicalism staffed and populated by people dedicated to the overthrow or, at least, the radical alteration of our society, Canadian universities are very much products of the society in which they are located and which supports them. In many ways, universities are very conservative places although the values they are dedicated to preserving reflect the competitive and achievement-oriented premises of a liberal society. Universities have rarely been "open" to all comers and have traditionally reinforced societal pre-judices. The inhabitants of the ivory tower in Canada have taken up many "liberal" causes and most of them would be shocked if asked to consider policies which discriminated on the grounds of race or ethnic origins. Since the majority of academics are men, however, they tend to view the low level of female participation in their own enterprise or the segregation of those women who do attend in a few "suit-able" disciplines to be "natural" or the result of a lack of desire and commitment on the part of the women involved. The young women who attend university, therefore, enter an environment which is almost exclusively male. They are primarily taught by men who want their meals cooked for them, their socks mended for them and their children ten-ded for them by women in the "natural way". These same women share classes with male students who, while less committed to the traditional division of labour between the sexes, also tend to see women as cooks, sock-menders and baby tenders. Since many of these same women themselves harbour a sneaking suspicion that they too would be disappointed if the "natural female roles" were denied them, the atmosphere of the academic world tends to reinforce rather than contradict societal norms and prejudices.

There are many possible roads a young woman may follow in pursuit of a more liberated life-style. For the Canadian girl from a middle-class background, the acquisition of a university degree and perhaps also professional or advanced technical training often seems the most promising. While few Canadian women as yet see the relationship between higher education and their potential ability to aspire to positions of authority, many do see such credentials as providing the basis for economic independence if and when they choose to pursue a life-style at variance with or in addition to the still dominant wife-and-mother role. Given this gradually growing awareness, it is important to realize that most members of the blue jeans brigade will either not finish their university programs or will obtain a basic degree which would permit them to teach school (if jobs are available) or to enter the business world where the first question they will be asked is "Can you type?" Clearly, then, we must examine more than simple participation rates at this level. We must also examine the kinds of university programs women choose or into which they are steered.

There is considerable evidence that a sizable portion of the increase in undergraduate enrollment in Canadian universities over the past two decades can be attributed to an increase in the rate of female participation.[4] It is also evi-

[4] See T.H. McLeod (ed.), *Post Secondary Education in a Technological Society* (Montreal & London, 1973), Table 8, p. 20. A 23% increase is noted for the 1955-65 period.

dent that this increased rate of female participation has not
included working-class women in any significant measure.[5]
Regardless of the fact that this increase in participation has
been limited in class terms and despite our belief that the
achievement of the appropriate credentials may well not
result in an appropriate "pay-off" even for upper-status
women, nonetheless it clearly represents an important de-
parture for Canadian women.

Although education is touted as the key to advancement
in the North American ideology, marriage rather than independent achievement has been traditionally offered as the
route for the advancement of women. To some degree, in
fact, university attendance for women was seen and is still
seen by many as a way of ensuring that marriage involved
upward mobility or at least not a drop in status. Increasingly, however, women are coming to see economic *independence* as more desirable than the economic *security*
sometimes gained through marriage. And, while they have
been slow to aspire to roles in which they would exercise
societal power directly and slow to recognize the realities
of how the system of privilege operates, they are increasingly aware that higher education is more than a personal
adornment. More and more young women are recognizing
the fact that higher education is often required to gain
admission to interesting and "worthwhile" jobs and the
quality of one's daily work is of greater concern as more
women contemplate an active work life of forty or even
fifty years rather than a few years prior to marriage and
perhaps a decade "after the children are grown". Many
young women are also increasingly aware of the value of
higher education from the point of view of personal development and self-esteem. As the female life-cycle changes

[5]See Robert M. Pike, *Who Doesn't Go to University—And Why: A Study on
Accessibility to Higher Education in Canada* (Ottawa, 1970).

because of more reliable contraception, less secure marriage relationships, and the diminished amount of time required to care for home and family, the value of higher education is enhanced even for those women who will continue to choose to marry and rear families.

The rate of female participation in university education *at the undergraduate level* in Canada has increased from 16.3% of the total enrollment in 1921 to 39.4% in the 1971-72 academic year.[6] In fact, the current rate of *participation* is somewhat higher since the 1971-72 percentage indicates first degrees (bachelors and first professional degrees) *granted*. In addition, Canada has recently experienced a great proliferation of post-secondary institutions of various types in a number of provinces in which women also obtain post-secondary diplomas and certificates if not degrees.

Despite this rather considerable increase in the *rate* of female participation in higher education, the quality and scope of that participation within the universities has not improved substantially in the sense that female undergraduates still tend to be restricted or to restrict themselves to a relatively small number of disciplines and fields which are traditionally female preserves and to others which do not give access to the higher professions or to occupations with high status and high levels of remuneration. The effects, therefore, of the increased rate of participation are significantly diminished.

In discussing the participation of women in the universities at this level, it is essential first to distinguish between discrimination, prejudice and sexual stereotyping. There are relatively few instances of explicit discrimination in Canadian universities which might be remedied by legislative action. Prejudice exists at many levels and while it

[6]See *Report/Status of Women* and Table 1.

causes discomfort can be tolerated if it is not accompanied by behavioural manifestations which would constitute active discrimination. Rather more serious is the fact that our society is permeated with a set of conceptions or stereotypes which express the dominant view concerning appropriate activities for men and women. These stereotypes are particularly difficult to eliminate because most young women continue to accept them and impose them on themselves. Although it is now completely acceptable for middle-class women to *attend* university in terms of societal norms, what they will study when they do attend is still conditioned by these stereotypes. It is significant that despite the wide-spread acceptance of the values of the women's liberation movement among female undergraduates, the proportion of women enrolled in scientific and professional courses and obtaining degrees in these areas remains very small. (See Tables 1 and 2.)

The continuing effects of sexual stereotyping whether self-imposed or not are evident when we consider the distribution of female enrollments in different areas and when we consider the fields in which women obtained first degrees. If we examine enrollments in the 1969-70 academic year, we can see that there were somewhat more than half as many female as male undergraduates enrolled in the various arts and science programs. (See Table 2.) Most of these women were enrolled in arts and a relatively small proportion (approximately 15%) were enrolled in science programs.

If we examine the distribution of women in terms of degrees awarded in the 1971-72 academic year, the fact that female participation is severely limited in scope and that female potential is likewise limited is even more evident. (See Table 1.) Women are under-represented in seventeen of the twenty-eight categories within which degrees granted are reported. They are seriously under-represented in the categories which represent the higher professions: architecture (10.8%), commerce and business administration (7.9%), dentistry (3.8%), engineering (1.3%), law (12.1%), medicine (17.3%), optometry (14.6%), religion and theology (20.8%) and veterinary medicine (12.3%). Women are over-represented in categories representing traditionally "female" fields which bring substantially lower status and levels of remuneration: education (55.9%), fine and applied arts (58.8%), household science (96.2%), library and records science (67.8%), music (60.6%), nursing (97.2%), secretarial science (100%) and social work (64.8%). Women are over-represented in only two fields which do not traditionally bear a female stereotype: pharmacy (50.3%) and rehabilitation medicine (87.6%).

The "male" fields in which women receive few degrees are generally the higher or senior professions which are self-regulating and entrepreneurial in nature. The women who do qualify in these fields generally obtain employment in salaried positions rather than setting up in practice for themselves. The fact that slightly more than half of the degree recipients in pharmacy were women is an interesting illustration of this point. The older pattern of small drug stores owned and operated by a pharmacist has changed considerably in recent years. This previously entrepreneurial profession is now largely a salaried profession because of the development of large chains which employ pharmacists on a salaried basis. A similar pattern is evident in other fields which were traditionally entrepreneurial but which now provide fewer opportunities for professional ownership and more salaried positions. Very few of those women who do manage to qualify in the higher professions end up in anything other than salaried positions. The fact that few women could obtain the financial backing required to establish practices for themselves or in female partnerships is a further result of sexual stereotyping.

The problem of sexual stereotyping affects every woman involved in higher education but it is a more serious problem for the relatively few women from working-class and immigrant families who do manage to gain access to university education. In a situation of scarce resources, female education remains a matter of low priority. Working-class families and many immigrant families with strongly-held views about the unsuitability of higher education for women will tend to allocate their resources for the education of male children and to expect female children to enter the labour force as early as possible. Even if women from these backgrounds do enter university, they are generally unable to contemplate or be able to finance lengthy or expensive professional education. Nor can they realistically expect to be able to enter the entrepreneurial professions which require some outlay of capital to establish a practice. There is perhaps more realism and less acceptance of societal stereotypes in these groups but the effects are essentially the same.

The ways in which these stereotypes are enforced are too numerous to explore fully but a few examples can be given. Young women entering university have already absorbed notions of "appropriate" careers for women. Every institution in our society from the family upwards is involved in the socialization of young women and the reinforcement of these stereotypes. Young girls rarely see women performing anything other than auxiliary or helper roles. To most young children, working women are teachers and nurses, not doctors or engineers. High school career counselling directs women into particular fields and often high school teachers fial to discourage young women from the easy course of avoiding mathematics and science.

Once in the university, women must contend both with the attitudes of their male counterparts and instructors and with their own attitudes. Some disciplines and programs are noted for their unwelcoming or even hostile attitudes towards female students. A young woman intending to study engineering, for example, will be forced to overcome a number of barriers—her own sense that engineering is not an "appropriate" female profession, the attitudes of parents and friends, her advisor's realistic advice that few engineering firms will employ women, the advice of well-meaning professors that she couldn't handle the heavy equipment or the unsavoury language, even the absence of a women's washroom in the building in which the engineering departments are housed. In short, it requires a profound commitment to a chosen career made early enough to ensure proper preparation at the secondary-school level to overcome these barriers and it is little wonder that few young women succeed in bucking the stereotypes even if they are inclined to do so. Of course, a male student aiming at a career in nursing or household science would encounter many similar barriers. The difference is that the female fields are relatively few in number and commonly neither well paid nor of high status. The resulting limitations for male students also limited by stereotypes are, therefore, far less in scope. In addition, some male students buck the stereotypes quite successfully and generally obtain positions in female professions superior to those of their female counterparts!

Perhaps one of the greatest problems female students encounter in their undergraduate years is the relative absence of female models in the university world. The original idea of the university involved a monastic life in which women were absent and sexuality was sublimated. Many of the values of contemporary universities continue to reflect this origin. The deep sense of inferiority many young women bring with them to the university is scarcely lessened by the study of a male-dominated society in which they are lectured to by men for whom the word "man" is generally easier to say than the words "human beings". According to the criteria which "count" in the university, women are often judged collectively as members of a sex which has sat on its collective derrière for hundreds of centuries and produced nothing of note other than children.

Many women encountered in the universities are unwilling or unable to counteract the man's-eye-view of the world they themselves have absorbed during their own education. Few of them are in senior and respected positions, especially in the "prestige" institutions and disciplines. Only recently, for example, have female academics begun to concern themselves with the collective history of their sex. The "women's courses" which have appeared in Canadian universities, moreover, are often viewed disparagingly as something which panders to a passing special interest and which should not occupy the time of serious students and academics.

Sexual *rivalry* permeates the world of undergraduates as much as it does society in general. The university presents for the bright female undergraduate the inevitable (in our society) dilemma of choosing between the roles society wishes to impose on her—attractive female object and/or worthy wife-and-mother—and the role for which her talents equip her. Academic competition takes on a distinct overtone of sexual rivalry which the well-socialized young woman recognizes as potentially damaging to her relationships with her male contemporaries. The brighter she is and the further she advances in her studies, the more painful the conflict becomes.

Many female undergraduates often seem to be their own worst enemies in the academic context—an observation frequently made by male instructors and a testament to the effectiveness of the socialization process. The norms of female passivity and inarticulateness, especially with regard to such topics as politics which are generally considered part of the male preserve, often make female students less willing and less able to compete in the academic context. They tend to defer too readily to the views of others and the student who produces a brilliantly written paper will often be reluctant to display her intellectual superiority in a more public way. The assumption that it is better to be bed-worthy than brain-worthy is clearly not erased by entrance to the university!

To some degree, the picture we have outlined is undergoing change. This is particularly noticeable among male and female students enrolled in arts courses where the ratio between the sexes is more nearly equal. The MRS degree continues to have its allure but increasingly marriage and motherhood are not seen as signals to drop out of university. These changes raise a host of new problems within the university context, involving such things as support, accommodation and child care, but they could quite easily be solved with a reasonable degree of flexibility and goodwill on the part of those involved in the administration of the university.

The existential problems female students face are similar to those faced by male students but always with an extra dimension. Support must be found, summer jobs obtained, decent accommodations sought and so on.[7] Generally women are less prepared and less permitted to contract debts for whatever purpose. This general reluctance to accept female indebtedness reflects the assumption that women will not be financially independent following graduation, or that their income will be far less than that earned

---

[7] In the summer of 1970, 88% of the female undergraduates seeking summer employment found jobs, in contrast to 92% of the male students. See Department of Manpower and Immigration, "Summer Employment Survey of Post-Secondary Students in Canada" (Ottawa, 1970), Table 2.2.

by their male counterparts. Banks tend to view young women as probable baby-machines who will drop out of the paid employment force or be forced out because of the current economic climate. (In present circumstances, these reservations are probably based as much on fact as prejudice!) In the area of publicly-funded grants and loans, however, there are fewer horror stories except in the case of part-time students in most jurisdictions and in the case of some women engaged in post-graduate training whose right to the "married" supplements granted to male students is still often denied.

While female undergraduates encounter only slightly more difficulty in finding summer employment than their male counterparts, the salaries earned are significantly lower.[8] The sexual stereotyping involved even in summer jobs handicaps female undergraduates. The common pattern for male undergraduates is to obtain either trainee jobs with government or in private industry or to obtain manual labour which while difficult is often well-paid. Female undergraduates are usually limited to working at poorly-paid clerical jobs or in summer camps and resorts.

Other existential problems faced by female undergraduates are more basically related to their sex and the role society expects of them. Male undergraduates do not drop out because of pregnancy and rarely because of marriage. These are still the two most common reasons why women discontinue or interrupt their studies.

Until recently in Canada, it was assumed that the university bore no special responsibility to provide married residences or day-care facilities although both were common in the universities in the United States. To some degree, this attitude is changing. A recent study indicated that seventeen out of the forty-five Canadian universities sur-

[8] *Ibid.*

veyed had some kind of day-care center. Twenty universities reported that no such facility existed on their campus.
Plans to create such facilities were in progress in three
institutions and five did not respond to the question.[9] Of
the seventeen universities in which there were day-care
facilities, however, only a small percentage bore any share
of the costs beyond providing space. In some cases the
facility was available only to the children of academic
staff, although this was not generally true since students
themselves have been the most active in the establishment
of the facilities. In one case, only the children of "lawfully
married" students were reported to be eligible for admission!
Changes in policy at the level of the provincial government
with regard to the general provision of day-care services
are clearly needed and have already taken place in several
instances. The financial control exerted by provincial governments over Canadian universities makes it virtually
impossible for them to provide necessary but expensive
services without the support of provincial ministries.

While the provision of such services as day-care centres
and married residences and the improvement of support for
students with family responsibilities can lessen the drop-
out rate among female undergraduates, many women will
still decide to interrupt their education hoping to return at
a later time or to continue their studies on a part-time basis.
This raises the very complex problem of the attitudes of the
Canadian university community towards "mature" and
part-time students and toward the whole area of continuing
education. (Data for part-time undergraduate enrollment
appears in Table 3.)

Except in Ontario and Quebec, female part-time undergraduate enrollment exceeds that of male part-time enrol-

[9] Information from a study by Ms. Linda Mitchell for the Canadian Association
of University Teachers, 1973.

lment. In every province the female/male ratio is higher in part-time than it is in full-time programs. But despite the demonstrated eagerness of women (and of many men) to undertake higher education on a part-time basis many universities are inhospitable to part-time students of either sex.

Provincial formulas for financing part-time programs are often at the root of the problem. If part-time programs are financed at a lower rate than full-time programs, the universities tend to "spend" less on them in terms of the provision of services and especially in terms of the quality of staff provided. Yet the general attitude is not entirely explained in these terms. Part-time students, especially if they appear at night, are considered to be little more than a nuisance. In some institutions, part-time programs are kept quite distinct from "regular" programs. Students are rarely permitted to undertake professional training on a part-time basis in any case. Often the courses offered are "extension" or "continuing education" courses and cannot be used for credit towards a degree. Evening courses are disliked by "regular" faculty and are often fobbed off on part-time lecturers, the newest professor, or someone out of favour as a punishment. Even student associations manage to pretend that evening students do not exist despite the fact that they collect fees from those who have been described by one student association president as "interlopers".

Because of a series of policies, it has rarely been possible for part-time students to apply to the usual sources for grants and loans, although there is some sign of change in this regard. One can in fact argue that it is because part-time and evening classes have so often been the only form of higher education open to women and to working-class men that the universities have been allowed to treat this large constituency in such a consistently shoddy manner.

One must, in this generally gloomy picture, praise those institutions which have acted positively to provide equal educational opportunities for part-time students.

To summarize, the opportunities for women to participate in higher education at the undergraduate level are limited in many ways and by a variety of factors. The ability and willingness of those who nominally control the university sector of education in Canada to effect the changes required is doubtful. Because of the almost total dependence of Canadian universities on government funding, however, changes can be stimulated by governments. Governments who deliberately used their control of the public purse to force changes would, of course, be accused of failing to respect the autonomy of universities and a series of head-on collisions would result. It is, however, unlikely that many substantial changes in university policy and practice will occur without the sort of governmental pressure which has been applied in the United States. Clearly, the problems resulting from the sexual division of labour and the sexual stereotyping of occupations and professions are not easily solved by government action. But it does not seem impossible for governments to make some effort in this area.

Women in Canadian Universities: Graduate Education

Although Canadian universities now have a fairly high percentage of women enrolled in undergraduate programs, the picture is substantially different at the graduate level. (See Tables 4 and 5.) The direction of female undergraduates into terminal first-degree programs is very common and those women who do enroll in graduate programs are much more likely to drop out than their male counterparts. If we assume that a Ph.D. is now considered the basic requirement for the academic profession, moreover, the fact that only

9.3% of the doctorates awarded in 1971 were awarded to women suggests that the academic profession itself is a predominantly male preserve. This is particularly disturbing when we recall that the *Report of the Royal Commission on the Status of Women* indicated that the proportion of women obtaining doctorates had declined substantially since the 1920s.[10] In fact, the picture is not quite as gloomy as the over-all statistics suggest since female participation is once again concentrated in particular disciplines. (See Table 6.) While the percentage of women obtaining doctorates in science and engineering is small (engineering and applied science: .4%, mathematics and physical science: 4.4%) the proportion obtaining doctorates in the humanities (19.8%), in education (11%), in fine and applied arts (50%), in the social sciences (14.7%) and in the health professions (15.2%) are all above the average.

It is quite clear, however, that the increase in participation among women at the undergraduate level is not repeated at the graduate level. Just as the low rate of female participation in the professions has a long-range effect on the future status of Canadian women, the relatively low rate of female participation at the graduate level will perpetuate many of the problems now faced by female undergraduates because of the small number of women active in the academic profession itself.

The problems women face as students at the graduate level can be divided according to the purpose pursued by the individual student. Of course all female graduate students face the existential problems we have already discussed and face the problem of negative attitudes. At the same time those who in their pursuit of graduate education are bent on an academic career are faced with somewhat different problems which will be discussed in the next section.

[10] *Report/Status of Women, op. cit.*

For those students who do not intend to pursue academic careers, graduate work at the master's level often represents additional professional training which is unavailable at the undergraduate level. This is true in some provinces and at some institutions in such fields as library science, social work, public and business administration and education. In other areas, master's level degrees can give women an additional qualification which ensures that they will have a slight edge over male applicants with undergraduate qualifications. This is true in such fields as journalism, for example. The master's degree is also resorted to by the young woman who cannot obtain employment with her undergraduate degree and simply decides to attend school for one further year in the hope that two degrees will dissuade more potential employers from making the perennial inquiry about her typing abilities. (See Table 8.)

In each of these cases the female graduate student discovers that competition for places and support has increased and, particularly if she has married and begun a family, that graduate education is geared to the "normal" or male life cycle. She experiences increasing pressure resulting from conflicting roles regardless of her life pattern since the older she becomes the more those around her expect her to give up this "playing at being a student" and either get married or, if she already is, to go home and tend to her husband and family. She is constantly suspected and accused of not being serious and of wasting time, space and money. If, on the other hand, it is obvious that she is serious, she constitutes an offense to many people's expectations about what she should be doing!

Women in the Academic Profession

Female participation in the academic disciplines at the doctoral level suggests that the academic profession is somewhat less attractive or receptive to women than the medical profession. Moreover, it is argued that the decline in the rate of female participation since the 1920s reflects the increased attractiveness of the profession to men. Certainly, grants and scholarships have increased in number and size. Levels of remuneration in the profession generally have improved. As a result competition for graduate places, support and academic jobs has increased substantially *despite* the fact that the number of places and jobs and the amount of support have also increased. As has happened in other fields undergoing improvement, women are in danger of being squeezed out.

In general, female graduate students beyond the master's level are highly qualified and highly motivated. They have to be to have successfully penetrated through the lower levels of the system. The existential problems and the problems raised by negative attitudes and sexual rivalry remain and even intensify but they are perhaps more easily faced as assurance and motivation increase. It is often difficult for female graduate students to establish relationships with faculty members and with their male counterparts and in many instances the pattern of being a "loner" is established and perpetuated. Both married and single women face problems because of their sex and because the female life-cycle raises various expectations in the minds of others. The problems faced by each group present difficulties which are somewhat different but equally troublesome.

At the graduate level, female students begin to learn that they will be more or less welcome in the profession *if* they accommodate themselves to the established (male) patterns of behaviour. They are effectively de-sexed except in social situations. They are expected to absorb and master the male view of the world. They will learn that "serious" academics are those who have internalized the norms of the academic profession, and that "taking time out" for other things marks you as less-than-serious. They will often discover that part-time doctoral studies are just not allowed. In short, they will find themselves tolerated as long as they are prepared to play the game according to a set of rules which have been made to suit the male life-cycle.

It is not surprising that the drop-out rate among female doctoral students is quite high. While many of those who do drop out probably plan to return as quickly as possible, re-entry at the graduate level is often made difficult by such things as time limits within which degrees must be completed. Furthermore, as has already been mentioned, the option of part-time graduate study is often not available. It is, however, our impression that many casualties do not drop out because of family responsibilities. Financial problems are often serious for female graduate students and are made worse by the policies of some granting agencies which assume that female students at this level can live on less than their male counterparts or that the children of female doctoral students need not or should not be supported through grants. Many other female doctoral students find the pressures of competition and of trying to conform to the academic mould to be "not worth the candle". The problem is, of course, as we are always being told, that women have a "respectable alternative"! In addition, there are clearly psychological problems faced by many talented women which have been described extensively in terms of their "fear of success".

The participation of women at the professorial levels in Canadian universities reflects such marked differences among disciplines and different types of institutions that overall generalizations are difficult to make. (Table 9 shows the female/male ratios by fields and median salaries for men and women for the 1969-70 academic year.) Only in the humanities do we find a relatively high level of female participation in core academic disciplines. Most notable of course, is the almost complete absence of women teaching in the fields of pure and applied physical science. As one engineering professor put it to the author, "We don't have a woman problem. We don't have any women."

Another important point is that our data indicate a spread of at least a thousand dollars between male and female median salaries. It is difficult to attribute this entirely or even partly to discriminatory practices without more detailed data and more extensive analysis. The median salaries for female academics could be lower for a number of reasons—inferior qualifications, few publications, slow promotion, the fact that many female professors are relatively young, or the inclusion of para-academics in the data.

In part, the female life-cycle for the married academic may result in relatively slow progress in the first decade of her career. Women may be slower to complete dissertations and slower to publish. They are also often less mobile and hence cannot play the "university A has offered me a better job" game to extract promotion or a higher salary—a common tactic of male academics in a favourable job market. Still experience indicates that female academics are often brought in at a lower starting salary than their male counterparts—perhaps because they don't bargain as well but also because they are both less secure and less mobile; that is, they are vulnerable and can rarely bargain from strength. They are also more likely to accept lower paying and insecure para-academic and part-time positions for the same general reasons. Their insecurity and lack of mobility can also persuade them to carry heavy work loads which in turn slow down their career progress. Some of these problems do not apply to single women without family responsibilities, but they too often find that their presence is tolerated at best and that their bargaining power is limited. Especially in a tight job market in which the question of redundancy may be raised, the sentiment that women "don't really need the job" is often heard. Certainly in this particular context militant action will be necessary to prevent the carrying out of policies implied in this point of view.

The female graduate student who has successfully completed her program will find that entrance to the profession in terms of getting a teaching job presents another high hurdle to scale. She will often be faced with a subtle and somewhat mysterious hiring process in which the "old-boy network" operates. Although some Canadian universities have ostensibly instituted open hiring with committees and advertisements, it is still true that personal contact and recommendations are generally essential in acquiring a position. Ability and qualifications are still the criteria for hiring academics, but in the current market there are so many excellent candidates in most areas that personal contacts and recommendations take on more rather than less weight than before.

Female academics tend to raise uneasy feelings in the minds of members of hiring committees for a variety of reasons. Mobility, for example, is often a problem. Will she come if her husband can't get a job here? Will she leave if she marries or if her husband is transferred? Academic couples often present difficulties. Despite the policy statements of the Canadian Association of University Teachers and the provisions of human rights codes, some universities still apply an anti-nepotism rule which often results in the hiring of the husband and the acquiring of the wife's cheap services on a part-time basis. Certainly many universities resist "package deals" and many hiring committees feel entitled to explore fully the personal circumstances of female candidates whether married or single. Some institutions in small, conservative communities are reluctant to hire single, separated or divorced women as professors.

Prejudice against female academics certainly enters into the picture in some instances. Although it was previously felt that opening up the hiring process and developing more regularized procedures would eliminate this, our impression is that it has failed to do so. It is not unusual for a hiring committee to sit around a table and explore in explicit terms the question, Do we really want a (or another) woman around? One suggestion which has been made to improve the situation is the establishment of university-wide hiring review committees which would scrutinize hirings and to which a rejected candidate could appeal if he or she felt that discrimination had been involved.

The academic professional associations have begun to turn their attention to problems in the area of fair hiring policy. At the moment they seem unprepared to hear cases concerning potential faculty members who have been refused employment. It is likely, however, that the threat of such a recourse would have as salutary an effect on the hiring process as it has had on the process of granting tenure in most institutions.

Certainly the general social biases with regard to women are rather strongly held by many male academics who while "liberal" in their attitudes toward such things as racial and class discrimination are often very reactionary in their attitudes toward women. This is partly the result of the dominance of "establishment" men in the universities. Certainly the internal power structures of universities and university departments reflect this dominance and the middle-class ideal of the "proper" female role.

Once a female academic has obtained a teaching position her problems have scarcely begun. Except for a few highly

productive individuals—largely those without family responsibilities—the female faculty member will often find
advancement slow, remuneration lower than for her male
counterparts, and higher than usual work loads imposed
upon her. She must conform to the time-table (which presents pressures even for male faculty), complete her qualifications, and achieve a respectable publication record. If
we assume that female academics should not be forced to
choose between career and some family life (though many
do choose a single life for personal or professional reasons),
it is necessary to rethink the time-table and to consider
family responsibilities not as excuses but as legitimate and
demanding activities which, while they may slow down
career progress for five to ten years, do not disqualify
women from making superior contributions as teachers
and scholars.

Women who have dropped out before completing graduate school or who have found the combined pressures of
full-time employment and family responsibilities too great
often join the large cadre of part-time faculty. These individuals perform the teaching function but are exploited in
terms of salary, are generally not eligible for tenure and
promotion, and are generally unprotected by academic
faculty associations. In some disciplines—especially the
sciences—highly qualified women are dead-ended in para-
academic jobs which do not provide the salaries, security,
and prestige of regular academic appointments. In fact,
women, whether they are fully qualified or are trying to
make a come-back after raising a family, are exceedingly
vulnerable. Women in all these situations are difficult to
organize, and internal university politics with its concern
for "higher matters" is difficult to penetrate with specific
demands for the improvement of these conditions. Arguments for improving the circumstances in which women

work are considered special pleading. Cases involving almost any other kind of discrimination are considered "higher matters".

Despite the many existential problems female academics face, perhaps the most difficult problem is psychological. Success requires a commitment to operate by male rules. But when this behaviour presents a perceived professional threat, the female academic is attacked as "aggressive", that is, "unfeminine". Relationships with female colleagues suffer in the process. The Aunt-Tom attitude—"I made it despite the problems. So can you if you are any good"—is all too common among female academics. The same attitudes colour their relationships with students, but it is difficult even to discuss this kind of problem with female colleagues. It is not surprising that women insecure in the academic context will ape the attitudes and behaviour of male academics even to the point of openly deriding women judged less "serious" than themselves. Instead of pressing for better arrangements for female students, the female academic is often less sympathetic than her male colleagues. In short, the de-sexing process has been successful enough to create a situation in which women are alienated by their experiences and aspirations from members of their own sex. Most men encountering a woman in the university context will assume that she is either a secretary or a student. But women engage in this sexist put-down too. Many women are afraid of becoming involved in "women's" courses (if you are going to make it, you must be concerned with "universal" issues) and avoid raising issues involving sexual prejudice for fear of threatening their own position in the group. Most female academics act from a sense of inferiority and vulnerability and the disparagement of other women is part of this syndrome.

Female academics have been almost as invisible in university politics as they have in the politics of the country generally. For various reasons—pressure of responsibilities, passivity, or fear of rocking the boat—women rarely achieve administrative positions in the university, rarely serve on important university committees and rarely participate in professional associations beyond mere membership. The power structures within universities and academic associations are still dominated by men out of all proportion even with the small female contingents in each context. Because it has been deemed "unprofessional" until recently to press for an improvement of female participation in the universities (but not unprofessional to fight on behalf of Negroes, Indians, or the poor) women have rarely used the little political leverage they do have to change the situation for future students and academics. Many academic women have, in fact, made their sexual characteristics invisible so as not to call attention to what they perceive as an inferior claim to the position their talents have earned them.

Solutions?

Several basic themes have been followed in this article. First, the assertion was made that Canadian universities are not generally outposts of enlightenment with regard to the situation of women and that they are social institutions which reflect the norms and prejudices of the society in which they are located. Second, it was observed that the quality of female participation and its scope is limited by sexual stereotyping and by the imposition of assumptions appropriate perhaps to the male life-cycle but inappropriate to the lives of many if not all women.

It cannot be assumed that the problems identified may be solved by making female lives identical to male lives, that is, that the problems would disappear if we all gave up marriage, families and our concerns for our personal lives.

Certainly changes in the assumptions about responsibilities as shared by the sexes and such things as the provision of day-care centers and more and better part-time programs would help enormously but acceptance in the university world must not depend on the intellectual de-sexing of women. Many of us, at least, do not want to be de-sexed. It should be as possible and as natural for women with a great variety of personal life-styles to participate in higher education as it is for men. It should be as proper and acceptable for the academic disciplines to concern themselves with female achievements and problems as it always has been to study "man's".

I have not argued that the entire social structure must be changed before any positive changes can be made in the position of women in higher education. Certainly the biggest nut to crack is the problem of sexual stereotyping and it is likely that substantial changes would have to occur in many other social institutions before the problem is eliminated completely within the university. There are, however, many kinds of changes which are within the power of the universities themselves to effect.

The basic change (beyond the elimination of as many of the existential barriers to female participation as possible) involves a major attitudinal change within the university community. The universities must stop simply responding to societal changes. They must begin innovating. They must stop assuming that women should adapt to current rules and norms and be prepared to adapt the rules and norms to some degree to fit the needs and aspirations of women. The same holds true for members of other disadvantaged groups many of whom are currently excluded from participation.

Although changes in attitude are essential, both on the part of individual members and of the academic community in general, they are also likely to be the most difficult to achieve. It may therefore be better tactics to begin by attempting to effect practical changes in the hope that the process will help to generate attitudinal changes.

The provision of excellent facilities for part-time studies at the undergraduate and graduate levels alike is a prime need. Many women and an increasing number of men wish to undertake higher education on a part-time basis, but are confronted by few programs, sometimes less qualified staff and the difficulty of obtaining financial aid. Contrary to some opinion, the university's performance of its functions would not suffer because of an increased emphasis on part-time students. Many protests against the "high cost of higher education" might disappear if more segments of society were offered the opportunity of pursuing a higher education.

The provision of adequate and subsidized day-care facilities and of more married student residences would aid many female day students. The university could provide catch-up programs designed to help women who have been out of touch with their disciplines for a period of time, especially in those characterized by rapid theoretical developments. Programs providing preliminary courses in mathematics and science would help many women whose basic abilities are suitable for scientific work but whose high school education has not included these subjects. Much more flexible rules with regard to financial help for students enrolled in these catch-up programs would also be required. It may be argued that positive discrimination in favour of women to counteract years of sexual stereotyping fails to attack the problem at its roots. Certainly structural change within the university context is not the only kind required but as it is more manageable such change could be implemented in the immediate future.

The question of quotas in fields with a low rate of female participation raises problems of a somewhat different order. Quotas alone, especially in the pure and applied sciences, might result in drastically lowered enrollments—raising a financial problem no university could face in the present economic and political climate. Quotas plus the provision of catch-up programs would be more effective, but upon completion of these courses women would still encounter enormous barriers against obtaining jobs in the "self-regulating" professions. Clearly, only some kind of regulation of the professions which are currently protected male preserves can begin to solve the final problem of permitting women who wish to participate fully in the professional and political life of society.

The question of quotas or positive discrimination in the academic profession itself raises many problems and great hostility. There are certainly other approaches which could be tried first. Academic women, for example, can and must press for more equitable hiring practices and procedures, and for the elimination of salary discrepancies where they exist. They can and must energetically undertake political activities within their departments, universities and academic associations. They must also concern themselves with the effects of current rules, policies and attitudes on their female students. They should also press for better conditions and more protection for part-time and para-academic staff and for a fairer deal for part-time students at all levels. Certainly women in the university must begin to offer support to one another and must reject the tendency to join the establishment in the sense of forgetting the needs and aspirations of members of their own sex.

One tends to feel, however, that the task may be too large and too complex to be handled in this manner. Certainly it would require enormous goodwill on the part of male academics and administrators. One suspects that it will ultimately be necessary to impose Affirmative Action on the universities and on other social institutions, as has been done in some countries. This prospect, of course, involves explicit political action and the risks attached to government intervention in the internal life of the universities. It may well be that we cannot avoid taking the risks.

TABLE 1

BACHELOR AND FIRST PROFESSIONAL DEGREES GRANTED IN CANADA BY SEX (1971-72)-ACCORDING TO AREAS OF SPECIALIZATION

Specialization	Total	No. Men	No. Women	% Men	% Women
Agriculture	617	564	53	91.4	8.6
Architecture and Lands Arch.	249	222	27	89.2	10.8
Arts	28,930	15,808	13,122	54.6	45.4
Arts or Science	776	511	265	65.9	34.1
Commerce and Business Admin.	3,623	3,338	285	92.1	7.9
Dentistry	398	383	15	96.2	3.8
Education	14,665	6,460	8,205	44.1	55.9
Engineering	4,200	4,147	53	98.7	1.3
Environmental Studies	350	305	45	87.1	12.9

Table 1 (cont'd.)

Specialization	Total	No. Men	No. Women	% Men	% Women
Fine and Applied Arts	498	205	293	41.2	58.8
Forestry	90	87	3	96.7	3.3
Household Science	600	23	577	3.8	96.2
Journalism	54	28	26	51.9	48.1
Law	2,152	1,892	260	87.9	12.1
Library and Records Sc.	152	49	103	32.2	67.8
Medicine	1,550	1,282	268	82.7	17.3
Music	449	177	272	39.4	60.6
Nursing	1,156	32	1,124	2.8	97.2
Optometry	48	41	7	85.4	14.6
Pharmacy	461	229	232	49.7	50.3
Phys. and Health Ed.	1,354	857	497	63.3	36.7
Rehabilitation Medicine	241	30	211	12.4	87.6
Religion and Theology	600	475	125	79.2	20.8
Science	8,788	6,576	2,212	74.8	25.2
Secretarial Science	33	—	33	—	100.0
Social Work	349	123	226	35.2	64.8
Veterinary Medicine	138	121	17	87.7	12.3
Others	43	17	26	39.5	60.5
TOTAL	72,564	43,982	28,582	60.6	39.4

Source: Statistics Canada Publication #42202-514 (June, 1973) titled "Degrees, Diplomas and Certificates Awarded by Canadian Degree-Granting Institutions", Table 4.

TABLE 2

FULL-TIME UNDERGRADUATE ENROLLMENT BY
FACULTY AND SEX (Regular Winter Session, 1969-70)

Faculty	Males	Females	Female/Male Ratio*
Arts	47,436	37,849	0.80
Pure Science	25,563	7,170	0.28
Arts and Pure Science Reported Together	5,664	3,831	0.68
TOTAL	78,663	48,850	0.62

*The ratio is derived by dividing female by male numbers.
If equal numbers, the ratio is 1.0.

Source: D.B.S. publication # 81-204, "Survey of Higher
Education", Part I, 1969-70, Table 5a. In June
Adam, "A Profile of Women in Canadian Universities", mimeo, prepared for AUCC, Table 10a,
p. 28.

TABLE 3

PART-TIME UNDERGRADUATE ENROLLMENT BY
PROVINCE AND SEX (Regular Winter Session, 1969-70)

Province	Males	Females	Female/Male Ratio
Newfoundland	861	1,129	1.31
Prince Edward Island	268	539	2.01
Nova Scotia	710	1,129	1.59
New Brunswick	1,211	2,213	1.83
Quebec	13,342	7,619	0.57
Ontario	17,521	15,350	0.88
Manitoba	2,319	2,539	1.10
Saskatchewan	1,494	1,789	1.20
Alberta	1,843	2,882	1.57
British Columbia	1,308	1,653	1.26
TOTAL	40,877	36,842	0.90

Source: Adam, "Profile", Table 10b, p. 29. Derived from
D.B.S. publication #81-204, 1969-70, Table 7B.

TABLE 4

LEVEL OF DEGREE GRANTED IN CANADA IN 1971-
1972 BY SEX

Level of Degree	Total	No. Men	No. Women	% Men	% Wome
Bachelor, First Professional Degrees	72,564	43,982	28,582	60.6	39.4
Undergraduate Level Diplomas	5,330	2,433	2,897	45.6	54.4
Undergraduate Level Certificates	2,693	1,382	1,311	51.3	48.7
Master's	10,258	7,715	2,543	75.2	24.8
Earned Doctorates	1,724	1,564	160	90.7	9.3
TOTAL	92,569	57,076	35,493	61.7	38.3

Source: Statistics Canada Publication #42202-514 (June
1973) titled "Degrees, Diplomas and Certificates
Awarded by Canadian Degree-Granting Institutions", Table 1.

TABLE 5

FULL-TIME GRADUATE ENROLLMENT BY FACULTY
AND SEX
(Regular Winter Session— 1969-70)

Faculty	Males	Females	Female/Male Ratios
Arts	7,306	3,003	0.41 (0.80)*
Pure Science	6,101	1,004	0.16 (0.28)
Arts and Science reported together	163	48	0.29 (0.68)
TOTAL	13,570	4,055	0.30 (0.62)

*Comparative Female/Male ratios for full-time undergraduate enrollments appear in brackets.

Source: Adam, "Profile", Table 11a, p. 32. Derived from D.B.S. publication # 81-204, Part I, 1969-70, Table 5a.

TABLE 6

FULL-TIME GRADUATE ENROLLMENT BY PROGRAM
AND SEX IN SELECTED PROFESSIONAL FIELDS
(Regular Winter Session, 1969-70)

Program	Males	Females	Female/Male Ratios
Architecture	96	19	0.20 (0.10)*
Law	132	20	0.15 (0.12)
Medical Studies	1,272	293	0.23 (0.21)
Commerce and Business Admin.	1,833	37	0.02 (0.07)
Engineering & Applied Sc.	3,163	54	0.02 (0.01)
Pharmacy	80	25	0.31 (not included
Dental Studies	83	8	0.10 (0.22)

*Comparative Female/Male ratios for full-time undergraduate enrollments appear in brackets.

Source: Adam, "Profile", abstracted from Table 11a, p. 32.

TABLE 7

EARNED DOCTORATES IN CANADA IN 1971-1972 BY SEX

Specializaion	Total	No. Men	No. Women	% Men	% Women
Education					
Education (all fields)	109	97	12	89.0	11.0
Fine and Applied Arts					
Music	6	3	3	50.0	50.0
Humanities and Related	202	162	40	80.2	19.8
Social Sciences and Related					
Social Science all except	24	18	6	75.0	25.0
Commerce	6	6	—	100.0	—
Economics	21	18	3	85.7	14.3
Law	10	8	2	80.0	20.0
Linguistics	4	4	—	100.0	—
Psychology	109	92	17	84.4	15.6
Social Work	1	1	—	100.0	—
Sociology and related	34	30	4	88.2	11.8
Geography	22	20	2	90.9	9.1
Total	231	197	34	85.3	14.7
Agricultural and Biological Science					
Agriculture (all fields)	52	48	4	92.3	7.7
Biochemistry	17	14	3	82.4	17.6
Biology and related	159	142	17	89.3	10.7

Table 7 (cont'd.) Specialization	Total	No. Men	No. Women	% Men	% Women
Household Sc. and related	1	1	—	100.0	—
Veterinary Med. and related	11	11	—	100.0	—
Total	240	216	24	90.0	10.0
Engineering, Applied Sciences					
Engineering	258	257	1	99.6	.4
Forestry	3	3	—	100.0	—
Total	261	260	1	99.6	.4
Health Professions					
Dental Studies and Research	4	3	1	75.0	25.0
Medical Studies and Research	134	114	20	85.1	14.9
Pharmacy	7	7	—	100.0	—
Public Health	6	4	2	66.6	33.3
Total	151	128	23	84.8	15.2
Mathematics and Physical Science					
Chemistry	221	208	13	94.1	5.9
Geology and related	56	56	—	100.0	—
Mathematics	97	93	4	95.9	4.1
Physics	132	129	3	97.7	2.3
Metereology	5	4	1	80.0	20.0
Oceanography	10	8	2	80.0	20.0
Other	3	3	—	100.0	—
Total	524	501	23	95.6	4.4
Total All Fields	1,724	1,564	160	90.7	9.3

Source: Stats. Can. Publication # 42202-514, Table 6.

TABLE 8

EARNED MASTERS IN CANADA IN 1971-1972 BY SEX

Specialization	Total	No. Men	No. Women	% Men	% Women
Education					
Education (all fields)	1,721	1,245	476	72.3	27.7
Fine and Applied Arts					
Fine and Applied Arts (all fields)	97	40	57	41.2	58.8
Humanities and Related					
Humanities all except Library	1,844	1,266	578	68.7	31.3
Science	402	97	305	24.1	75.9
Translation and Interpretation	16	5	11	31.3	68.8
Total	2,262	1,368	894	60.5	39.5
Social Sciences and Related					
Social Sciences all except	371	255	116	68.7	31.3
Commerce, Bus. Admin. etc.	1,135	1,104	31	97.3	2.7
Health Admin.	44	35	9	79.5	20.5
Economics	318	297	21	93.4	6.6
Law	28	24	4	85.7	14.3
Linguistics	50	27	23	54.0	46.0
Social Work	522	210	312	40.2	59.8
Military Studies	2	2	—	100.0	—

Table 8 (cont'd.) Specialization	Total	No. Men	No. Women	% Men	% Women
Psychology	375	238	137	63.5	36.5
Sociology and related	514	421	93	81.9	18.1
Total	3,359	2,643	746	77.8	22.2
Agricultural and Biological Sciences					
Agriculture (all fields)	149	130	19	87.2	12.8
Biochemistry	32	20	12	62.5	37.5
Biology and related	318	234	84	73.6	26.4
Household Sc. and related	18	4	14	22.2	77.8
Veterinary Med. & Sc.	27	27	—	100.0	—
Total	544	415	129	76.3	23.7
Engineering and Applied Sciences					
Architecture	25	19	6	76.0	24.0
Engineering	962	940	22	97.7	2.3
Forestry	39	39	—	100.0	—
Total	1,026	998	28	97.3	2.7
Health Professions					
Dentistry	15	15	—	100.0	—
Basic Sc. Medicine	104	71	33	68.3	31.7
Medical Specializations	33	32	1	97.0	3.0
Paramedical Sciences	37	27	10	73.0	27.0
Nursing	41	1	40	2.4	97.6
Pharmacy	30	21	9	70.0	30.0
Public Health	19	10	9	52.6	47.4
Rehab. Med.	13	2	11	15.4	84.6
Total	292	179	113	61.3	38.7

Table 8 (cont'd.)

Specialization	Total	No. Men	No. Women	% Men	% Women
Mathematics and Physical Science					
Mathematics and related	428	375	53	87.6	12.4
Chemistry	190	162	28	85.3	14.7
Geology and related	105	96	9	91.4	8.6
Meteorology	11	10	1	90.9	9.1
Oceanography	9	7	2	77.8	22.2
Physics	214	207	7	96.7	3.3
Total	957	857	100	89.6	10.4
TOTAL FOR ALL GROUPS	10,258	7,715	2,543	75.2	24.8

Source: Stats. Can. Publication #42202-514, Table 5.

TABLE 9

FEMALE/MALE RATIOS AND MEDIAN SALARIES OF
FULL-TIME UNIVERSITY TEACHERS
(By Division, 1969-70)

Division	Female/Male Ratio	Median Salary Male	Female
Pure Humanities	0.24	$12,209	$10,310
Applied Humanities	0.23	12,456	11,212
Pure Social Science	0.10	12,883	11,250
Applied Social Science*	0.28	13,589	11,597
Pure Biological Sciences	0.12	14,600	11,590
Applied ” ” **	0.24	16,322	10,325
Pure Physical Sciences***	0.06	13,676	10,800
Applied ” ”	0.01	14,137	11,850

* Includes Education, Household Science, Physical &
    Health Education & Social Work.
** Includes Nursing, Physio/Occupational Therapy.
*** Includes Mathematics

Source: Abstracted from Adam, "Profile", Tables 17-20,
pp. 53-56. Data drawn from D.B.S. #81-203,
"Salaries and Qualifications of Teachers in Universities and Colleges: 1969-70", Tables 8-11.

Bob Anderson - Photo Features

Grace Hartman is president of the Canadian Union of Public Employees. Her ascendancy in the public service unions began when she joined the staff of the borough of North York as a secretary in 1954. She held a series of offices in the old National Union of Public Employees and then with CUPE after it was formed in 1963. She became its national secretary-treasurer in 1967 and held that post until 1975 when she was elected president. She was appointed to the Federal Status of Women Council in 1973, an independent board established in response to a recommendation of the Royal Commission on the Status of Women, and is past president of the National Action Committee on the Status of Women.

Women and the Unions

Grace Hartman

"The time will come, we hope, when women will be economically free . . . when women will receive equal pay for equal work, and have all avenues of activity open to them."

An ad which ran recently in women's magazines shows a man operating a swtichboard and has the caption: "This phone company wants more operators like John Jones." Although this seems to indicate the company's enlightened hiring policies, what is going to happen to the next woman who applies for the traditionally female job of telephone operator? If the company wants more operators like John Jones she may very well be passed over for a man. And if she does get the job, will she and John be making the same pay, will they get an equal opportunity to be supervisors or to receive the training for management jobs? Chances are good that they won't. That is the reality of women in the work force.

Someone once defined woman as "a *side*-issue at Creation". While the validity of that statement must be left to Biblical scholars, my experience as a representative of Canadian working men and women has proven that women are very much pushed to the side today.

To a frustratingly great extent working women occupy

the low status, low-paying jobs with little chance for advancement. Despite the fact that the percentage of women in the total Canadian work force increased from 25.8 percent in 1960 to 33.2 percent in 1972, women are still doing the same kind of "supportive" jobs they've always done. They are secretaries not executives, assembly-line workers not foremen, stewardesses not pilots, and teachers not principals. There is nothing wrong with any of these jobs, but too often women are doing them because other occupations are not open to them. And too often they are doing them at a depressed rate of pay because they are women. When it is sex, not ability or inclination which determines who will do a job and how much they will be paid for doing it, something is wrong.

Even in occupations in which women are in the majority, it is still often considered essential that the top position be held by a man. In Edmonton, for example, the director of nursery schools is a man although nursery school teachers are invariably women. And of course women's wages are lower in almost all sectors of industry. The most glaring examples of this occur in the garment and rubber industries—two areas in which the majority of employees are women.

Myths alleging that women are the "weaker sex", that working women have higher rates of absenteeism than men, that women job-hop more than men, must be permanently buried. One government myth offered to explain the unexpected jump in benefits paid under unemployment insurance was that some housewives were making temporary forays into the labour force for periods just long enough to qualify for UIC benefits. But according to the Women's Bureau of the Federal Department of Labour, the average unemployment rate for men aged twenty-five years and over from January to September 1972 was 5.1 percent compared with 5.2 percent in 1971. The average rate of unemployment for women aged twenty-five years and over for 1972 was 3.6 percent compared with 3.3 percent in 1971.

Federal Department of Labour statistics also showed the employment record for women claiming benefits is better than that of men. Only 1.9 percent of women claimants had worked just eight weeks before receiving benefits compared with 2.5 percent of men.[1]

Rates of absenteeism, long a favourite excuse of employers to limit women, have proven to vary insignificantly. Federal Department of Labour statistics for 1973 (the last full-year figures available) show that for absences of more than one week, more work-time was lost by men than by women. Random sampling done by the federal government showed that of the 3.8 percent of the work force off work for more than one week, only 1.8 percent were female.

One of the myths that has persisted longer than most is that women are too emotional, that they tend to burst into tears in the board room. It seems more likely that any woman who has fought her way to the top in a society like ours in which it takes more skill, more energy, more qualifications and more determination for a woman to reach that level than it does a man, will have few tears left by the time she gets there. In any case, better that she burst into tears under stress than have a heart attack behind her executive desk.

Canadian unions have pushed for a more enlightened attitude. They've had to push governments, employers, and their own membership—both men and women. Despite these efforts, however, we have just begun to make the changes necessary to bring about real equality for working women.

Unions must be concerned with recruiting more women and encouraging them to become actively involved in union

[1]Sylva Gelber, Director, Women's Bureau, Canada Department of Labour, Ottawa.

activities: drawing up collective agreements, running for office and speaking out on behalf of women within the trade union movement itself.

This will have to be achieved through organization, through the education of union men to the fact that the contract doesn't protect the female employee as well as the male employee. It will be assisted by giving women special treatment within unions for an interim period allowing them to catch up after generations of discrimination.

Women make up one third of Canada's total labour force, yet only 23.5 percent of them are union members. This number, however, is steadily increasing: eight years ago, only 17 percent were union members.

There are many reasons why women have been slow to enter unions and to become active within them. Ignorance about unions is common. All too often an uninformed person, whose ideas about unions derive from misinformation she received at school and from sensational newspaper reports, complains that unions are run by criminals operating from the United States, greedy, and the cause of all the economic ills besetting the country. Her image of union activity is one of strikes, violence and corruption. We call this the "Hoffa syndrome". Attitudes such as these are difficult to eradicate.

The 95 percent of collective agreements settled without a strike don't get into the newspapers. A democratically run local union in which the members make their own decisions and oversee the spending of the dues money is a facet of unionism unknown to many women.

Similarly, the elimination of "male" and "female" classifications in collective agreements; the demand that day-care facilities be provided at the work place; the winning of promotion systems that prevent sex discrimination; the end to archaic maternity leave rules—none of these union activities can compete for news value with volatile picket lines.

Women also do not become involved in union activity because their husbands are opposed to it. They feel they almost need his permission to become active in their local unions.

At the risk of arousing the wrath of my union brothers, I suggest that another reason more women don't become active in unions is that the sexist nature of our society is at least partially reflected in the labour movement itself.

In my own career I have encountered discrimination almost every day. Most men don't know how to deal with a woman on an equal basis; they see her only in terms of her sex. I once made a presentation to the Alberta government on a pertinent labour matter. At the conclusion I was congratulated by a union "brother" who said, "It was a pretty good presentation for a woman."

The *Report of the Royal Commission on the Status of Women* reinforces my personal experience. Says the commission report: "Although labor unions have made contributions toward better working conditions for all employees, women have not as yet obtained equal opportunities with men at work in all sectors or acquired full representation in labor unions." According to a study prepared for the commission, "when unionists discuss women at work, it is never in quite the same way they discuss men at work. There always seem to be implications, in the conversation, that woman's role is elsewhere."

At Dare Foods Limited in Kitchener, although men were a minority in the bargaining unit they endorsed a contract that would give them higher pay than their women co-workers. The women voted against the contract and a long strike ensued. And in Winnipeg the seniority rights of two women were overlooked by McGavin Toastmaster Limited and the Bakery and Confectionery Workers International Union of America. The two workers claimed they had been laid off because they were women, without regard to their seniority. They said the union had refused to assist them. The Manitoba government intervened and ordered both company and union to pay $500 compensation to the women. The company was also ordered to provide equal opportunity for both sexes and to post one single and corrected seniority list.

It is an undisputable fact that unions have not done as much for working women as they could have. With some exceptions they have not led the fight for improved day care, maternity leave with pay, abortion on demand, and equal pay for equal value. These are regarded as low priority items by unions which tend to reflect male values.

Unions, like all other institutions in society, are made up of individuals who suffer from years of misguided conditioning. We have all been affected by the crippling myth of woman's inferiority, the one that designates her "natural role" as man's subordinate. The indoctrination has been thorough. And women have accepted it. A cultural conditioning that begins as a child when she is given a toy broom and her brother a rocket ship, and continues throughout her life, teaches a woman to expect less from life.

Women are consistently represented in the media as morons, concerned only with their deodorants or talking to genies who come out of cleaning bottles. It is clear the kind of role society has chosen for them. Should there be any doubt, Dr. Benjamin Spock, grandfather of pediatricians, is quick to add, "I believe that women are designed in their deeper instincts to get more pleasure out of life . . . when they are not aggressive. To put it another way, I think that when women are encouraged to become competitive too many of them become disagreeable." Despite Dr. Spock, more women should be encouraged to become competitive, and if necessary, disagreeable.

Undoubtedly their reluctance to compete is one of the major factors which discourages women from reaching the senior levels in unions, as in industry, even when they are in the majority. The Canadian Union of Public Employees, which represents 200,000 hospital, municipal, school board, public utilities and CBC employees, has a female membership approaching 40 percent. Despite this and despite the fact that CUPE is growing fastest in the areas of clerical and technical employees, only four members of the seventeen-member national executive board of CUPE are women. And CUPE has probably a better record of recognizing the disparities and moving to correct them than any other union operating in Canada.

As of December 1971, there were 720 executive board members of unions in Canada. Of this figure eighty—about 11 percent—were women. The national unions had the best record with sixty-one out of 405 executive board members. Government unions—PSAC and provincial associations—were next with thirteen women out of 209, and the internationals were a dismal last with six women out of 106 executive members.

No doubt the unions are partly responsible for the relatively small proportion of working women involved in unions at any level. Unions should have been organizing in the personnel agencies, insurance companies, department stores and banks. Unionization in these areas has of course been difficult. Management here has taken an extremely hard-line approach against union organization. Because of the unskilled nature of the work, it has been possible to fire "agitators" and replace them relatively easily with untrained women.

Union organizers must use different methods when operating in these areas. Plant-gate distribution which spelled success for organizing factory workers doesn't work with clerical and technical employees. They require a more sophisticated approach. Perhaps by specifically setting aside sufficient funds annually for organizing clerical and technical employees, the labour movement, through the Canadian Labour Congress, can begin to organize in these areas in the future.

Unions have won many things for working women but faster and greater change will only be forced on employers and on society in general by unions in which women are more active. There is much to be done.

As a beginning, legislation must be passed to implement the most basic and overdue reforms—equal pay for equal value, equality on the job and equal opportunity for advancement. This simple beginning won't be easy because the vast majority of our legislators are men.

In 1951 the International Labour Organization passed its monumental bill number 100. This document confirmed the principle that discrimination should not be made on the basis of sex with regard to remuneration in any form payable to workers for work of equal value. Canada is a member of the International Labour Organization, yet for twenty-one years our legislators refused to ratify that document. Four days before the 1972 Canadian federal election, then Labour Minister Martin O'Connell grandly announced that the federal government had the agreement of the provinces to approve the equal remuneration clause. In the announcement, Mr. O'Connell managed to avoid saying that the Canadian government was poised to ratify an article most other countries had ratified twenty-one years before.

Even though women have had the vote in Canada for half a century, there are only nine women sitting in the House of Commons. This means men will decide the fate of the recommendations from the Royal Commission on the

Status of Women, including adoption of the four underlying principles:

1. Women should be free to choose whether or not to take employment outside of their homes.
2. The care of children is a responsibility to be shared by the mother, father and society.
3. Society has a responsibility for women because of pregnancy and childbirth, and special treatment related to maternity will always be necessary.
4. In certain areas, women will for an interim period require special treatment to overcome the adverse effects of discriminatory practices.

CUPE does take the status of women seriously. It has adopted a special policy on the status of women in the union. It says no CUPE collective agreements should tolerate sex discrimination.

It is unlikely, however, that the Canadian Manufacturing Association or the Chamber of Commerce will follow suit. But even with CUPE's policy, it is not easy to eliminate sex discrimination. Many of the employers with which the union negotiates tenaciously hang onto their own prejudices. CUPE is determined to change this, but traditions die hard.

Employers can be pushed only so far. Members often have to decide if they will strike to end discrimination or suffer with it until the next round of negotiations. Strike, and we're accused of being too militant and destructive. Settle, and we face the charge of having abandoned the cause of equality for women.

The case of the Town of Dauphin, Manitoba, was one of the worst examples of blatant discrimination CUPE has encountered. The town had a policy which in contract language said: "The town reserves the right to continue its longstanding practice whereby it may terminate the employment of any female employee upon her marriage." CUPE vigorously opposed this clause. The town refused to yield.

Finally, the Manitoba Human Rights Commission, which now has some bite, stepped in and ordered the town to desist.

The contract with Manitoba Hydro states that where a husband and wife are both employed in the same northern location, only the husband is entitled to northern allowance. The City of Saskatoon is another employer which persists in discrimination. Two members of one family cannot work in the same department. If a husband and wife happen to be assigned to the same department, the woman must resign or move to another department.

Employees of the City of Calgary and the City of Regina are entitled to one maternity leave. Should a woman become pregnant a second time, she must resign and lose her seniority. In other words, a woman may commit the error of pregnancy only once.

Another example of long-standing sex discrimination occurred in Ontario hospitals. In the past orderlies had been paid more than Registered Nursing Assistants. Yet RNA's are more highly skilled, having undergone special training for nearly a year. Orderlies receive only on-the-job training. The basis for the wage disparity was that orderlies are men, perhaps able to do heavier lifting, and considered to be family heads.

CUPE is winning this fight. There are now eight hospitals in Ontario in which RNA's are paid more than male orderlies. Thirty-eight CUPE contracts stipulate equal pay. And now in only two hospitals with CUPE representation do RNA's receive less pay than orderlies. In New Brunswick hospitals this injustice has been ended.

Women must work from within their unions to eliminate the inequities which are guaranteed by discriminatory collective agreements. Jobs designated by sex, earlier retirement age for women, different pension rates for women, "rug ranking" of secretaries' salaries according to the position of their boss, different rates of pay for the same work, are all supported by the collective agreements between employers and trade unions. All union contracts must be carefully scrutinized and all such discriminatory clauses removed.

Even where a collective agreement seems straightforward, however, there may be pitfalls. I was once a union nominee on an arbitration board dispute which centred around a female employee who had been off work to have a baby. The contract guaranteed her six months maternity leave without pay. Under the terms of the contract she was also entitled to three weeks paid holiday annually. However, when she applied for the holiday management refused, stating that because she hadn't worked for six months she wasn't entitled to the full three weeks.

Employers are often capable of inventing ingenious schemes to circumvent contract terms or employee demands. When forty part-time female employees at the Welland County Separate School Board approached CUPE to represent them, the board countered by "firing" all the women and "hiring" Office Overload. Technically this meant that the same employees would continue on the same jobs at the same rate of pay—$2.34 an hour—but the employer would be Office Overload, not the school board. It also meant that in order to organize the forty women, CUPE would have to organize a majority of all employees sent out by Office Overload—an impossible task. Fortunately, the board's absurd plan failed. The union filed charges under the Ontario Labour Relations Act claiming that the secretaries were really employed by the school board and not Office Overload. The Labour Relations Board agreed.

Women who work for the temporary employment

agencies—such as Dot, Drake, Office Overload—face a special problem. These agencies place office workers in temporary jobs usually for short periods of time. They make their profit by charging the employee an hourly rate. There are usually no benefits, no paid holidays, and no assurance when each job ends that another will be forthcoming. Because of the very nature of these employment agencies, it has been virtually impossible for unions to organize this "secretarial proleteriat".

Legislation, when it is passed, can lull us into thinking things are improving. Most provinces now have laws on the statute books which guarantee equal pay and maternity leave, and prohibit sex discrimination in hiring. The problem is that they are not always enforced or enforceable. It wasn't until September 1972 that Manitoba became the first government to prosecute sex discrimination in Canada.

In the case already cited concerning Registered Nursing Assistants in Sudbury, the Ontario Employment Standards Branch which compared their working conditions and wages with that of the orderlies could not intervene directly to correct the disparities they discovered but merely suggested they should be adjusted through future negotiations.[2]

It is imperative that unions be unrelenting in bringing pressure on governments, on business and on management in general, and even on some of our own fellow unionists, to recognize the rights of women and work to ensure that these rights are, in fact, a reality for all women.

As unions begin to speak out for working women, they will naturally attract the woman who has avoided involvement in the past. There are already some encouraging signs that the process is beginning. One of the main factors in

[2]Sylva Gelber, Canada Department of Labour.

[3]Letter from R.C. Cain, Regional Manager, Employment Standards Branch, to Annette Taylor, President, CUPE Local 1023, May 18, 1972.

the 1972 strike at Toronto's Western Hospital was the differential between male and female employees—as much as $80 a month for general help. It was obvious that the female employees were settling for nothing short of parity.

The Royal Commission's Report on the Status of Women and the Ontario government's proposed report on opportunities for women suggest that all levels of government, if for no other reason than to set a good example, will hire more women in the future. This will be in addition to the ever-increasing growth of public services which we can expect for many years to come.

Each year, more women are entering the labour force. Economic necessity is no doubt the prime motivation but many women are working because they want to, and because society's expectations for women in all situations are changing rapidly.

As women take their rightful place in the labour movement and make their contributions, they will reap the benefits. But they will have to do it for themselves. If the labour movement, and women within the movement, are going to achieve success, women must be willing to carry their own load and more.

This is "the best of times and the worst of times" for today's working women. Although there are many struggles to come, it is also a most exciting time for women to enter the labour force. Women are now doing jobs they didn't know existed ten years ago. They are beginning to demand the rights that have been long denied them, and they are finding support and gaining strength from other women.

Women today are embarking upon a revolution that will alter not only the working world, but the quality of life for both men and women. After several thousand years of civilization, society has awakened to the fact that women are more than a side-issue. And it is women in the trade unions who must drive home the wedge of this new consciousness.

Graeme Gibson

*Born in Ottawa in 1939 Margaret Atwood is one of Canada's fore-
most poets and novelists. She has published six volumes of poetry
including* The Circle Game *for which she won the Governor General's
Award in 1967, two novels,* The Edible Woman *and* Surfacing, *and
the seminal and controversial critical work* Survival: A Thematic
Guide to Canadian Literature. *She has taught at York University,
the University of British Columbia, Sir George Williams University,
the University of Alberta, and was Writer-in-Residence at the University of Toronto in 1972-73.*

Paradoxes and Dilemmas: The Woman as Writer

Margaret Atwood

*"I knew ... what a writer can be at his best ...
an interpreter, a revealer of secrets. ..."*

I approach this article with a good deal of reluctance. Since promising to do it, in fact, I've been procrastinating to such an extent that my own aversion is probably the first subject I should attempt to deal with. Some of my reservations have to do with the questionable value of writers, male or female, becoming directly involved in political movements of any sort: their involvement may be good for the movement, but it has yet to be demonstrated that it's good for the writer. The rest concern my sense of the enormous complexity not only of the relationships between Man and Woman, but also of those between such other abstract intangibles as Art and Life, Form and Content, Writer and Critic, and so forth.

Judging from conversations I've had with many other woman poets and novelists in this country, my qualms are not unique. I can think of only one fiction or poetry writer I know who has formal connection with any of the diverse organizations usually lumped together under the titles of women's liberation or the women's movement. There are even several who have gone out of their way to disavow even fellow-feeling. But the usual attitude is one of grudging admiration, tempered with envy: the younger

257

generation, they feel, has it a hell of a lot better than they did. Most writers old enough to have a career of any length behind them grew up when it was still assumed that a woman's place was in the home and nowhere else, and that anyone who took time off for an individual selfish activity like writing was either neurotic or wicked or both, derelict in her duties to some man, child or aged relative. I've heard stories of writers so consumed by guilt over what they had been taught to feel was their abnormality that they did their writing at night, secretly, so no one would accuse them of failing as housewives, as "women". These writers accomplished what they did by themselves, often at great personal expense. In order to write at all, they had to defy other women's as well as men's ideas of what was proper, and it's not finally all that comforting to have a phalanx of women—some younger and relatively unscathed, others from their own generation, the bunch that was collecting china, changing diapers and sneering at any female with intellectual pretensions twenty or even ten years ago—come breezing up now to tell them they were right all along. It's like being judged innocent after you've been hanged: the satisfaction, if any, is grim. There's a great temptation to say to feminists, "Where were you when I really needed you?" or "It's too late for me now." And you can see, too, that it would be fairly galling for these writers, if they have any respect for historical accuracy, which most do, to be hailed as products, spokeswomen, or advocates of the women's movement. When they were undergoing their often drastic formative years there *was* no women's movement. No matter that a lot of what they say can be taken by the theorists of the movement as supporting evidence, useful analysis, and so forth. Their own inspiration was not theoretical; it came from wherever all writing comes from. Call it experience and imagination. These writers, if they are honest, don't want to be wrongly identified as the children of a movement that did not give birth to them. Being adopted is not the same as being born.

A third area of reservation is undoubtedly a fear of the development of a one-dimensional Feminist Criticism, a way of approaching literature produced by women that would award points according to conformity or non-conformity to an ideological position. A feminist criticism is, in fact, already emerging. I've read several reviews, and I'm sure there will be more, in which a novelist was criticized for not having made her heroine's life different, more active and directed, even though that life was more typical of the average woman's life in this society than the reviewer's "liberated" version would have been. Perhaps feminist reviewers will start demanding that heroines resolve their difficulties with husband, kids, or themselves by stomping out to join a consciousness-raising group or get a job, which will be no more satisfactory from the point of view of literature than the legendary Socialist Realist romance with one's tractor. However, a feminist criticism need not necessarily be one-dimensional. And—small comfort—no matter how narrow, purblind and stupid such a criticism in its lowest manifestations may be, it cannot possibly be *more* narrow, purblind and stupid than some of the non-feminist critical attitudes and styles that have preceded it.

There's a fourth possible factor, a less noble one: the often observed phenomenon of the member of a despised social group who manages to transcend the limitations imposed on the group, at least enough to become "successful". For such a person the impulse—whether obeyed or not—is to disassociate him/herself from the group and to side with its implicit opponents. Thus the black millionaire who deplores the Panthers, the rich *Québécois* who is anti-Separatist, the North American immigrant who changes his name to an "English" one; thus, alas, the Canadian writer who makes it in New York and spends the rest of his life decrying provincial dull Canadian writing. And thus the women with successful careers who say, "*I've* never had any problems, I don't know what they're talking about." Such a woman tends to regard herself, and to be treated by her male colleagues, as an honorary man. It's the rest of them who are inept, brainless, tearful, self-defeating: not her. "You think like a man," she is told, with admiration and unconscious put-down. For both men and women, it's just too great a strain to fit together the traditionally incompatible notions of "woman" and "good at something". And if you *are* good at something, why carry with you the stigma attached to that dismal category you've gone to such lengths to escape from? You should rock the boat only if you're still chained to the oars. Not everyone reacts like this, but this factor may explain some of the more hysterical opposition to the movement on the part of a few woman writers, even though they may have benefited from it in the form of increased sales and more serious attention.

A couple of ironies remain; perhaps they are even paradoxes. One is that in the development of modern Western civilization writing was the first of the arts, before painting, music, composing, and sculpting, which it was possible for women to practice; and it was the fourth of the job categories, after prostitution, domestic service and the stage, and before wide-scale factory work, nursing, secretarial work, telephone operating and school teaching, at which it was possible for them to make any money. The reason for both is the same: writing as a physical activity is private. You do it by yourself, on your own time; no teachers or employers are involved, you don't have to apprentice in a studio or work with musicians. Your only business arrangements are with your publisher, and these can be conducted through the mails; your real "employers", the readers, can be deceived if you choose by the adoption of an assumed male name: witness the Brontës and George Eliot. But the private and individual nature of writing may also account for the low incidence of direct involvement by woman writers in the movement now. If you are a writer, prejudice against women will affect you *as a writer* not directly but indirectly. You won't suffer from wage discrimination, because you aren't paid any wages; you won't be hired last and fired first, because you aren't hired or fired anyway. You have relatively little to complain of, and, absorbed in your own work as you are likely to be, you will find it quite easy to shut your eyes to what goes on at the spool factory, or even at the university. Alas, paradoxically, the same conditions that allowed female participation in the first place may discourage militant attitudes now.

Another paradox goes like this. As writers, female writers are like male writers. They have the same professional concerns, they have to deal with the same contracts and publishing procedures, they have the same need for solitude to work and the same desire that their work be accurately evaluated by reviewers. There is nothing "male" or "female" about these concerns and needs; they are just attributes of writing as an activity. As biological specimens and as citizens, however, women are like other women: subject to the same discriminatory laws, encountering the same demeaning attitudes, burdened with the same good reasons for not walking through the park alone after dark. They too have bodies, the capacity to bear children; they too eat, sleep, bleed and go to the bank. In bookstores and publishers' offices and among groups of other writers, a woman writer may get the impression that she is "special", but in the eyes of the law, in the loan office, in the hospital and on the street she's just another woman. She can't wear a sign to the grocery store saying "Respect Me, I'm a Woman Writer". No matter how good she may feel about herself, bigoted strangers who aren't aware of her shelf-full of volumes with cover blurbs saying how gifted she is will still regard and treat her as a nit.

We all have ways of filtering out aspects of our experience we would rather not think about. Woman writers can keep as much as possible to the "writing" end of their life, avoiding the less desirable aspects of the "woman" end. Or they can divide themselves in two, thinking of themselves as two different people: a "writer" and a "woman". Time after time, I've had interviewers talk to me about my writing for a while, then ask me, "As a woman, what do you think about [for instance] the woman's movement?" as if I could think two sets of thoughts about the same things, one set as a writer or person, the other as a woman. But no one comes apart this easily; categories like Woman, White, Canadian, and Writer are only ways of looking at a person and the person herself remains whole, entire and indivisible. Thus Woman and Writer are often treated as separate categories; but in any individual woman writer, they are inseparable.

One of the results of this paradox is that there are certain attitudes and conditions, some overt, some concealed, which women writers encounter *as* writers, but *because* they are women. Here are a few of these.

Reviewing and the Absence of an Adequate Critical Vocabulary

Cynthia Ozick, in the American magazine *Ms.*, says, "For many years, I had noticed that no book of poetry by a woman was ever reviewed without reference to the poet's sex. The curious thing was that, in the two decades of my scrutiny, there were *no* exceptions whatever. It did not matter whether the reviewer was a man or a woman; in every case, the question of the 'feminine sensibility' of the poet was at the centre of the reviewer's response. The maleness of male poets, on the other hand, hardly ever seemed to matter."

Things aren't this bad in Canada, possibly because we were never thoroughly indoctrinated with the Holy Gospel according to the distorters of Freud. Many reviewers manage to get through a review without displaying the kind of bias Ozick is talking about. But that it does occur was demonstrated to me by a project I was involved with at York University in 1971-72.

One of my student groups was attempting to study what we called "sexual bias in reviewing", by which we meant not unfavourable reviews, but points being added or subtracted by the reviewer on the basis of the author's sex and supposedly associated characteristics rather than on the basis of the work itself. Our study fell into two parts: i) a survey of writers, half male, half female, conducted by letter: had they ever experienced sexual bias directed against them in a review?; ii) the reading of a large number of reviews from a wide range of periodicals and newspapers.

The results of the writers' survey were perhaps predictable. Of the men, none answered Yes, a quarter Maybe, and three-quarters No. Of women, half were Yeses, a quarter Maybes and a quarter Nos. The women replying Yes often wrote long, detailed letters, giving instances and discussing their own attitudes. All the men's letters were short.

This proved only that women were more likely to *feel* they had been discriminated against on the basis of sex. When we got round to the reviews, we discovered they were sometimes justified. Here are the kinds of things we found.

i) *Assignment of Reviews*

Several of our letter-writers discussed the mechanics of review assignment. Some felt books by women tended to be passed over by book-page editors assigning books for review; others that books by women tended to get assigned to women reviewers. When we started toting up reviews we found that most books in this society are written by men, and so are most reviews. Disproportionately often, books by women were assigned to women reviewers, indicating that books by women fell in the minds of those dishing out the reviews into a special "female" category. Likewise, woman reviewers tended to be reviewing books by women rather than books by men (though because of the preponderance of male reviewers, there were quite a few male-written reviews of books by women).

ii) *The Quiller-Couch Syndrome*

This phrase refers to the turn-of-the-century essay by Quiller-Couch, defining "masculine" and "feminine" styles in writing. The "masculine" style is, of course, bold, forceful, clear, vigorous, etc.; the "feminine" style is vague, weak, tremulous, pastel, etc. In the list of pairs you can include "objective" and "subjective", "universal" or "accurate depiction of society" versus "confessional", "personal", or even "narcissistic" and "neurotic". It's roughly seventy years since Quiller-Couch's essay, but the "masculine" group of adjectives is still much more likely to be applied to the work of male writers; female writers are much more likely to get hit with some version of "the feminine style" or "feminine sensibility", whether their work merits it or not.

iii) *The Lady Painter Syndrome, or She Writes Like A Man*

This is a pattern in which good equals male, bad equals female. I call it the Lady Painter Syndrome because of a conversation I had about female painters with a male painter in 1960. "When she's good," he said, "we call her a painter; when she's bad, we call her a lady painter." "She writes like a man" is part of the same pattern; it's usually used by a male reviewer who is impressed by a female writer. It's meant as a compliment. See also "She thinks like a man," which means the author thinks, unlike most women, who are held to be incapable of objective thought (their province is "feeling"). Adjectives which often have similar connotations are ones such as "strong", "gutsy", "hard", "mean", etc. A hard-hitting piece of writing by a man is liable to be thought of as merely realistic; an equivalent piece by a woman is much more likely to be labelled "cruel" or "tough". The assumption is that women are by nature soft, weak and not very talented, and that if a woman writer happens to be a good writer, she should be deprived of her identity as a female and provided with higher (male) status. Thus the woman writer has, in the minds of such reviewers, two choices. She can be bad but female, a carrier of the "feminine sensibility" virus; or she can be "good" in male-adjective terms, but sexless. Badness seems to be ascribed then to a surplus of female hormones, whereas badness in a male writer is usually ascribed to nothing but badness (though a "bad" male writer is sometimes held, by adjectives implying sterility or impotence, to be deficient in maleness). "Maleness" is exemplified by the "good" male writer; "femaleness", since it is seen by such reviewers as a handicap or deficiency, is held to be transcended or discarded by the "good" female one. In other words, there is no critical vocabulary for expressing the concept "good/female". Work by a male writer is often spoken of by critics admiring it as having "balls"; have you ever heard anyone speak admiringly of work by a woman as having "tits"?

Possible antidotes: Development of a "good/female" vocabulary (wow, has that ever got womb . . ."); or, preferably, the development of a vocabulary that can treat structures made of words as though they are exactly that, not biological entities possessed of sexual organs.

iv) *Domesticity*

One of our writers noted a (usually male) habit of concentrating on domestic themes in the work of a female writer, ignoring any other topic she might have dealt with, then patronizing her for an excessive interest in domestic themes. We found several instances of reviewers identifying an author as a "housewife" and consequently dismissing anything she has produced (since, in our society, a "housewife" is viewed as a relatively brainless and talentless creature). We even found one instance in which the author was called a "housewife" and put down for writing like one when in fact she was no such thing.

For such reviewers, when a man writes about things like doing the dishes, it's realism; when a woman does, it's an unfortunate feminine genetic limitation.

v) *Sexual Compliment/Put-down*

This syndrome can be summed up as follows:

She: "How do you like my (design for an airplane/mathematical formula/medical miracle)?"

He: "You sure have a nice ass."

In reviewing it usually takes the form of commenting on the cute picture of the (female) author on the cover, coupled with dismissal of her as a writer.

Interviewers and Media Stereotypes

Associated with the reviewing problem, but distinct from it, is the problem of the interview. Reviewers are supposed to concentrate on books, interviewers on the writer as a person, as a human being, or, in the case of women, as a woman. This means that an interviewer is ostensibly trying to find out what sort of person you are. In reality, he or she may merely be trying to match you up with a stereotype of "Woman Author" that pre-exists in her/his mind; doing it that way is both easier for the interviewer, since it limits the range and slant of questions, and shorter, since the interview can be practically written in advance. It isn't just women who get this treatment: any writer may get it. But the range for male authors is somewhat wider, and usually comes from the literary tradition itself, whereas stereotypes for female authors are often borrowed from other media, since the ones provided by the tradition are limited in number.

In a bourgeois, industrial society, so the theory goes, the creative artist is seen as acting out suppressed desires of the audience; thus we get certain Post-Romantic male-author stereotypes, such as Potted Poe, Bleeding Byron, Doomed Dylan, Lustful Layton, Crucified Cohen, etc. Until recently the only personality stereotype of this kind was Elusive Emily, otherwise known as Recluse Rosetti: the woman writer as aberration, hiding behind doors or looking at life through the wormholes in a shroud, neurotically denying herself the delights of sex, kiddies and other fun. The twentieth century has added Suicidal Sylvia, a somewhat more dire version of the same thing. The point about these stereotypes is that attention is focused not on the actual achievements of the authors, but on their lives, which are distorted and romanticized; their work is then interpreted in the light of the distorted version. Stereotypes like these, even when the author cooperates in their formation and especially when the author becomes a cult object, do no service to anyone or anything, least of all the author's work. Behind all of them is the notion that authors must be more special, peculiar or weird than other people, and that their lives are more interesting than their work.

The following examples are taken from personal experience (mine, or interviewers); they indicate the range of possibilities. There are a few others, such as Earth Mother, of which I have no personal knowledge.

i) *Happy Housewife*

This one is almost obsolete: it used to appear on the Woman's Page. The questions were about what you liked to fix for dinner; the attitude was, "Gosh, all the housework and you're a writer too!" Writing was viewed as a hobby, like knitting, that one did in one's spare time.

ii) *Ophelia*

The writer as crazy freak. This is a female version of Doomed Dylan, usually with more than a little hope on the part of the interviewer that you'll turn into Suicidal Sylvia and *really* give them something to write about. Questions tend towards "Do you think you're in danger of going insane?" It's useless to point out that most mental institutions are crammed with people who have never written a word in their life. "Say something interesting," one interviewer quipped. "Say you write all your poems on drugs."

iii) *Miss Martyr, or, "Movie Mag"*

Read any "movie mag" article on Liz Taylor, translate it into writing terms and you've got the picture. The writer as someone who *suffers* more than others. Why does the writer suffer more? Because she's successful, and you all know Success Must Be Paid For. In blood and tears, if possible. If you say you're happy and enjoy your life and work, you'll be ignored.

iv) *Miss Message*

The interviewer who believes in Miss Message is incapable of treating your work as what it is, poetry and/or fiction.

There's a great attempt to get you to say something about an issue and then make you into an exponent, spokeswoman or theorist. The interviewer is unable to see that putting, for instance, a nationalist into a novel doesn't make it a nationalistic novel, any more than putting in a preacher makes it a religious novel. The interviewer is rigidly one-dimensional and judgmental, and expects you to follow suit. Rare indeed is an interviewer who regards writing as a respectable profession, not as some kind of magic, madness, trickery or evasive disguise for a message; and who regards an author as a person engaged in a professional activity, not as a witch, boor, sufferer or messiah.

Other Writers and Rivalry

Regarding yourself as an "exception", part of an unspoken quota system, can have interesting results. If there are only so many available slots for your minority in the medical school/law school/literary world, of course you will feel rivalry, not only with members of the majority for whom no quota operates, but especially with members of your minority who are competing with you for the few coveted places. And you will have to be better than the average majority member to get in at all.

Woman-woman rivalry does occur, though it is surprisingly much less severe than you'd expect; it's likely to take the form of *wanting* another woman writer to be better than she is, expecting more of her than you would of a male writer, and being exasperated with certain kinds of traditional "female" writing.

What a woman writer is often unprepared for is the unexpected personal attack on her by a jealous male writer. The motivation is envy and competitiveness, but the form is often sexual put-down. "You may be good writer," one older man said to a young woman writer who had just had a publishing success, "but I wouldn't want to fuck you." Another version goes more like the compliment put-down noted under Reviewing. In either case, the ploy diverts attention from the woman's achievement as a writer—the area where the man feels threatened—to her sexuality, where either way he can score a verbal point.

I've been trying to give you a picture of the arena, or that part of it, where "woman" and "writer", as concepts, over-lap. But, of course, the arena I've been talking about has to do largely with externals: reviewing, the media, relation-ships with other writers. This, for the writer, may affect the tangibles of her career: how she is received, how viewed, how much money she makes. But in relationship to the writing itself, this is a false arena. The real one is in her head, her real struggle the daily battle with words, the language itself. The false arena becomes valid for writing itself only insofar as it becomes part of her material and is transformed into one of the verbal and imaginative struc-tures she is constantly engaged in making. Novelists and poets are not propagandists or examples of social trends or preachers or politicians. They are makers of novels and poems, and unless they can make these well they will be bad writers, no matter what the social validity of their views.

At the beginning of this article, I suggested a few reasons for the infrequent participation in the movement of Can-adian woman novelists and poets. Maybe those reasons were the wrong ones, and this is the real one: no good writer wants to be merely a transmitter of someone else's ideology, no matter how fine that ideology may be. The aim of pro-paganda is to convince and to spur people to action; the aim of fiction and poetry writing is to create a plausible and moving imaginative world, and to create it with words. Or, to put it another way, the aim of any political movement is to improve the quality of people's lives on all levels, spiritual and imaginative as well as material (and any political movement that doesn't have this aim is worth nothing). Imaginative writing, however, tends to concentrate more on life not as it ought to be, but as it is, as the writer feels it, experiences it. Writers are eye-witnesses, I-witnesses. Political movements, once successful, have historically been intolerant of imaginative writers, even those who initially aided them; in any revolution, writers have been among the first to be lined up against the wall, perhaps for their intransigence, their insistence on saying what they perceive, not what, according to the ideology, ought to exist. Politicians, even revolutionary politicians, have traditionally had no more respect for writing as an activity valuable in itself, quite apart from any message or content, than has the rest of the society. And writers, even revolutionary writers, have traditionally been suspicious of anyone who tells them what they ought to write.

The woman writer in Canada, then, exists in a society that, though it may turn certain individual writers into revered cult objects, has little respect for writing as a profession, and not much respect for women either. If there were more of both, articles like this would be obsolete. I hope they become so. In the meantime, it seems to me that the proper path for a woman writer is not an all-out manning (or womaning) of the barricades, however much she may agree with many of the aims of the movement. The proper path is to become better as a writer. Insofar as writers are lenses, condensers of their society, her work may include the movement, since it is so palpably among the things that exist. The picture that she gives of it is altogether another thing, and will depend, at least partially, on the future course of the movement itself.

Postscript 1975

I wrote the above article in the early part of 1973. Since then, things have changed enough to warrant a brief postscript. Although there continue to be small, relatively active, politically-oriented groups of women who call themselves Feminists, feminism has broadened its base considerably. It's now not so much a political movement as a climate of opinion, one which is transforming the attitudes of men towards women and of women towards themselves, less radically and dramatically perhaps, but also less defensively, less faddishly and with more quiet determination. There are now a number of female writers who don't mind the word "chairman", who did not become actively involved in CR groups or marches, who toe nobody's ideological line, but who are nevertheless dealing in their work with women's experience, in all its diversity, without the sense of apology they might have had a few years back. And there's a new awareness on the part of capital-F Feminists that such writing, since it voices the hitherto repressed lives of half the human race (not a minority group, though it's been treated like one) is *de facto* revolutionary. Telling it like it is and has been is as valuable as telling it like it should be; it's an articulation of the previously inarticulate. Seeing our own images gives us heightened confidence in our own existence.

The diversity of these images is a healthy sign. For centuries—especially the nineteenth—men have appeared in the pages of men's books as individuals, women as something called Woman. Men existed in their own right, women, with a few usually comic exceptions, as a gender, an eternal abstraction; or, at best, as a handful of symbols defined by their function *vis-à-vis* men: Mother, Wife, Sister, Virgin, Whore, Goddess, Witch/Bitch. Nourishers or threateners, valuable for what they promised to provide in the way of food or pleasure, feared for their imagined powers to blight the wheat or to deprive a man of his genitals. Since most books were and still are written by men, these images have had a long life and many incarnations, and we haven't seen the last of them yet.

But the work of serious women writers in Canada has been heading in the opposite direction. If the fictions of Margaret Laurence, Marian Engel, Alice Munro, Audrey Thomas, Adele Wiseman, Sylvia Fraser, Marie-Claire Blais, Anne Hébert, Gwen MacEweeb, Jane Rule, Sheila Watson, Phyllis Gottlieb, Gladys Hindmarch, Gabrielle Roy and Ethel Wilson (to name a few) have anything in common—and formally they don't—it's the abolition of such categories. Women in their books are no longer relegated to the shadowlands of either/or. They proclaim, if anything, their right to be fully human, to nurture without being Earth Mothers, to curse without being witches, to suffer without being Little Nell the loveable victim, to copulate without being the Scarlet Woman. *Woman* as a homogeneous gender has become obsolete; women as human beings, on and off the page, are flourishing as never before.

So are women writers, though the story is by no means over. For instance, Canada has a higher proportion of women writers who are taken seriously as writers than does, for instance, the United States; yet in several poetry anthologies I sampled, the work of women still accounted for a third or less of the total, and if you check the bestseller list week after week the percentage is about the same. It's better than for politicians or miners, but not proportional to the population. Even in 1975, it's evidently more imaginable for a man to become a writer than for a woman, and the woman writer is still a kind of exception, an anomaly. I continue to be asked why there are so many good women writers in Canada, yet such questioners haven't stopped to think: by "so many" they mean "some", and the question betrays its own prejudice. There really aren't that many of us; not yet.

Maryon Kantaroff was born in Toronto of Bulgarian parents. She received an honours degree in art and archaeology at the University of Toronto in 1957 and in 1959 went to England on a Canada Council grant to continue her studies in American ethnology and in painting, drawing and sculpture. During the next ten years her work was widely exhibited in London and other European centres. Since her return to Canada she has become one of the country's best known sculptors. Her work has been shown in galleries across Canada and she has received many commissions and awards.

Breaking Out
of the Female Mould

Maryon Kantaroff

"Life conspires to keep a woman tangled in trifles."

The usual reaction when people learn I am a sculptor is interesting and predictable: they are surprised, impressed and often awed. These reactions arise from certain misconceptions.

The first, I think, is the idea that "art" is a man's domain. If a woman does something men have always done, she is considered extraordinary, somehow more than just a mere woman. And this misconception no doubt originates in the relationship between art and religion. God, the prime creator, is, after all, regarded as male. When Western religion began to disintegrate, art inherited a number of its functions, mainly the power to consecrate. An art object has become something to be worshipped, something pregnant with eternal power and meaning. Such an object made by a woman must be unseemly, if not downright blasphemous. This may explain why women's reactions to me convey a certain sense of alienation. In some way I am regarded as a superior being, somehow akin to a male. The same, I might add, is true of men's reactions, except that their discomfort is experienced as threatening rather than alienating. In a very real sense I am no longer a woman in their eyes. Thus the female sculptor is de-sexed by her activity—a real

275

woman wouldn't be doing a man's job. It is absolutely amazing how many people assume that I am a lesbian because I am a sculptor. This is not so much because they suspect that I may love women, but rather that they suspect I must be like a man.

Before I became a feminist all this disturbed and mystified me. I sensed this distance from other women while knowing that I wasn't being accepted by men in my field. Our society goes to great lengths to keep a woman in the female mould; if she steps out of it for whatever reason she is subjected to suspicion, alienation and sometimes total social rejection.

The activity of "making art" is itself generally viewed with suspicion, whether engaged in by a man or a woman. It is seen as a threat to established societal norms and values. The artist's job is to observe—to question, probe, reevaluate—in some ways, the artist is the conscience of society. In this sense, creative activity is allied to the traditional female role: that of the sensitive guardian or nurturer of society. In order to escape the stigma of "femaleness" attached to creative sensitivity, the male artist has become increasingly virile in his work, assuming the pose of judge or authority—the patriarchal arbiter of taste. The female artist is placed in several binds. She is exiled from society not only in her role as artist, but in her role as woman artist. Further, she is exiled from artistic society which is dominated by male aesthetics and male power. And I haven't yet touched on the woman artist's personal relationships with men, in which she is expected to conform to the requirements of her feminine "obligations" (as housewife, mother, cook, hostess, sex partner). When all of this is taken into account, one can see why women artists in Canada are in a dilemma. Their social role, to which they have been conditioned, is always at odds with their creative activity, both being extremely demanding, and forcing these women into a perpetual state either of exhaustion or guilt, or both.

Women in Canada—as in other countries—grow up under the influence of a predominantly male culture. All our values, including those of church, state, school and media, derive from male institutions. This male culture is overlaid on our own deepest experiences as women. Without fully realizing it, women artists become involved in male aesthetics—the basis of contemporary art modes—which are at odds with their own female experience. When women default in the art world, they blame their lack of talent or application. They judge themselves, finally, by the standards of what is essentially an alien culture—a culture from which they are profoundly excluded by definition of their sex. There have always been a number of women artists who have been able to achieve some success in this male world, but they have done it by accepting and imitating male aesthetics. Actually, a more accurate word would be politics, rather than aesthetics, for the quality I am referring to in male art is that of power.

I am speaking from experience, for I produced male sculpture myself for a number of years. Of course I didn't realize what I was doing until some time after my feminist involvement. My work was generally characterized by strong assertive forms and rigid lines of tension. Some of my female experience did enter into my earlier work, but I fought against it. "Soft" or "warm" shapes seemed weak and flabby to me and I used these terms pejoratively, my tastes well-honed by and respectful of masculine values. Anything that had a symbolic association with the female I automatically experienced as inferior and therefore rejected. I was using male standards against myself, reflecting and reinforcing them in an attack on female standards. I shudder when I think of it now.

The bizarre aspect of all this mimicry of masculinity was

that none of it reflected in my personal life. I was just as intensely "feminine" in my everyday behaviour as I was anti-feminine in my sculpture. Male artists, like female artists, are forced to hustle and compete and generally make their presence known. However, my femininity made this most necessary procedure almost impossible for me. This kind of aggressive self-promotion is second-nature to most male artists, as it is a direct application of learned sex role patterns. The female artist, on the other hand, finds that aggressive and assertive behaviour is in direct contradiction to her conditioning and is next to impossible to assume.

Any individual is to a large extent the product of his or her environment and the social values reflected in it. A woman artist cannot possibly escape the deep-rooted prejudices with which she has been inculcated since birth. What have we been surrounded by during our formative years? Women (the grown-up versions of us) involved in the traditional female world—the kitchen, the nursery, the whole domestic life of the unpaid but willing housewife. Or, we have seen them working in the fields, scrubbing floors for other people, or in boring, dead-end jobs undertaken as alternatives. They have been teachers to male principals, secretaries to male executives, nurses to male doctors—or just generally extensions of some male: wife, hostess or someone's date. Whoever heard of great women doctors or politicians or scientists—least of all artists? Women give birth to great artists, they serve great artists, they slave for great artists—but they seldom *are* great artists! How would a young girl conceive of the idea that she could someday become a great artist? There are just no models to aspire to.

In a very real sense, women are outsiders in society, their existence is viewed as peripheral. They have no direct influence on events. The indoctrination of femininity has been a useful tool in keeping us politically passive.

An obvious analogy can be made with native people in Canada. They, too, have been relegated to the periphery by a kind of "femininity". They can be easily distinguished from white people by their physical characteristics and by their own cultural patterns of behaviour. These differences become the rationale for maintaining power in the hands of the white man. Land was taken away from native people in exchange for the dubious security of being cared for on reserves by big white daddy. Native people were effectively incarcerated in a kind of purdah. When women marry they give up their rights and freedoms for the same kind of "security". Just as the native people have lost their dignity and culture, so we lose ours.

Where are the great native artists and achievers? The answer will be the same as it is for women. What they do achieve, is achieved on their own cultural terms and cannot be compared to the products of an alien culture. Native people have come from a hunting culture and cannot be judged by a technological one which excludes them. Similarly, women have come from a domestic culture and are expected to continue in it and define themselves by it. The artistic achievements of both women and natives are relegated to the inferior status of craft. We each have our "cultural slot" and we will be happily tolerated only as long as we stay in it. The real art world is consecrated ground for the superiors—men—and white men at that.

If approached, I suspect that the vast majority of Canadian women artists would deny that they were discriminated against, in fact if married would consider themselves lucky to have the financial support of their husbands. The problems of sex-role playing are so subtle that it is often very difficult to pin-point them for others. The male artist, no matter how suspect he may be in the eyes of society in general, has the full support of his male colleagues, the full backing of the powers that be in the art world and most important personally, perhaps, the full support and backing of his wife and family. Everything in the family is geared to his activity. The woman artist, on the other hand, often has none of these areas of support open to her. Certainly she is excluded from rapport with other artists (unless she is personally attached to a male artist) and she is most definitely seen as an anomaly in the art world generally. But most damaging, perhaps, is the lack of support she is likely to find in her personal life. However much her husband may value her artistic activity, he will still be considered the prime breadwinner, while her primary function will be to support him domestically and emotionally. For this reason, many Canadian women artists are invisible in the art world. They are busy creating, all right, but they are squeezing in their art between thousands of fracturing domestic chores. As they can fall back on the financial support of their husbands they rarely exhibit much incentive in trying to sell their work.

I don't see extremely talented women artists promoting and competing in the art marketplace. I do see many mediocre male artists doing just that. Women artists seem to share the same deep sense of inadequacy experienced by most women in our society—a society that views men as primary. The married woman artist's basic reality is one of available time and energy. Our society almost makes marriage mandatory for women and marriage almost makes professional creative production impossible. I don't think it is accidental that the only well-known Canadian women artists were unmarried. The painter Emily Carr lived a life more akin to a gypsy's than to that of a typical Canadian woman. And as for the two sculptors Florence Wylie and Frances Loring, there is no doubt they too completely rejected the traditional feminine sex role. Our society encourages women to gain their status and sense of identity from the men they live with, not necessarily from their own chances of achievement. To live without a man is to choose to be alienated from society. No male artist is expected to forgo a family because he wants to create; he can in fact expect to be serviced by women whether in or out of marriage. The same is obviously not true of women.

The entire situation regarding women in art is problematic when one considers the close association made between creativity and femininity. Certainly it is part of the female role to encourage sensitivity which is a necessary part of creativity. Our contemporary mystique says that women are creative because they bear children—then goes on to say that for this very reason women have no need to create art. This is a politically useful confusion of biological with intellectual function. There is considerable evidence now emerging to suggest that women in ancient cultures played an extremely active role in the arts, but information about their early contributions have not come down to us in the history books written by men. Consequently, it is widely thought and taught today that women as a group were never of much significance in the cultural activities of past societies. People ask, "Why were there no great women artists?" with the happy assumption that there were none.

The fact is that there were many great women artists— but they were never publicized, they were little known in their own day and have remained virtually unknown today. The paleolithic cave paintings until recently were attributed to men and were recognized as great art. Now that modern scholarship can attribute them to women artists, it will be interesting to see if they will still be regarded as "great".[1]

---

[1] See *Art and Sexual Politics*, edited by Thomas B. Hess and Elizabeth C. Baker (Toronto: Macmillan, 1973).

One of the acknowledged greatest masterpieces of the Middle Ages, the Bayeux tapestry, was designed and executed by women—but the fact that the artists were nuns was not broadcast. In the thirteenth century Sabina von Steinbach carved the most important sculptures, "The Church" and "The Synagogue", on Strasbourg Cathedral, thus surpassing the work of her father. But no one bothered to mention it. The museums of the world are filled with Marietta Tintoretto's paintings happily attributed to her father Jacopo. Judith Leyster's work in the seventeenth century was attributed to Frans Hals. Constance Marie Charpentier's work in the 1800s was credited to the great neoclassic master, J.L. David. If these women's work was good enough to be attributed to the great male masters, obviously it deserves the term "great". But who knew any of this before it was unearthed by feminists? I spent four years at a reputable Canadian university studying art history, and the first woman I came across in my studies lived in the late nineteenth century. I call that male-biased education.

In examining our views of women and art, it is most important to look at the two most powerful past influences on Western culture today. The first influence was, of course, the classical culture of ancient Greece. The Greeks were openly homosexual and excluded women in all important areas. They used women for procreation or for erotic satisfaction, but were culturally homosexual in that love was a concept reserved for men. Thus the highest form of love was seen as that between men, whether consummated sexually or not. Aristotle wrote: "The female is a female by virtue of a certain lack of qualities. We should regard the female as afflicted with a natural defectiveness." From what we can see in Greek political structures and in their literature, it would appear that Aristotle was not alone in his contempt for women.

The second major influence on Western culture was the Christian church. It viewed woman as the root of all evil, accepted and embellished Greek thought on women, and formed the values that are the basis of most of our social and moral attitudes today. In its medieval period, the church burned as witches the most creative women of that time—women numbering into the millions. Both ancient Greece and the Christian church thus clearly expressed male supremacist attitudes to the point of open inhumanity towards women. Discussing women's lack of achievement during their reigns in history is a meaningless exercise, rather like discussing the reasons why no Jews became popes. The concepts are mutually exclusive.

Modern Western culture, therefore, has inherited an extreme anti-female bias. It is basically homosexual in the sense that real value is vested in the male. Hence the occurrence of strong male bonding in our society—clubs, sports, business, politics. If a man in our society is to love a woman, he must first elevate her in his imagination, make her an exception to the inferiority of all other women. This need is the basis of the false and romantic illusions perpetuated in our society with regard to love. Romanticizing the woman makes her worthy of the man's love or respect. This attributed value makes her a suitable subject for the artist; the woman (subject) is romanticized while real value remains vested with the male (artist). It is interesting to note that even women artists in the past have romanticized their female subjects (e.g., Constance-Marie Charpentier's portrait of Charlotte du Val d'Ognes).

I remember that during my own postgraduate studies, the majority of our models were women. All my professors of sculpture were men, and they arranged for the models. At the time, this didn't seem odd. Even while I was studying sculpture I suspected darkly that there was something wrong with me or I wouldn't be so involved in an activity in which no other woman I knew of was or had been involved. I was further encouraged in this prejudice by my professors. When I complained to one of them that he never talked seriously about art with the women students, he answered that as none of us would ever become professionals there wasn't much point in bothering. Interestingly, every one of my female contemporaries did go on to become professional sculptors—with the exception of one, the only one who was married. As for myself, I was only able to take my work seriously once I had made the political connections in regard to my sex. Society has always allowed women a creative outlet—but only to the degree of dilletante. It is positively unwomanly to be professional, even in our own so-called modern times.

North American culture is predominantly male; all power structures are male and the world of ideas is considered the male prerogative—as opposed to feelings, which are the female prerogative. A female who tunes into the culture at any level must take on male value systems. For example, the university educated woman becomes an intellectual extension of the male. She has studied male writers, male philosophers, male historians, male scientific research, male design, male everything. And if she becomes part of this culture and adds to it, she will be making primarily a male contribution to male culture. A rather frightening example of this is the woman Freudian analyst. These women accept the distortions about their own sexuality and continue to conform to male authority in an area which should rightly be their domain. Their "thinking" on the subject is in direct contradiction to their feeling or experience, which must, in fact, be totally negated. By cutting off experience, the female can become totally male-identified in her "thinking". The same applies to aesthetic values. Male aesthetics have come directly out of the experiences and perceptions of male artists, just as Freud's "thinking" was an extension of his experiences as a man, and not as an asexual observer. When a female artist therefore works out of male aesthetics, she is denying the reality of her perceptions as a woman/person and is cutting herself off from her deepest and most meaningful creative sources.

I would like to trace through my own experiences in this connection. From my earliest days as a postgraduate sculpture student I was preoccupied with two subject areas. The first dealt with integrating male and female symbols into one aesthetic concept—that is, going beyond the two distinct forms into the whole. The other was a preoccupation with flight. Neither of these recurring themes were conscious, even though I have referred to them as preoccupations. These themes persisted in emerging during composition classes, even though I was consciously trying to work in totally abstracted forms. The first subject area reflected my deep sense of alienation from the male, and the sculpture was an emotional and symbolic attempt to make the two come together, to find a solution to the dilemma. The flight theme was, I believe, a straightforward way of expressing both escape from oppression and a search for freedom. Both themes were coming directly out of my experience as a woman in society. I did not value either and I constantly strove against their emergence in my work.

Even though I was not successful in completely repressing the subject matter, I was far more successful in my stylistic treatment of it, which helped to camouflage the ideas. From the moment I left art college and began having exhibitions, I made concerted efforts to move closer and closer to a male aesthetic. My style became progressively more strident, sharp, anguler—in short, "stronger". I even remember making a decision to get rid of all textured surfaces because I thought they were too seductive and sensual. I wanted hard, glossy, cold surfaces with rigidly defined forms. I wanted what I thought was intellectual clarity, without feeling (which I identified as confusion).

The change began with my return to Canada after almost ten years of living and working in Europe. Culture shock probably started the process, for I was suddenly able to see the workings of Canadian society somewhat as a "foreigner" and therefore more objectively. In a few weeks I realized the cultural distortion I was confronted with on my return came from a sexist base. I became deeply involved in the feminist movement and through my experiences was able to come to an understanding and acceptance of my womanhood. Naturally this meant a total re-evaluation of the male culture of which I was a product, and the eventual rejection of it and all its implications in my life.

During this time my changing attitudes toward myself were of course directly reflected in my work. Interestingly, though, it was more than a year before I recognized that my work was being affected by my new political awareness. My work was beginning to lose its rigidity and was becoming more fluid. The forms were less forcefully defined. Every shape began to undulate, as if looking for its own natural rhythms. My relief constructions, which at one time had been contained within a picture-like frame, began breaking free of confining edges; they became totally free-flowing. Another vast change was in my use of colour. Just as I had previously used low-keyed, "sophisticated" colour schemes, now the work became bright, optimistic, no longer held back or frightened of feelings. The three-dimensional sculpture often began to relate to my earliest lovers groups, but the male and female forms were no longer read specifically. The hard lines of definition between the male and female were gone. They now ebbed and flowed in and out of each other, reflecting, loving, caressing, interchanging, free of confinement and restriction.

Possibly most important was the emergence of the egg. The oval form had always been present, almost as if hanging around the periphery of my consciousness. Now it was fully apparent. It emerged as a symbol of the beginnings of life, the essence of life, the seat of all potential, awareness, and then would change into the head—the centre of all consciousness. It became a belly, pregnant with life—or with an idea. All allusions to phallic shapes which were so evident in my earlier work (the thrusting forms) have increasingly been replaced by the celebration of the egg. The unconscious is really most marvelous. Waiting there ready to be tapped is all knowledge, all feeling, all understanding. The artist has only to respect it and let it out.

For a woman artist that means respecting herself and her own experiences. As long as she allows the male aesthetic to overpower her own, she effectively chokes off the flow of her own creative wealth. When we consider what is known today about social expectations, subtle indoctrination and role guilts, this is a very tall order for any woman living in this world. I must admit, however, to a deep optimism where women and the arts are concerned. This could be due to desperate wishing, or to the number of times I have encountered women who no longer view the women's movement as a terrifying threat. Somewhere, somehow, we're beginning to contact each other—or rather, more women are listening to what other women are saying. Not much is happening yet, I can't pretend to that. But we are *beginning*.

Rosemary Brown was born in Jamaica in 1930. She attended McGill University and the University of British Columbia where she received a master of social work degree in 1964. In 1970, after several years as a social worker in Vancouver, she was appointed ombudswoman of the Status of Women Council of British Columbia, and in 1972 was elected to the B.C. Legislature. She has served on several standing committees in the Legislature and has received a United Nations Human Rights Fellowship and the National Black Award of Canada. Her near successful campaign for leader of the New Democratic Party in 1975 and her outspoken commitment to both socialism and feminism have made her nationally prominent.

A New Kind of Power *

Rosemary Brown

> *"Men have had the control of affairs for a long time, long enough perhaps to test their ability as the arbiters of human destiny."*

Sisters, Friends and Colleagues:

It is a very special pleasure to be here with you this evening. I am filled with joy at this happening and I accept it as further proof of the determination of the women of this country that the *Report of the Royal Commission on the Status of Women* will not be allowed to gather dust on parliamentary shelves in Ottawa.

I have searched my soul a million times over to find just the right things to talk to you about on this historic occasion, because the truth of the matter is that the whole idea of women and the political sphere fills me with so much excitement that I could probably go on for hours. I won't, of course, because one of the first things I learned as a fledgling politician was that it is more blessed to listen than to be listened to. So I will be brief.

Before I actually launch into my formal address I would like to tell you that at first I was tempted to share with you some of my experiences as a new naive politician. I was tempted to talk to you about the panic that gripped me when I had to make my maiden speech and decided that it would be woven around the fact that I am a feminist and

*Address to Women for Political Action, May 1973.

as such felt that I had a responsibility to declare my position, and issue a plea to our new government for a better deal for all people including women. I imagined what it would be like to stand there in that august chamber surrounded by persons who were for the most part male, and wondered if this time I was not testing the outer limits of society's acceptance. And I thought that I might share with you the sense of peace that came over me as I heard my words and came to fully understand that I was not flaunting society, but rather that I was encouraging society to be its own best self and to recognize that "the full use of human resources is in the national interest".[1] But I did not want to bore you with my ruminations. So I thought instead I should share with you some of the little irksome experiences that touch the life of a woman in a sector of society dominated by men; then I decided that as women in politics you had experienced these things yourself, and anyway it would not be political for me to discuss them publicly. (Perhaps after I am dead I will publish my memoirs.) So, finally I decided to share with you my fears, in the hope that together we might work them through to ensure that they never come to be.

I have two fears that are centered around the role of women in politics. One, that we might make the same mistake that the suffragists made, and after some token victory retire thinking that we had won the war when really we would only have won one battle. The other, that we might find after having achieved 50 percent representation in the political arena that nothing else had changed; that poverty and despair would still be the lot of most of the women of this country, and that the exploitation of people and resources and our environment would still be raging un-

---

[1] *Report of the Royal Commission on the Status of Women* (Ottawa, 1970), p. xii, Terms of Reference No. 6.

checked in a competitive, ruthless society which destroyed all but those most conditioned to cope with it. It is my hope that somehow you and I and all of us will be able to ensure that these fears will never be realized.

If we accept Webster's definition that "politics is the art of government", we realize that to talk of politics is to talk of the care, nurturing and utilization of power. Yet to talk of power and to talk of women is to talk of the absence of power as we understand it today. This fact was brought home very forcefully to women in Canada when the Royal Commission Report was published. Many women in different parts of the country realized that one of the ways of dealing with this dilemma would be to play a more active role in the political arena and indeed strive for more equitable representation in the halls of government throughout the land.

This was a very simplistic one-two-three decision which evolved without any real knowledge or understanding of the power structure of society or the herculean task which we were trying to perform. So, many women went forth and bravely challenged the political structure on all levels, and in most instances they were defeated. It could be said that this was good—good because it forced us to return to point one, forced us to analyze and understand the politics of power and to decide how, and if, we can or are willing to operate either in or outside of the structure as it is presently constituted.

Kate Millett quite rightly deals with dominance when she deals with politics. She explores the structure of our patriarchal society which is built on the dominance of the female by the male and of the younger male by the older male. She deals with the fact that "the military, industry, technology, universities, science, political office and finance —in short every avenue of power within society including the coercive force of the police" is entirely in male hands.[2] What this means is that when we speak of power we speak of power as it is defined by males. If we accept the thesis that politics is this kind of power, then how are we going to deal with the fact that what we are trying to do when we work to become more actively involved in the political arena, and when we strive for equitable representation in the halls of government, is a challenge to the very structure on which this society is based? I have met various women in the political arena who have never thought about why they were there, or what they were really doing in politics. At some time in their lives they had thought that more women should be in politics so they became involved, or else they decided to follow in their father's footsteps, or their husband's footsteps or their brother's footsteps. Consequently over the years many of these women contributed very little to the struggle for the liberation of women, or indeed even to the liberation of themselves. They accepted male models as their models, male values as their values, male goals as their goals, and the male definition of power as their definition of power.

I suggest this is no longer good enough. Women in politics now have a constituency. There are now women ready to support the bid of their sisters to participate more fully in the political arena. But these women will, and must, support only those women who understand fully what more women committed to the struggle for liberation will mean to the thrust and direction that society will take as a result of their participation.

There is really no law that says that women must accept the male definition of power. There are reasons why they do, but no law that says they must. There is really no reason why we as women cannot struggle to establish our

[2]Kate Millett, *Sexual Politics* (New York, 1970), p. 25.

own definition of power even as the black people in this and other countries are struggling to establish their own definition of beauty and truth and dignity. Indeed by definition we must have a different perspective. We must see the world differently. Very few of us have ever known power in the male sense. And it is my belief that whenever we have the opportunity to participate in government, if we would refrain from aping the male fraternal order with its worship and admiration of domination, we could conceivably change things. If women in politics endeavoured to act like themselves rather than the way they think they should act in order to "fit in"—then we could probably break down the old competitive, control-oriented dominance system prevalent in politics today.

A woman who enters the political arena is often assumed to be aggressive. By whose definition is she aggressive? Who decides that entry into an arena as vital to our survival as politics is an act of aggression rather than an act of courage? Who decides that a woman who enters the political arena is unfeminine? The great Canadian feminist Nellie McClung once wrote, "Women who set a low value on themselves make life hard for all women." The truth of this statement is still being recognized by such women as Judith Niles, for example, who in the February 1973 issue of *Ms.* commented on "widows and soft-spoken women who have come and gone over the years, changing neither attitudes about women in power, nor the rigid procedures of Congress itself".

Why cannot power be seen as a creative force? Why cannot the creative use of resources be power? Why cannot cooperation be seen as power? Why use the term "power" at all?

Is there really an insurmountable reason why political involvement has to mean the replacement of one type of power for another? It is my belief that politics can be the evolution of a different way in which people relate to each other. In its present manifestation politics is a power-structured relationship in which some groups of people are controlled by others. This is the kind of political relationship that Nellie McClung attacked in *In Times Like These*, referring to it as "male statecraft" which because of its "one-sided" nature has made "human welfare lag far behind material welfare".

For these reasons, therefore, it is crucial that women entering politics today see themselves not as individuals alone, but as members of a constituency working for and dedicated to change. These are the reasons why we must learn from the mistakes of our ancestors. These are the reasons why we must not fall into the trap which weakened the achievements of the suffragists. They thought that the vote would mean that women could take their place as equals in society. Yet today, more than fifty years later, we are meeting to discuss our role in politics, cognizant of the fact that there are indeed fewer of us in the political arena now than there were twenty or twenty-five years ago. This ironical situation can be explained by the fact that when women obtained the vote they did not use it ideologically, but individually. In the case of both suffrage and prohibition, women acted as individuals, not as members of a group.

I know that there will be those of you who will not agree with me on this issue. I know that there are those of you who will say that there are reasons why we accept the male definition of power, and I know very well that "to those that plays the game goes the spoils". I also know that those who do not are reprimanded. But these reasons are not insurmountable, they can be dealt with. I have often heard from women in the professions, as well as from women in the world of business, and of politics, that they "made it" despite being women. *Well, my philosophy is and has always been, that until all of us have made it, none of us has made it.*

There is no woman anywhere in this country today who can look at me and tell me she has made it, because she hasn't—not according to my criteria. I must confess that my criteria are tinged by the fact that I am a socialist, by the fact that I am not impressed by individualism, by the fact that I believe in collective responsibility, and that as such I am not without bias. This is by way of saying that it is not the quantity of women in politics that will change things, but rather that it is the qualitative philosophy that women bring to politics which will decide if change will occur. Fifty percent of the House of Parliament occupied by women committed to the male concept of power means only that to my continued oppression will be added my sense of betrayal.

I remember attending a conference on women at the University of Oregon last spring, and in particular one workshop which dealt with minority group women and the feminist movement. And I remember quite clearly these black and Chicano women saying that it made no difference to them whether they were oppressed by white males or white females, that it was the oppression that hurt. And that indeed if the women's liberation movement meant that white women were fighting for the right to be able to oppress them equally with white men, then it made little sense to ask them to participate in this struggle. I do not want to repeat myself, but I feel that I cannot stress too strongly that if we are going to do things the same way that the men have been doing them, then there really is no point to the struggle after all. If our participation in the public and political sector cannot force a confrontation with poverty, then there is really no point to the struggle after all. If our participation in the public and political sector cannot force a change in thinking on wars, on pollution, on the exploitation of our fellow human beings, on the need to respect each other and our environment, if our participation in the public and political sector does not challenge the concept that might is right, and that competition is the basis for survival, then there really is no point to the struggle after all.

The Watergate horror is living proof of what happens when the struggle for power goes beyond the realm of reason, when it passes the point of power for the ability to deal with issues to the point of power for power's sake, even to the edge of insanity. As Gene Errington, the ombudswoman for The Status of Women in Vancouver, said, "Watergate shows what happens when a man sends a man to do a man's job."

So it is my hope that in our deliberations we will have the courage to come to grips with some of the tasks which involve women in politics; that we will examine and try to learn from earlier liberation movements why they failed, so that we may protect this movement from dying before it has achieved its goals. Surely we do not want the struggle for women's rights to be a cyclical phenomenon that occurs like the eclipse of the sun at regular or irregular intervals.

I am hoping that even as we discuss our struggle to get more women elected to Parliament and the Senate, and on boards of governors, that we will come to terms with the fact that change when it occurs must include the more than one million women in this country who live below the poverty line. I am hoping that we will explore the statement of Judith Nies, "that women who are effective, cause great disruption in the fraternal order of political business; and this order includes many of the traditional allies of women

—the liberal press, liberal politicians, and radical intellectuals". I am hoping that as our discussions progress we will try to see whether it is possible that coming from different political philosophies we can work together for the same things for this movement. One of the myths that has existed around the movement for a long time has been that no matter what, we are all women together and that's what counts. Well, in the political arena if that is true, is it political?

For those of us who have chosen to enter the political and public arena, the responsibility is ours to understand fully the workings of the present political structure. To do less would be irresponsible. We can no longer use naiveté and innocence as a method of sliding through. We can no longer sit quietly in the arena and hope that we will not make any ripples. As the old saying goes, "Silence is not always golden; sometimes it's just plain yellow."

We can no longer refuse to accept the commitment which we must have to the feminist movement. And if in order to ensure that our worst fears are not realized, and that indeed fifty years from now our female descendants will not be standing here debating and discussing the same issues that we are today, then we will have to be willing to work for real changes. In the words of a poem I learned in grade school and whose origins I can hardly remember, *We are not here to play to dream to drift/We have hard work to do and loads to lift.*

The doors through which we walked when we entered politics were opened for us in large part by women who had the courage to fight for the right to take their place alongside the statesmen of their day. Their initiative and work left us a legacy of social legislation which has served to make life a little bit more meaningful for all of us. We can do no less. We must open doors, and we must see to it they remain open, so that others may pass through. But we cannot, and will never be able to do that as long as we are willing to "wait our turn" and run the risk of that turn never coming. We have to be prepared to turn the system around. We have to be prepared to have it work for people first. And we have to be prepared even to sacrifice our personal ambitions (if we have any) in the interest of achieving these goals.

All of us, I'm sure, have read *Up the Organization* and other books of this nature which tell us how to succeed in the male-oriented climb up the ladder of success. We all know the rules. The question is, do we play by those rules? And if we do, for how long? We must bear in mind that the longer we play by those rules, and the more adept we become at making those rules work for us, the harder it will be for us to decide, or work, to change them.

As a socialist I find that my political philosophy with its emphasis on people responsibility dovetails into my commitment to the other liberation struggles in which I am involved. And I find that being a feminist makes it possible for me to work with women of different philosophies in their struggle for liberation. I know that we, as women in public life, must support the struggles of women in every walk of life.

It is my hope that if this conference achieves nothing else, this at least it must do. It must bring home to us the knowledge that when we reach out across this country and touch each other we draw strength from each other. And in this strength lies our success—and without this, without this working together—fifty years from now our children may not even know the surge of energy which came from the women and threatened to engulf this country in the 1970s.

Thank you.

Lynne Teather grew up in the Niagara Peninsula and received degrees in history from Brock University and the University of Toronto. She has taught women's history and women's studies courses at the University of Toronto and Brock and has been an active participant in women's groups in Toronto. Currently she is preparing for a degree in museum studies from Leicester, England and is pursuing research in women's social history as well as the international women's movement.

The Feminist Mosaic[1]

Lynne Teather

*"In Canada we are developing a pattern of life
and I know something about one block of that
pattern. . . . we who make the patterns are not
important, but the pattern is."*

A letter received in the winter of 1974:

Dear Ms.:

As a student in a course at a local college, I have chosen
to write an essay on the women's movement in Canada.
I have tried to find information from various sources
but up until now the material has been difficult to find.

Having read the few Canadian and several American
books, I still feel frustrated that there is no work that
outlines the current women's movement in Canada.
Could you make any suggestions?

Such letters are received regularly by women's groups. They
are written by women, whether inside or outside the "movement", who are demanding knowledge about their own
heritage. In groups and centres, women seated cross-legged
around postered rooms exchange personal experiences
and statements of strong belief mixed with discussions
about the state of the "women's movement". We alternately

[1]The present study is based on varied research: a survey of women's centres,
women's groups, a series of interviews, a study of documents (newsletters,
magazines, journals, books), and visits to conferences, meetings, courses, etc.
Special acknowledgement is given to the many women who assisted in this
study, especially Gwen Matheson, Angela Miles, Helen Tucker and Dorothy
Curzon.

express hopes for a new non-sexist society and fears of failures and "splits". We try to sort out the seemingly confused scenario of women's groups, labels and trends. In these searching letters and heated discussions, and elsewhere in the debates in status of women's groups, in consultations of advisory councils, in consciousness-raising sessions, women are urgently voicing their need for answers, analysis, and action.

This urgency is heightened by the occasion of International Women's Year, long anticipated and planned for by women around the world. It seems, therefore, especially appropriate during this historic year to take a comprehensive and informed look at the women's movement in Canada, to explore its relationship to past decades and to develop an analysis for the future.

The women's movement in Canada exists as a unique and influential mosaic of groups, councils, centres, committees, and ultimately of individuals spread across the breadth of Canada. It is unique because it is multi-faceted and ethnocentric, like the country itself; the Canadian movement has, in addition to the problems basic to the women's movement in most countries, the special necessities of regionalism, geographical diversity, and multi-cultural character, all of which hinder easy communication. It is strong because of the one-to-one contact possible in groups in the decentralized *ad hoc* formation. The flexibility of structure allows local women to set up their own groups based on their needs. One outcome of the mosaic is variability: groups mentioned in this article may not be operating in six months while others will be newly formed; and the many that are not mentioned here because of limits of space and available information will be going about their daily business.

But there are weaknesses in the mosaic which make this a critical time for its growth. The heterogeneous format hinders contact with people in other regions. Toronto groups hardly know what's being done in Toronto let alone in British Columbia; few understand the developments in Quebec. Centres and groups disappear with no record of their activities, inhibiting continuity in the movement. There is a lack of a unified presence to pressure governments and business, for governments don't take notice of silent, if effective grass-roots activity. There is finally, as in many other countries, an absence of theoretical or practical ana-lysis of the feminist experience needed to give direction and to prevent the co-optive process.

Yet the women's movement is still a force to be con-tended with in Canadian society. It is at a critical stage dramatized by the focus of International Women's Year: a stage when, as the suffragist experience demonstrated, the basic concerns of women in Canadian society could fade in the overexposure of government conferences. Or it may be that in future years, 1975 will mark the turning-point when Canadian women came together to remedy the fundamental inequalities of women in Canada and the world.

The Past

The revival of the women's movement in Canada in the sixties is often claimed to be an outgrowth of the civil rights movement or leftist student politics in the United States or Britain.[2] What has been overlooked by histor-ians[3] and is only slowly being rediscovered by women is the unique heritage of Canadian women's experience. In the voices of women of earlier periods in Canadian history can be heard the eerie echo of current problems and

[2] For examples, see the introduction to *Women Unite!* (Toronto: Women's Educational Press, 1969), pp. 9–13.

[3] See Ramsay Cook's introduction to C. Cleverdon's *The Woman Suffrage Movement in Canada* (Toronto, 1974), pp. vi–xxiv.

conflicts: from pioneer days to the present "rebirth of feminism", a women's tradition appears. A basic fact often egnored is that these experiences, lived out in a Canadian environment, determine the nature of women's actions and the awareness of their problems as women. The Canadian women's experience in the nineteenth century was one of life in a British colony set against a rugged frontier landscape; in the twentieth century, it is one of participation in a modern nation of 23 million people distributed over a vast and varied country. The result has been a decentralized women's movement—a feminist mosaic.

In early settlements in frontier communities or the backwoods, the difficulty was to maintain the female roles determined by European culture. The records of individual women such as Madame de la Tour, the heroine of Fort La Tour in Acadia, Laura Secord, the heroine of the War of 1812, Susanna Moodie and Catherine Parr Trail, to name only a few, outline the impact on their lives of nineteenth-century cultural values. Ideas about woman's "separate sphere" and its corollaries of gentility, submissiveness and respectability, were re-rooted in the Canadian land of extreme cold, rough housing, and premature aging. There began an account of the trials and difficulties inherent in the feminine role which led to questioning, awareness, and ultimately to organization:

> I have caught myself wishing an old forgotten wish that I had been born of the rougher sex. Women are very dependent here, and give a great deal of trouble; we feel our weakness more than anywhere else.[4]

However, Anne Langton, the author of these lines, who came to Sturgeon Lake, Ontario in 1837 at the age of thirty-three to live with her brother, was not able to reach the

[4]Eve Zaremba (ed.), *Privilege of Sex* (Toronto, 1974), p. 17.

point of feminist criticism. Following this sensitive description of the hardships of women's life, she continued:

> This I cannot but think, has a slight tendency to sink us, it may be, into a more natural and proper sphere than the one we occupy in overcivilized life, as the thing I mean that still operates as a safeguard to our feminine virtues, such virtues as the Apostles recommended to us.[5]

There were exceptions to this ambivalence. In *Winter Studies and Summer Rambles in Canada, 1838,* Anna Jameson understood the difficulties of her sex with an analytic strength reminiscent of Mary Wollstonecraft, and predictive of current feminist analysis. Married to Robert Jameson in 1824 (attorney-general of Upper Canada) and later separated, she spent her life travelling, studying, and writing. In her work on Canada, Jameson outlines an almost feminist view:

> Unless we women take some courage to look upon the evil and find some help, some remedy within ourselves, I know not where it is to come from.[6]

But Jameson is not always consistent and her vision of the female role is debatable.[7] Does she see the remedy as a rejection of sex roles, or does she suppose that in time the required changes will somehow occur—a prophecy which has yet to be fulfilled? In any case, these women's ideas indicate the sources of later suffragist and feminist thought.

There are other recorded evidences of women's growing awareness before the suffragist period which have yet to be explained, and many still to be uncovered. One example is the attendance in 1852 and 1854 of some Canadian women

[5]*Ibid*, p. 17.

[6]*Ibid*, p. 37.

[7]*Ibid*, p. 5—7.

at a Seneca Falls convention in New York State, where four years earlier the "Declaration of Sentiments" was drawn up marking the beginning of the American suffrage movement.[8] Our history books record neither the origins nor sentiments of these women.

Of course, most of the research on Canadian women has concentrated on the suffragist movement, and particularly on its political aspects, leaving the broader social issues to await analysis.[9] The Canadian suffrage movement differed in several ways from the British or American models. As has been pointed out there was little militance among Canadian women. Particularly significant to the later movement is the fact that there was also a more decentralized organization, reflecting the conditions of geographic isolation. The Canadian movement was organized on a provincial or local basis, with the exception of the Dominion Women's Franchise Association, the National Council of Women, the Women's Christian Temperance Union and the Women's Institutes, most of which were also decentralized.

Because of this diversity, each province followed its own time-table. In the Maritimes, issues were second to the more basic aspects of development; therefore, suffragist activities were more subdued than elsewhere and were later in development. Ontario was the first to have suffrage discussions but also the first to bog down in political problems. In the prairies, the organization was more widespread because there was a smaller population to reach and groups such as the Grain Growers' Association supported suffragist efforts.[10] The regional divergence has been repeated in the contemporary movement, perhaps as a heritage from the

[8]C. Cleverdon, *The Woman Suffrage Movement in Canada* (Toronto, 1974), p. 16.

[9]See Deborah Gorham's article in this book, "The Canadian Suffragists", p. 23.

[10]*Women Unite!*, pp. 22-23.

earlier suffrage organization, or as a result of the basic societal patterns in the history of Canadian federalism.

Federal structure meant specifically that the provinces regulated provincial suffrage while the federal government regulated federal elections: Canadian women could win only provincial not federal voting rights by changes in provincial legislation, and hence had the burden of mounting a dual campaign.[11] In the United States, in contrast, the states regulated both state and federal suffrage for elections; there, a national women's organization organized a central campaign to increase the number of states which allowed women to vote in state and federal elections. The ironical result in Canada was that the federal vote was finally granted as much as a result of federal political needs and significant contributions of women in the war effort as for suffragist activities, while provincial voting privileges had still to be won separately in some provinces. In Quebec, the vote was not won until 1940.

There remains a great deal of work yet to be done to bring to light the regional experiences of the suffragists, if they are not already lost to history. Research on suffragist history in the Niagara Peninsula indicates its divergent and particular nature.[12] Mrs. Gertrude Knapp, now ninety, has reported that from 1910 to 1918 there was very little suffragist activity in that region other than the circulation by one or two women of a petition brought down from Toronto. Mrs. Knapp herself had been introduced to the suffragist cause through an American newspaper published by Carrie Chapman Catt. Her philosophy regarding the women's vote is direct: "Of course women are equal to men." In the peninsula area, there was no local movement and there was a great deal of apathy to the issue of suffrag-

[11] Cleverdon (*op. cit.*), p. 4.

[12] An interview with Gertrude Knapp, May 1974.

ism. Mrs. Knapp walked miles up and down country roads knocking on doors and gathering signatures. She was often met by those comments familiar to early champions of women's rights, such as, "Why aren't you at home looking after your children?" Similar remarks are still heard today.

The Interim, 1919-1960

In 1879, one suffragist wrote as follows:

> Let no confident friend of the movement anticipate too great results from such success. That it will be followed by great disappointment to many—happy disappointment to those who fear, and unhappy to those who hope—there can be little doubt. It will effect far less change then is generally fancied; at first scarcely any. All social evils will not be voted down; nor the offices all filled with saints at the next election thereafter. It will not be found the *panacea* for all human, or *all* womanly ills. It will simply be the opening of another door—the passage into a larger freedom. . . . But to work out her complete womanhood vastly more is required than the right of suffrage.[13]

This quote was a forecast of the period between 1919 and 1960 in Canada: the opening of doors but not the winning of solutions.

During this period of the women's movement, some organizations such as the Imperial Order of the Daughters of the Empire (IODE), the Women's Institutes, the Young Women's Christian Association (YWCA), church clubs, and social groups following the suffragist example took some constructive actions for women; but without the single issue of the vote which had provided a focus for groups before 1918, each worked in isolation from the other bringing little fundamental change for women. As before, group activities depended on regional problems determined by

[13]R. Cook's Introduction to *The Woman Suffrage Movement in Canada*, p. xx.

local membership. Moreover, the problem of reaching a majority of Canadian women, which had curtailed suffragist efforts, had not been remedied. Individual groups attempted to follow the philosophy behind the vote but the overall realization was that in this period as in the last, the vote had not proved to be "the panacea for all ills".

Many contemporary women's groups were active in the interim period and their record of achievement is not to be denied. During this time, the YWCA (founded in 1894), in addition to supplying traditional services for women, sponsored education programs on woman's role. In what must have been a forerunner of consciousness-raising groups, the YWCA Convention of 1919 suggested that girls when clustered together at the end of classes should discuss issues such as "Should every girl have men friends?" or "What is my future?". The parallel of current studies and submissions were reports like that of Winnifred Hutcheson in 1935 which presented the details on the female needle trades in Toronto to the Parliamentary Committee on Price Spreads and Mass Buying.[14] At a later date, 1950, twenty-one YWCA's set up Public Affairs Committees centering on anti-discrimination and equal pay for equal work, formed a Women's Electoral Association, and made resolutions to set up a Women's Bureau in the Department of Labour.[15]

The Canadian Business and Professional Women were also part of that tradition of activism and women's rights. Formed in 1930 at the height of the Depression, the "B and P's", as they are sometimes called, supported programs promoting social legislation and reform of legal inequities, and were concerned with the largely overlooked claims of unemployed women workers of all classes but especially those of the "white collar" type: they asked that "any

[14]J.P. Harshaw, *When Women Work Together* (Toronto, 1966), p. 168.

[15]*Ibid.*, p. 170.

legislation which might be introduced in respect thereof shall apply equally to men and women". A number of resolutions and petitions were delivered to Ottawa by personal delegations. Several suggestions were followed by governments: a Female Employees Remuneration Act was passed first by Ontario then followed by other provinces and the federal government; a Women's Bureau was set up in the Department of Labour in 1954; a Royal Commission on the Status of Women was established in 1967.

Elsie Gregory MacGill, an engineer and a member, summed up the situation on New Year's Day, 1941, the day that the suffrage act for women was put into effect in Quebec. She was asked by a reporter:

> Since women have had equal rights for so long, why are none of our national figures women? Why have we no "king-size" women in Canada?

Elsie's response was:

> Because no women are in the "king-size" jobs yet. It is the job that gives a man a chance to furnish public proof of his ability, raises him to national status and makes him "king-size" in the public eye. No one can be "king-size" in a little job.[16]

In the history of the Canadian women's movement, individuals have often been the mainstay of the struggle. Helen Tucker, now secretary of the National Action Committee on the Status of Women, was a lecturer on the "church circuit" during the postwar period, when she discussed such topics as "The Death of Romantic Love". The late Margaret (Peggy) MacLellan, president of the Canadian Federation of University Women, spoke on the status of women through the fifties. She was later to write a report on the history of women in Canada for the Royal Commission. Thérèse

[16] From an interview with Helen Tucker, May 1974.

Casgrain was a central figure in the Quebec movement, both before and after the winning of the vote.

Women of the left were also active in the interim period. Women had helped defend those arrested in the 1919 Winnipeg General Strike and were involved in other labour struggles; the Women's Labour League, many of whom were new immigrants, fought for many years for better wages and living conditions especially in the "Hungry Thirties"; women such as Mary "Ma" Flanigan, who had started work at age eleven in a cotton mill went on the "On-to Ottawa Trek", a march by the unemployed in 1930.

After World War II, Housewives' Consumer Associations of the 1930s were revived. And out of these grew the Congress of Canadian Women as a branch of the Women's International Democratic Federation (WIDF). The Congress of Canadian Women (CCW) was supported by women in ethnic groups, such as the Association of Ukrainian Canadians, Federation of Russian Canadians, Hungarian, Bulgarian, and Finnish associations and other groups representative of pioneer immigrant families. They organized on issues that concerned them, such as high prices. And in Quebec, despite threats of police action, a group of women fighting high prices gathered together to hear their president make this statement:

> We must remind These Members of Parliament, They are not our Masters, They are the Servants of the People.[17]

Since then the CCW have, in the words of one of their members, "worked to educate women in world affairs and activities for peace". They have sent briefs to the government on education, immigration, and the status of women. Occasionally some of their activities have been regarded by

[17] Canadian Congress of Women, "Canadian Women in International Women's Year", Pamphlet, 1974, p. 7.

the Canadian and particularly the American governments as controversial because of their political affiliations. But they remain a dedicated and active although small group.

If the activities of these groups and individuals cannot be denied, neither can their problems. Many of the basic issues first approached by Emily Stowe and Nellie McClung remained paramount. For example, from 1919 to 1960 the record of women in politics was not encouraging. Charlotte Whitton, later to be mayor of Ottawa, said in 1946, "We remain the most inert, in the consciousness of use of our power, of women in the nations the world over."[18] A study in 1949 showed Canadian women's performance in politics was behind that of women in the United States and Britain, let alone countries like Japan where women were elected to one-tenth of the legislative seats.[19] The Royal Commission Report showed that from 1917 to June 1970, there were 134 federal and provincial elections and of the 6,845 elected, sixty-seven were women. Further, the expansion of women's wartime opportunities was curtailed when 90,000 Canadian women lost their jobs between 1945 and May 1946 as government and industry simultaneously excluded married women from employment.[20] Women returned to the home: the era of the suburban housewife and the "Feminine Mystique" had begun.

Still, some women's rights supporters saw a slow improvement in women's situation. As Anne Francis, later chairperson of the Royal Commission on the Status of Women, stated in 1949, women had tasted power especially in their wartime activities and they had begun to become aware of their potential.

[18]Cleverdon, *op. cit.*, p. 267.

[19]Cleverdon, *op. cit.*, p. 269.

[20]Cleverdon, *op. cit.*, p. 279.

By 1960, despite the activities and hopes of some groups and individuals, many of the same problems which the suffragists had not been able to overcome were still with us. True, there was an active Canadian women's movement which was generic to Canadian culture, but women's groups still worked in isolation from one another and with only limited success. Meanwhile, during the sixties, the proportion of women working increased and a new awareness grew which portended the revival of the women's movement. But once again the movement was determined by the format of its environment—it was to be a mosaic.

The Revival of the Women's Movement in Canada

The 1960s, the decade of student strikes, separatism and the War Measures Act in Canada, of assassinations, civil rights and anti-Vietnam protests in the United States, witnessed as well the emergence of a somewhat different and stronger Canadian women's movement. The special circumstances of the decade plus the active, if unspoken and certainly unsung, heritage from the earlier periods created a "movement" of women, by very definition a loose myriad of concerned women allied in Women's Rights, Women's Liberation or Feminist groups.[21] As a movement is not an organization, so the women's movement was not an organization—not unified, singular, nor impervious to "splits" or divisions. It was in the sixties that the philosophy of the loosely organized women's groups was worked out for a recasting of the sex roles which would make substantial if not revolutionary alterations in the world, whether through legislative, economic or psychological change.

If the movement itself was complex so were the causes. The most profound effects came as a result of the changes in sex roles. The increase of industry brought more women

[21]The definition of these terms will follow.

into the labour force, but it also created dramatic disparities in status. In 1951, 24.5% of the labour force were women; in 1961, the figure was 29.3% and in 1967, 33.8%.[22] But the percentage of women in professions or high status jobs was low and in some cases, such as in university teaching, the percentage was lower than in previous decades.[23] The baby boom of the fifties combined with the fact that more women were in the work force, meant that despite the lack of child care facilities more married women with small children were working and experiencing the resulting pressures and frustrations. The establishment of conferences on woman's role reflected the changing consciousness. In May 1961, a two-day conference entitled "Women at Work" was held at the Montreal YWCA to study the impact on individuals and on the community of the increase in the number of working wives. As a result of this conference a "Roles of Women" study was initiated in October 1962. In September 1962, 500 delegates attended a CBC conference in Toronto titled "The Real World of Women" which was held for the purpose of determining what the average Canadian woman of 1962 was thinking and doing.[24]

Canadian women were influenced by the activist American culture. The Commission on the Status of Women established on December 14, 1961 was a catalyst which precipitated the demand by women's rights groups for a similar commission in Canada. In the New Left, women protested against the patronizing behaviour of their male counterparts and organized the Women's Liberation Movement. Betty Friedan's *The Feminine Mystique* (1963) was read by many

[22] *Women Unite!*, p. 126.

[23] R.A.H. Robson, "A Comparison of Men's and Women's Salaries and Employment Fringe Benefits in Academic Profession", No. 1, *Studies of Royal Commission on the Status of Women,* 1970.

[24] Harshaw, *op. cit.,* p. 171.

Canadian women and inspired personal changes for almost all who read it. Laura Sabia, chairman of the Ontario Status of Women Council and founder and former chairperson of the National Action Committee on the Status of Women, admits the role of the American model. She and other Canadian women met with members of the National Organization of Women to learn about what was being done by the American women. Later actions, however, were based on the special problems of Canadian women.

In many of these cases, in fact, although the American influence was present, it was not dominant nor necessarily even major. It acted rather as a catalyst for the Canadian movement. For example, the civil rights movement in the United States, which focussed on black rights, was a major impetus to the Women's Liberation Movement there.[25] In Canada, although black liberation was an important factor in terms of the questions it raised, other issues such as peace and internationalism, native rights and biculturalism were also important in leading to a focus on women's liberation.

International organizations were a socializing force for the women's movement as groups such as the YWCA, the United Nations Association, the Voice of Women and others prepared women, if not men, for the issues of the women's movement. The logic of a concern for peace, international harmony and human rights, engendered principles of freedom for all races, creeds, and of course eventually, both sexes. For example, the YWCA supported the United Nations and worked to protest Soviet nuclear testing in 1961, while the Voice of Women moved from peace issues, to human rights, to action on women's issues in recent years.

[25] J. Hole & E. Levine, *The Rebirth of Feminism* (New York, 1971), pp. 109–110.

An important catalyst for the organization of Women's Rights groups was the designation in 1963 by the United Nations of the year 1968 as International Year for Human Rights. The stated aim was to encourage nations to intensify efforts to realize full human rights for all citizens; women interpreted this as a chance to bring their concerns to the government and to set up an investigation, using the then popular format of a royal commission. ,

In Quebec, there is a relationship between theories of women's oppression and the problems of French-Canadian identity, and according to the separatist radical feminists, between their oppression as women and as French-Canadians. National women's groups have also been concerned with the rights of French-Canadians; for example, the Voice of Women, for a time led by Mme. Thérèse Casgrain, was involved in the establishment of the Commission on Biculturalism.

By 1966, the women's movement was on its way. Three years later Women's Rights, Women's Liberation and Feminist groups had emerged as separate branches of the movement.[26] By 1975, the regional mosaic was complicated by an ever-changing formation of groups, the demise of old ones, and the realignment around specific actions, issues, or new groups.

Women's Rights

The aim of Women's Rights groups is to achieve equality by working through the existing social system. Whereas Women's Liberation grew out of New Left politics, and Feminism from different sources, the Women's Rights

---

[26]The labels Women's Rights, Women's Liberation, and Feminism are used to facilitate identification of groups and because they are assumed within the women's movement itself. However, these terms are only labels and like any labels, are difficult to apply in practice as there is overlapping of groups, individuals and theories. Other labels could be applied.

groups originated from traditional political and social organizations earlier represented by the suffragists: i.e., business and professional bodies, service and church organizations, and government. The Women's Rights women might be called moderate or conservative feminists who often pursue political solutions to issues such as job discrimination, equal pay, and property laws and who speak of the "equality of persons". They are frequently middle-class married women of middle-age or over; some accept the traditional concept of women's separate sphere originating from the volunteer ethic and affiliation with older institutions, but often contradictions arise when equality of the sexes is sought based on the breakdown of separate spheres.

In the spring of 1966, Laura Sabia, president of the Canadian Federation of University Women, invited forty national women's groups to discuss the setting up of a government commission to study the situation of women in Canada. At this founding meeting, Ms. Sabia voiced the demand:

> We hope that the national organizations represented here agree that we work for a Commission on the Status of Women. We should go to the government and demand action NOW.[27]

The resulting Committee for Equality of Women prepared a brief which by September 1966 was endorsed by thirty-two national women's organizations (two million women). Issues were presented to the public via the media and to the government via delegations to M.P.s; Judy LaMarsh, Secretary of State, gave her outspoken support for the plan as she had long recommended such a national study.

In November, an appointment was arranged with Prime Minister Lester Pearson. Saying that he was unable to meet

[27]Cecelia Wallace, "How We Got the Royal Commission on the Status of Women", Atkinson, York University, April, 1972, p. 12.

the delegation, he sent instead Judy LaMarsh and Lucien Cardin, Minister of Justice. Women felt this was a slap in the face and so the confrontation began. Letters of protest were sent to the government. The misinterpretation by a *Globe and Mail* reporter of what was in reality Sabia humour resulted in the headline, "Women March on Ottawa". On February 4, 1967, the Royal Commission on the Status of Women was appointed with Anne Francis as head. From 1966 to 1969 the members listened to briefs and acted both as researchers and, unwittingly, as an amazing catalyst and focal point for various heretofore silent elements of the women's movement.

The report was tabled in the House of Commons in 1970 and was followed in 1973 by the acceptance of one of the recommendations: the establishment of the Federal Advisory Council on the Status of Women. However, many recommendations remain untouched, while others have been altered. The Federal Advisory Council, for instance, was to report to the House of Commons according to the recommendation, but as it is set up, the council reports to the government directly. Nevertheless, these concerted actions of the Women's Rights groups in the Committee for Equality, in the subsequent National Ad Hoc Committee, and finally in the National Action Committee on the Status of Women (NAC) which followed, are an active part of the movement. Increased potential for NAC, up until now bound by lack of funds and problems of regionalism, is the aim of members who at their 1975 annual meeting concentrated on four priority areas: equal pay, child-care services, birth control and abortion, and family property law. In Quebec, the Fédération des femmes du Québec was formed in April 1966 as an umbrella group for thirty-six women's groups. It followed a decision made by 400 women at a meeting in 1965, the twenty-fifth anniversary of the vote for women in Quebec. Since then it has been concerned with matrimonial property regime, equal pay and women and politics; it has set up conferences and forums and was instrumental in pressuring the Quebec government to set up a Council of Women.

Women's Rights groups approach the problems of women in a variety of ways: for some the focus on women is based on nineteenth-century concepts of women's special sphere, her role in the family or as special moral force; others are more adamant in promoting women's equal status. While within some groups such as the YWCA and the Canadian Federation of University Women some women are engaged in activist issues, the majority follow the policy of "boring from within", aiming at legal inequities and employment discrimination. The National Council of Women, for example, founded in 1893 by Lady Aberdeen and a member of the International Council of Women, is sometimes ambiguous in its philosophy of women's rights. At a recent annual meeting the council moved to deal with discrimination against women, but only because it was the logical outcome of a concern for the preservation of the family and the need to fulfil every member of the family, including the mother. The council's interest in women's rights is based on traditional values, the "application of the Golden Rule to Society, Custom and Law". Its statement of principle begins:

> We women of Canada, sincerely believing that an organized, non-sectarian and nonpartisan movement will best serve the highest good of the family and the state. . .

Yet the council in its concern for women's special role also supports the more radical issue of removal of abortion from the criminal code. The National Council of Jewish Women of Canada similarly supports birth control, abortion and day care but they also have as a basic tenet the promotion of family life, while their support of the Royal Commission applies to those recommendations which deal with principles and which do not seek "special treatment for women".

Within organizations such as the YWCA there are as many radical women as conservative. The "Y" has been an instrumental action group since its origin; since 1966, however, it has instituted special programs on a national and local level by establishing women's residences, counselling and information services, and women's centres on YWCA premises which have linked it with the women's movement. In June 1974, perhaps because of the involvement in women's issues of the YWCA locals in some areas such as Montreal, Toronto and Vancouver, a Special General Meeting of the YWCA and YMCA (Young Men's Christian Association) was held; 372 delegates responded to four proposals of change including one to unify the two associations. The vote followed months of debate; the American branch of the YWCA had gone through a similar confrontation in 1969 when it had voted to retain complete autonomy. The result in Canada was a compromise: formal cooperation with separate identities.

The YWCA structure follows the mosaic pattern: centres have been established in most communities. Services presented differ from community to community according to the needs of the locality. For example, in Toronto, the Metro YWCA is a very effective organization which offers a women's centre, resource materials, and programs and courses for women. In smaller areas such as the Maritime cities, the YWCAs are often the only contact centres for women interested in meeting together as women. In Whitehorse, Yukon, the YWCA provided the location for the recently established women's centre.

Although differences in viewpoint within the mosaic are blurred in practice, the Women's Rights groups basically are working from within society, and often show the ambiguities of such a position.

Women's Liberation

The Women's Liberation Movement evolved from student activism and formulated quite different analyses from those of the Women's Rights groups. Women were generally young, middle-class, and schooled in the campus politics of the New Left groups such as the Student Non-violent Coordinating Committee (SNCC) and the Student Union for Peace Action (SUPA). The theories of change arrived at by such groups were based on analyses of the basic oppression in society as experienced by blacks, by students, and by working classes. Inevitably, theories of oppression, like those of human and civil rights, led to an application of them by women to their own case, especially in the face of the powerlessness experienced in those very leftist bodies where the theories were learned. Soon, women established Women's Liberation groups in some cities. However, in the next few years as differences arose over analyses, women regrouped. These "splits" and "divisions" were sometimes accompanied by confrontations, accusations and ideological differences. But whether the word used is "splits" or "regrouping" the end result was that the Women's Liberation Movement evolved into another phase. Some groups underwent difficulties around 1968, others in 1971, others not at all, but difficulties did not signify the end of the movement.

From the outset there was a basic difference in approach: some saw the woman question as part of the greater struggle for socialist solutions; others viewed women's issues as primary and studied the oppression of women in its own right. The first group—the "politicos"—accepted the Marx-

Engels analysis which presented capitalism and thus the oppression of women as the historical result of the first division of labour, that between men and women. According to this view capitalism had evolved through the evolution of the monogamous family (wherein women submit to the supremacy of man in order that paternity is not questioned and wealth may be transmitted from generation to generation), private property and the state. The second group—the "feminists"—some of whom were to separate later into Feminist groups, assigned the cause of women's oppression to male-dominated society in which sex role stereotypes relegate more than one-half of the population to lesser status.

Although the difference between these two outlooks was basic and was later to create tension in various groups, it was not at first divisive. In the beginning all differences were submerged in the common cause of "sisterhood", the discovery of which was made in the face of growing disillusionment with the New Left. In Canada, women had been involved in civil rights organizations such as SNCC as part of the North American student activist culture. They were certainly aware of the 1964 paper written by R.D.S. Robinson on "The Position of Women in SNCC" which resulted in the now famous retort from Stokely Carmichael that "the only position for women in SNCC is prone".[28]

A Students for a Democratic Society (SDS) convention in 1966 set off a chain of events in Canada and the United States which crystallized in Women's Liberation. The SDS was formed around protest against capitalism, the arms race, the curtailment of civil liberties and the bureaucracies of institutions such as universities, but women at the convention in 1966, still experiencing "put-downs" in the

[28]For a history of the evolution of the Women's Liberation Movement in the United States see J. Hole and Ellen Levine, *The Rebirth of Feminism*, Chapter 2.

organization because they were women, wanted a plank added on women's issues. They were pelted with tomatoes while on the convention platform. Consequently, women's caucuses were formed in cities, including Toronto. Then, at a National Conference for New Politics held in Chicago in 1967 an *ad hoc* committee demanded a civil rights plank for women. Two women who were patronizingly patted on the head left the conference in a rage to form the first liberationist groups in Chicago and New York.

Simultaneously, a number of women in Toronto began to organize what was the first Women's Liberation group in Canada. In a paper presented to a SUPA membership conference, these women outlined their objections to women's roles in the organization as typists, fund raisers and community organizers, their purpose being "to maintain a stable, homey atmosphere which the radical man needs to survive" without having an identity in their own right. Their reaction was not just one of petulance but of basic theoretical disapproval:

> Perhaps the position of women in the sexual act most often lying underneath the man, illustrates the social and economic position of women in society. Women feel they are still on the bottom in all respects. The notion of human liberation is in direct opposition to the notions of efficiency, profit, the accumulation of possessions. The separation of man from women contributes to the maintenance of such a society.[29]

They would form their own groups because

> It is our contention that until the male chauvinists of the movement understand the concept of liberation in relation to women, the most exploited members of any society, they will be voicing political lies.[30]

[29] Bernstein, Morton, Seese, Wood, "Sisters, Brothers, Lovers . . . Listen . . .", *Women Unite!*, p. 33.

[30] *Ibid.*, p. 39.

Day care, working women, marital break-up, education, birth control information, abortion, and actions against "sexism" in any form were issues discussed in groups.

One of the more vivid protests staged by the Women's Liberation Movement (WLM) in Toronto was against the Miss Winter Bikini Contest in 1969. As a promotional gimmick, contestants wearing bikinis beneath fur coats were asked to parade in a downtown shopping concourse, the winner to be selected as Miss Winter Bikini. A WLM woman who had entered the contest opened her coat to reveal a well-covered, mini-dressed torso, much to the amazement of the judges, while her sisters picketed with placards and a window mannequin marked up in sections like a side of beef.

The period from 1968 to 1972 was one of extraordinary growth in the women's movement which was not limited to big cities: groups were formed and centres established in Regina, Saskatoon, Winnipeg, Hamilton, Kingston, and Halifax.[31] A conference was held in 1969 in Sudbury sponsored by the Canadian Union of Students, and another in Vancouver where the Western Women's Liberation Conference established Women's Liberation in the west. In 1970, the Abortion Caravan travelled from Vancouver through the country providing a forum for women to talk about different issues relating to their role and specifically about abortion. In May, the Abortion Caravan went to Ottawa where a number of women chained themselves to seats in the House of Commons to protest abortion policies.

Groups formed and disbanded on an *ad hoc* basis. The women worked in collectives, in non-structured associations; pride was taken in the lack of organization and of the "star syndrome" so often found in male groups. The collective format educated as many women as possible and developed

[31]See *Women Unite!*, Introduction.

their strength. But there was also as a result of non-structure a vulnerability to fragmentation.

Conferences brought out differences in strategy and analysis. In Saskatoon, at the Women's Liberation Conference in November 1971, an open split occurred. Some women rejected the formation of a broad movement around abortion or other "single issues" as weak from the point of view of broader political analyses. Instead, for example, they advocated the organizing of working women in accordance with leftist political theories.[32]

Two other conferences held in 1971 in Toronto and Vancouver furthered the division. They were originated by the Voice of Women to enable American women to make contact with Indochinese women who could not get into the United States. Canadian women at the conference have recorded their frustration. First, American women made the decisions while Canadians organized and performed the lesser tasks, duplicating the relationship that had existed in male-dominated groups. Second, the climate of American militance and fractionalism brought a crisis air to the conferences. This was the so-called "McCarthy" period in the American movement, an era of bitter recriminations and accusations when epithets such as "elitist" or "star" were used as reprimands or even to purge women's groups. However, the crisis climate brought Canadian women to important decisions on the very purpose of Women's Liberation. The question was whether to organize as women or to become involved in the wider political format. The result of the differences was the dispersal of Toronto and Vancouver Liberation groups.[33]

Around 1969 and 1970, the Women's Liberation Movement and the Feminist groups had to contend also with

[32] *Ibid.*, p. 11.

[33] *Ibid.*, p. 12.

"infiltration" which aggravated the divisions already present. Allegedly, attempted takeovers were made by leftist organizations such as the Young Socialist Alliance (YSA) and the League for Socialist Action (LSA) or others. It was felt that in some cases they aimed to take over centres, groups or conferences. An issue of *A Majority View* (August 23, 1970), the paper of the Vancouver Women's Caucus which was then the major group in Vancouver, discussed the increasing debates and fears that opinions presented by the women were decided in leftist organizations and not in the caucus with the other women:

> The Caucus has been defined by YSA/LSA as a priority because it is a group which they see as having potential for becoming a mass movement. . . . They define the limits of the Caucus. They believe we should not develop into a strong individual movement which can explain the total exploitation of women and give women the tools to analyze the world around us.

Some centres voted not to allow women who were also members of what were regarded as male-dominated leftist organizations on management boards; other women reacted by becoming more aware of political and organizational techniques as defence.

But it is important to note the difference between "politicos" women and women in radical leftist groups. The former while working from Marxist concepts are independent of leftist organizations and value that fact; they develop their own theory. The LSA/YSA, on the other hand, were centralized, disciplined groups firmly committed to the decisions and principles of their leftist organizations; it was they, therefore, who were accused of using the women's movement to their own ends. Many of the politicos women are working in other areas of the movement as the majority of Women's Liberation groups, per se, have disbanded;

some women are working in small, low-profile associations researching and studying or are involved in other movements—for example, the NDP or other existing political parties. Many women are working on theoretical analysis derived from experiences in the early movement, and to prevent what they view as the co-option process inherent in certain feminist approaches. The debate seems to hinge on the relationship of the central nature of economic theories of the family to a reworked Marxist-Engels theory. Peggy Morton sums it up: "A socialist who is not a feminist lacks breadth. A feminist who is not a socialist lacks strategy."[34]

The seventies have also seen the emergence of a new awareness among working women across Canada, and many developments in the labour movement have for the first time centered around women's issues. Several important strikes and protests, for instance, have aimed at better working conditions for women and featured women in a leading role. Examples are the Texpack Automotive strike concerning wage disparities, Dare Cookies on the issue of wages and washroom facilities, Wardair which opposed the exploitation and sex-objectification of stewardesses. Other groups composed mostly or completely of women, such as teachers, nurses, legal secretaries, and domestics have all played a part in demanding fairer treatment. A major step in the formulation of new policies regarding women workers was the document drawn up by Grace Hartman and others on the status of women in the Canadian Union of Public Employees (CUPE).

Several Women's Liberation groups exist in Saskatoon, Winnipeg, and Quebec. In Saskatoon and Winnipeg the groups are involved in the usual activities of women's centres, ie., resource and information, abortion and birth

---

[34] L. Briskin, "The Women's Movement: where is it going?", *Our Generation*, Vol. 10, No. 3, p. 26.

control information, but there is also a commitment to working class women and class analysis; for example, the Saskatoon Women's Liberation groups have a Working Women's Committee and have been involved in the struggle of the University Employees Union. Other groups of Feminist orientation often have had difficulty in reaching working women.

Women's Liberation had altered substantially from 1966 to 1974. Women had passed through the initial organization into various other fields of involvement as the women's movement evolved into new phases. Unfortunately, media images have failed to keep up with changes in the overall movement. The sixties' "Women's Lib" image of "crazy ladies running around burning their bras", a media fantasy, remains effective as a stereotype. Anyone involved in the women's movement has heard a man or woman say, "I'm not a women's libber, but I agree that women do suffer and maybe should do something about it." Women's Liberation had basically never proposed differently; nevertheless, the false image has become the bane of women.

Feminism

The word "feminism" is used in the movement in two senses. It can describe a concept espoused by women in history and in the current movement who believe that women should have political, economic and social rights equal to men; this applies to all women supportive of this idea whether conservative, moderate, or radical in application. But "Feminism" (Radical Feminism) is also used in a more specific way to represent women in the movement who work for what they see as radical solutions to the total oppression of women in a male-dominated society, whether economic or psychological. The confusion of terms is made more difficult by the fact that there is no systematic body

of feminist theory as there is to support the Marx-Engels
view of women. There are individual pieces, journals, magazines, newsletters, newspapers and books which together
form the body of feminism. Often the theory is to be found
most clearly in practice, and in the experience of feminism
itself—in consciousness-raising, in Women's Places, resource
centres and action groups. Consequently, most women in
the movement call themselves feminists in the first sense of
the word; but to Feminists, in the second sense, women are
not feminists unless they are "women defined women",
that is women who have attempted to analyze their personal
oppression as women and not as part of another group or
class.

The history of feminism used in the first sense is long,
but in the second sense it is a short if complicated story
which originated in the last decade. From the beginning of
the Women's Liberation Movement there were many women
who were not interested in studying the oppression of
women from the basis of Marxist economic ideology, but
preferred to study the actual experiences, the media stereotypes, and psychological oppression of women particularly
with regard to their sexuality and their relations with men.
When the politico/feminist divergence occurred many of
these women entered service groups and formed women's
centres and consciousness-raising cells in order to pursue
their ideals.

Feminists (or Radical Feminists), to quote from an early
theorist,

> are opposed specifically and centrally to sexism rather
> than capitalism differing from the Marxists, and would
> not be particularly concerned with "equal rights",
> "equal pay for equal work" and other major concerns
> of the NOW segment.[35]

[35] Bonnie Kreps, "Radical Feminism 1", *Women Unite!*, p. 75.

Feminist writing redefines the "Anatomy is Destiny" idea born of Western attitudes to women, and claimed to have been perpetuated by Freud, that the differences between the sexes are natural or inherent, and that the feminine role is defined by the female body. Radical Feminists would say that the differences between the sexes are, in the main, socialized, learned not inherited. Some writings are devoted to the rediscovery of women's history and culture to find examples and role models. Much writing and study has been done on sex-role stereotyping and the institutions which reinforce it. These writings are accompanied by analyses of actions, issues and tactics: media monitoring, lobbying, status of women groups, women's studies, women's centres, telephone "trees".

One of the founders of the Radical Feminist movement in Canada is Bonnie Kreps, currently editor of a column on women in *Chatelaine* magazine and creator of the film *Growing Up Female*. In June 1968, she presented a brief to the Royal Commission which contained the following excerpt:

> Radical feminism is called "radical" because it is struggling to bring about really fundamental changes in our society. We in this segment of the movement, do not believe that the oppression of women will be ended by giving them a bigger piece of the pie. . . . We believe that the pie itself is rotten. . . . "Separate but equal" will get us nowhere; we must eradicate the sexual division on which our society is based.[36]

The New Feminists in Toronto were the first organized group of Radical Feminists in Canada. In March 1969, some women separated from the Women's Liberation Movement in Toronto and joined with others to form the New Feminists. Some women had followed the by now familiar

[36]*Ibid.*, p. 75.

route of involvement in leftist politics to Women's Liberation and to Feminism, rejecting the economic theories of what they believed to be male-dominated organizations. They saw the individual analysis of their own lives as the first step toward raising the political level of women. The aim was "to awaken the consciousness of women as to the nature and extent of their oppression as women. That is to eliminate the sex roles of people through fundamental changes in our society."[37] The New Feminists were concerned with abortion, birth control, access to education for women, equal job opportunities, but also socialization and the family in relation to sex roles.

One of their actions was taken against *Maclean's* Magazine and its editor Charles Templeton for printing an article on Lionel Tiger, author of *Men in Groups*. Tiger, who applies theories based on ethnological studies of primates, presented a theory of male bonding which could be observed in primates and as he thought in contemporary society; the corollary of his theory was that females did not bond. The article discussed these theories, and added references to women which were viewed as unnecessary and even male supremacist. The New Feminists picketed the *Maclean's* office on University Avenue in Toronto with signs reading, "Men are not born superior, they are raised privileged," and "Our goal Maclean's for every trashcan." They asked for space for rebuttal of the article, but were refused. Among their many other projects was a protest against restricted dining-rooms.

The New Feminists disbanded in 1973; the women are still involved in various activities such as writing, teaching, and new women's groups based on the experience gained through those first years. (One of their main achievements, a small magazine titled *The New Feminist* and edited by

[37] An original statement of purpose by The New Feminists, 1970.

Valerie Perkins, survived for some time after the group's dispersal.)

The reason for the disbanding of the New Feminists, as in the case of many groups that have come and gone since 1968, may have been simply the logical and not necessarily undesirable development of women's groups whose aim is not an organization as an end in itself but rather an expression of contemporary needs. When the common concerns alter, members move on to another stage of involvement. It may also be that the problems of the New Feminist experiment reflected a more fundamental problem in its evolution as well as that of other women's groups: the lack of analysis and strategy to support their radical vision. The identification and articulation of women's problems is no more than a necessary first step in what must be a more complex process.

A number of other groups and centres formed across Canada. One format was the small consciousness-raising cell of six to ten women who came together to discuss their role in society under topics such as Love and Marriage, Women and Work, Sexuality and Sex-Role Stereotyping. There are no specifically titled "Feminist" groups now but feminist theory forms the basis of many women's groups and centres and is shared by many individual women.

As a result, some feminists see this as a dangerous time of "watering down", of "reformism", which is evidenced by so-called co-option of their part of the programs and sometimes of individuals by governments or institutional programs. The question now is whether Feminism, too, was just a passing stage, whether it will produce new and significant philosophies on the basis of work already done (such as that of the Americans Shulamith Firestone and Mary Daly[38]), or whether it will take entirely new directions.

[38] Shulamith Firestone, *The Dialectic of Sex: The Case for Feminist Revolution* (New York: William Morrow & Co., 1970); Mary Daly, *Beyond God the Father* (Beacon Press, 1974).

Current Developments and the Future

The Saskatoon *Women's Liberation Newsletter* of September 1974 carried an article by some women who had visited the different groups of the Vancouver women's movement. Noting the fragmentation of these groups which "has enabled them to concentrate on their respective areas" they also observe:

> In their fragmentation lies a discontinuity in the movement as a whole resulting in a lack of political togetherness. Without this solid base which is so essential to furthering the rights of women within our system, there lies a fruitless search for political equality and change. The words "Women Unite!" seem to apply to all women's groups . . . we've got a long way to go before you or we or Canada or even women across the world can effect the changes we're so desperately struggling for, for the sake of our kind.

Women may have an underlying orientation to Women's Rights, Women's Liberation or Feminism as outlined in preceding sections; but, in practice, it is becoming more difficult to talk about the women's movement as a single or even triple entity. The movement has diversified as women pass through the stages of discovery to consciousness-raising and study, to organization and reorganization on actions and issues. As a result, there are a number of disparate groups in each province which I have described here under the blanket term, the feminist mosaic.

Newsletters, papers, discussions, conferences of women's centres and status of women groups clarify contemporary concerns. They cover the spectrum of current women's issues: information and drop-in facilities, transition in marital break-up, rape crisis, health, law, consciousness-raising, lesbian women, Indian and ethnic women, women's studies, media and sex-role stereotyping, abortion, matrimonial property law, equal pay for equal work, and discrimination, to name a few.

In addition, women have organized groups with political aims. At the time of the July 1974 federal election the *Women's Vote* of Ottawa sent a questionnaire to women's groups in order to test local candidates' attitudes to women's issues. Women for Political Action (WPA), which was formed in February 1972, have stated their aim as:

> increasing the participation of women at all levels of the political process and educating women in the nature of political power and how to use it.

They support and put forward women candidates in elections and act as an educational and pressure group.

Women in the three political parties in Canada have been working to improve their status. They have done this both by raising the consciousness of party members as a whole and through their own individual achievements.

In the Progressive Conservative party, eight women candidates ran in the 1975 Ontario election. Two out of the three who were elected have since been promoted to positions in the cabinet: Dr. Bette Stephenson is minister of labour, and Margaret Scrivener is minister of government services; Margaret Birch has retained her post as provincial secretary for social development. It is the party's policy not to use women as "token candidates"; they are run in successful ridings on the same basis as the men. Although there are no special women's caucuses or committees within the party, there is a Progressive Conservative Women's Organization in Ontario which holds annual policy conferences. At the federal PC leadership conference in 1976, Flora MacDonald, M.P. for Kingston, will be a candidate for party leader.

Women in the New Democratic Party favour what they consider to be a more direct approach in the form of women's caucuses in some provinces with special programs for women's issues. These began operating in 1969 and a national NDP women's convention was held in 1974. The formation of the federal Women's Committee has noticeably changed the content and discussion at party meetings and conventions. As a result of experience in the Women's Committee and other areas more women are becoming vocal within the context of the party as a whole.

Rosemary Brown, M.L.A. from British Columbia, has become a national figure since her near successful campaign for New Democratic Party leader in 1975, a considerable feat given the present state of consciousness in the Canadian political scene. Brown is probably our most outstanding example of a socialist feminist (or feminist socialist) who sees the two causes as inseparable.

One reason for the presently higher status of women in the NDP may be the former efforts of women in the now disbanded radical off-shoot of the party, the "Waffle". A former activist in the Waffle Women's Caucus believes that the emphasis they put on "parity", that is, equal representation of women within the leadership of the group, along with the briefs they drew up on various women's issues, helped to draw attention to these issues in the party, a process which is still continuing.

In the Liberal party the Liberal Women's Federation was dissolved in 1973 and replaced by the Women's Liberal Commission. This latter group is an interim step on the way towards "integration" when it is hoped women in the party will gain sufficient influence to compete on an equal basis with men and no longer need guaranteed positions on the executive. In the recent Ontario election there were more Liberal women running as candidates than in either of the other two parties.

Religion is another field in which women in Canada have been making slow but steady progress. As a result of International Women's Year government funding is making possible two ecumenical women's conferences in the fall of

1975—one in Saskatchewan and the other in Ontario. The former, titled "Western Canadian Conference on Women in the Church", is being organized by Canadian Women and Religion, an interdenominational group whose objective is to promote the equality of women on all levels in the churches. A similar organization begun in Toronto in 1973 is The Friends of Hagar who use consciousness-raising techniques of the secular women's movement and hold week-end worship services for professional women. Christian feminists are beginning to bond together through newsletters and other sources of information. Valerie Dunn, assistant editor of *The Presbyterian Record,* notes that "the big question among women today is ordination". Although women have been allowed to be ordained to the ministry in the United church since 1936 and in the Presbyterian church since 1966, a proportionately small number have actually become ministers. In June 1975 the ordination of women to the priesthood was approved by the Anglican church, but there is still some controversy over the issue. In the Roman Catholic church a National Advisory Committee to the Bishops was formed about four years ago, but ordination is still in dispute. However, it has been pointed out that Catholic nuns, who are becoming increasingly non-cloistered, have perhaps more influence in the church than Protestant deaconesses.

Specific concerns among women in general are often determined by the special problems of the area or group, and especially the state of the women's movement in a particular location. In the Maritimes, the movement has so far taken a back seat to economic problems of development in the area; now, groups are forming, and active programs set up but they are shaped by the context of the more conservative Maritime society. British Columbia, with a dynamic movement and a women's centre in almost every city or town, has now formed a Federation. The B.C. and Western provinces are especially concerned with "Affirmative Action" as outlined by the Western Conference/Opportunities for Women held in May 1974, attended by 325 women from Manitoba, Saskatchewan, Alberta, British Columbia, the Yukon and the North West Territories. In their brief they stated:

> We do not want more sweet and empty words about rights from our Government; we want tough, effective, change-oriented legislation.[39]

In Saskatchewan, the Status of Women Network and other groups and centres are highly organized perhaps because there are fewer women or because of the tradition of grassroots organizations there. Ontario has one of the most active cities (Toronto), but there is little contact between groups within the province. At Crossroads '75, a conference jointly sponsored by the International Women's Year Secretariat and the Quebec Status of Women Council, 480 women from all ten regions of Quebec drew up recommendations and presented them to the law-makers.

The Women and Film project, which will begin its third year in 1976, is an organization which typifies the mosaic: it is a coast-to-coast network of independent regional and provincial projects. In 1974 the projects took the form of travelling vans which provided films by women, filmmaking equipment, and information, books and pamphlets on women's issues.

An ethnic women's group which plays a significant role in support of women is the National Women's Committee of the Association of United Ukrainian Canadians. Formed in 1922 as the result of the organizing of working and farm

[39]Brief to Minister of Labour, "Affirmative Action: Proposals Concerning Anti-Discrimination Legislation", submitted by Western Conference/Opportunities for Women, May 1974.

women of the Ukrainian Canadian community, this group has carried on humanitarian and cultural activities both within and outside the Ukrainian community, and has worked to end exploitation and discrimination. They have supported the Canadian women's movement in a number of ways and are currently concerned with the need for coopera- tion with other women's groups in united efforts to achieve practical goals.

The native Indian women of Canada have perhaps en- countered even greater problems than have immigrant women. The Status of Women Commission reports that "if it is true that large numbers of the poor in Canada are women, the poorest are the Indian, Métis, and Eskimo women".[40]

It is a significant commentary on the fate of the Cana- dian Indian that the Indian woman, especially among the Iroquois, was in her original society more liberated than her white sisters. But it appears that her decline in status began with the Indian Act imposed by the patriarchal white government. While imposing integration on the Indian it punishes the Indian woman who marries a non-Indian by denying her her status. This decline has been reinforced by the ambivalent attitudes of the government towards aid for Indian women and the dominance of men in many con- temporary Indian organizations.

The case of Jeanette Corbière Lavelle is a classic one in the struggle of Indian women for their rights. She is an Ojibway woman, presently director of the Nishnawbe Insti- tute and president of the Ontario Native Women's Associa- tion, who was the first to protest in the courts against the loss of her Indian status upon her marriage to a white man. Although she and her lawyer Clayton Ruby challenged the Indian Act on grounds of discrimination under the Canadian

[40] *Report of the Royal Commission on the Status of Women in Canada*, p. 328.

Bill of Rights, her case was finally lost by a decision from the Supreme Court of Canada in August 1973.

In a recent interview, however, Ms. Lavell stated that the National Committee on Indian Rights for Indian women will be making a special effort in 1975 to get the status decision changed through parliamentary procedures.

Indian women have been meeting together recently to discuss methods of achieving better conditions for Indian women, especially with regard to marriage, family life, housing, education, and culture. They also take part, according to Ms. Lavell, in issues that involve the women's movement generally, such as equal pay for work of equal value. However, she points out that the problems associated with being Indians as well as women necessitate their carrying on their own meetings and activities within the larger context of Canadian women's groups.

The Native Women's Association of Canada was formed recently to promote the interests of native women in Canada and to encourage them to assume more active roles in their prople's struggles. The word "native" in the official title was defined as "one who is a descendant of the original inhabitants of this country who are now known as Indian (Status and Treaty), Non-Status, Métis, Eskimo and Inuit". Their second annual conference was held in Ottawa in 1975 and had as its theme, "The Future Role of Native Women in Canada". Workshops were formed to discuss such subjects as employment, alcoholism and drug abuse prevention, and the need for more women's centres.[41] A strong stand was taken in a letter presented to Prime Minister Trudeau stating that "men still hold all positions of power

---

[41] A model for native women's centres exists in "Anduhyaun House" ("Our Home" in Ojibway) in Toronto. It is a non-profit, non-sectarian, non-political organization funded by Metro welfare, provincial government and private donations and supported by the Ontario Native Women's Association. The centre provides information, practical assistance and emotional support for young native women new to the city or in special difficulties.

and make all the decisions" in native organizations. They asked that the Native Women's Association of Canada be recognized as the voice of native women.

Among native women the Inuit (formerly "Eskimo") woman has received less publicity than her Indian sister, but significant changes have been taking place in her life also. Although white influences have to some extent weakened the traditional position of Inuit women as central influences in their families and equal work partners of their husbands, in recent years they have been taking a more formal responsibility in community affairs and have been actively involved in a revival of traditional skills in the arts and crafts. One young Inuit woman wrote to the French editor of *North/Nord,* a bimonthly publication of the Department of Indian Affairs and Northern Development: "Qu'est-ce qu'il faut a une femme pour être heureuse? Avant tout, je pense qu'elle a le droit naturel d'être reconnue comme un être humain intelligent."

An organization of black women in Canada, the Canadian Negro Women's Association, was founded in 1951. In 1973 they organized the First Black Women's Congress in Canada, a three-day conference which centred on the problems relating to immigrant women, single parents, education and youth. In 1974 the Montreal Coloured Women's Club hosted the Second Black Women's Congress. One of the workshops at the conference, entitled "The Triple Repression of Black Women", discussed how black women are repressed according to race, class and sex. (The same discussion might apply as well to other non-white women in Canada.)

Recent developments in the Canadian women's movement in general give evidence that the present time is a critical one of reformation and revision. One of these is International Women's Year 1975, declared by the United Nations on the advice of the UN Commission of Women (established since 1946) with the stated aims of "Equality, Development, and Peace". Internationally, the women's movement is undergoing many of the divisions experienced in Canada. To point to a few parallels, there are problems of diversity, complicated by international politics and the lack of contact with national groups, not the least of which is Canada. How many Canadian women, for example, know of recent World Population and Food Conferences where women began to caucus separately and to press for recognition of the fact that women's issues are basic to all world issues? Indeed, the future of the Canadian women's movement will undoubtedly become more involved with the international women's movement than it has been.

In Canada, the International Women's Year plans, plus the establishment by the federal government of an IWY Secretariat in Ottawa and the prospects of grants, have been a catalyst although not necessarily in the way the government might wish. Canadian women in the process of presenting projects have re-evaluated their own movement. Further, contacts with government personnel have sometimes uncovered a lack of sensitivity to women's issues and created a backlash against IWY. Women, brought together to advise the federal government, reacted against government plans for a series of regional conferences which seemed irrelevant to the majority of Canadian women; they prepared alternate plans. Also, they have been sensitive to government attempts to try to pacify women in IWY rather than deal with Affirmative Action. (Sylvia Gelber in the October 1975 issue of *Branching Out* warns, however, that "Affirmative Action" in Canada must take a different form from that in the United States.) Yet despite the protests, IWY has undoubtedly begun necessary dialogue even if it will not be the "panacea of all ills".

Approximately thirty-five Canadian women attended the

controversial International Women's Year Conference in Mexico City during the summer of 1975. The official delegation was led by Coleen Campbell, M.P., parliamentary assistant to Minister Marc Lalonde. According to Muriel Duckworth, member of the Nova Scotia advisory committee for IWY and past president of Voice of Women, the ten-member delegation generally played the usual Canadian role of conciliator between factions holding strongly opposing points of view. Campbell stressed "attitudinal barriers" as being the chief remaining obstacle to the progress of Canadian women—an approach which many Canadian women have criticized as too often characterizing government efforts during IWY in Canada. Instead they believe there must be more emphasis on positive and legal action. It was reported at the conference that the Canadian International Development Agency (CIDA) had recently announced that it was committed to giving high priority to the needs of women in its overseas programs. It will be interesting to see to what extent women do have policy-making roles in determining Canadian government actions which affect women both at home and abroad. Of course, talk about Canadian aid to women in developing countries is somewhat ironic in view of the existence of Canada's own "Third World": its native population and other depressed groups. This was vividly emphasized at the conference by Mary Two-axe Earley, vice-president of Indian Rights for Indian Women and one of a number of Indian women threatened with eviction from their reserves because they are married to white men. She received much support from the Canadian women in attendance and a telegram on behalf of these Indian women was sent to Prime Minister Trudeau.

Participation of Canadian women at the conference at least contributed to unity among women from all parts of Canada. However, the general division at the conference between women with socialist and feminist points of view was of course also reflected in the Canadian delegation. There was a wide range of opinion between the two positions with a number of women adopting both.

Perhaps the most positive aspect of the conference was the opportunity for women from all parts of the world to meet together and learn more about some of the horrendous problems with which they have to deal. For the first time "sisterhood" became a worldwide possibility.

There are several events of an organizational nature which show the evolution of the Canadian mosaic. First, within the provinces, women are unifying. In Montreal, a liaison of women's groups is planned. In Toronto, a Women's Information Exchange for groups is operating. The British Columbia Federation of Women was established in 1974 to "focus the energy that does exist throughout the province".

Second, following the creation of the Western Canadian Women's News Service (WCWN) the Feminist News Service (FNS) has been set up to facilitate the exchange of information, features and news stories on women. In March 1975 delegates from women's newspapers, newsletters, magazines and presses met for an organizational conference. There will be ten regional representatives and two national coordinators, and bilingual monthly news packets will be sent out to members. Their aim was clearly to remedy problems of regionalism:

> FNS was seen as an important factor in alleviating the problems of geographic, language and cultural isolation, and also as a balance to the bias of traditional news service against women's groups and news.[42]

Third, in March 1975 in Thunder Bay, representatives of women's centres and groups gathered to discuss the possibility of a national organization, as a response to difficulties

[42] *Women's Information Newsletter* (Toronto), March/April, 1975, p. 2.

experienced through the government's lack of consultation in planning International Women's Year. Although a national organization was thought premature, it was decided to form a grassroots communication network on a national and regional basis as an attempt to alleviate the fragmented nature of the movement. "Network Nellie" will be a telephone "tree" stretching from east to west. The first transmission of the network was made on March 7, the eve of International Women's Day, when the message—"Ahnee (Ojibway for "hello"). Network Nellie is alive and well and marching forward. Equality to all our sisters"—was sent from St. John's to the west. Further, a possibility which is gaining attention is that of setting up a women's information centre or clearinghouse or set of centres to house information, research and records of the movement.

Governments have instituted women's programs to provide grants for projects, as well as Affirmative Action programs both in government and business designed to go beyond equal pay laws to more basic causes of inequalities. The attitude of the women's movement is, however, often one of suspicion. Can a viable women's movement be maintained on piecemeal funds from government departments? And is there not a real danger of co-option, a natural tendency to reform the ideas of feminism in the face of the wheels of government? These are some of the questions being asked. For a number of women, the government programs offer a means to "bore from within"; for other women, as shown above, the plan is to continue to develop a base apart from government.

All the above evidence is proof of the changes in the women's movement which are being made in an effort to alleviate the isolation and powerlessness sometimes felt by women in decentralized groups; but the future success will also hinge on another factor—theoretical analysis. First, women must develop their own culture, through history projects, media, writing, theatre, women's studies. Second, national contact and coordination should continue; there can be nothing more helpful than sharing women's culture from Vancouver to Newfoundland. Third, we must further develop the theoretical base of the women's movement in Canada to clarify for other women the Women's Rights, Feminist, Marxist-Feminist, and socialist viewpoints. (It is sometimes difficult to differentiate sharply among these groups. Many women may be included in more than one "category" and many are not sure where their primary orientation should lie.) Although Canadian women such as Charnie Guettel and others in the movement have produced some theory, the need for more analysis and theory is being discussed at conferences, in groups and privately.

It is perhaps true that as Simone de Beauvoir wrote many years ago the realization of sexual oppression is a difficult and draining experience for women which does not leave much time or energy for philosophical theorizing on the universe.[43] However, the next stage may bring the evolution of a philosophy of the women's movement along completely new lines.[44] It is also possible that the theory will evolve mainly from the practice. Of course, there are those who prefer not to dwell on theory for fear of creating more splits and waste of energies.

What seems clear, however, is that both theory and action are essential. If we can preserve the strengths of the mosaic which lie in contact between small groups, while overcoming problems of isolation with national networks, the resulting movement would be an effective model for other

[43] Simone De Beauvoir, *The Second Sex* (New York, 1961).

[44] Some women are reading Mary Daly's book *Beyond God the Father* which deals with the relationship between feminism and religion.

national women's groups and the international movement. The resulting theories would also be relevant, and perhaps crucial in the task of heralding in a new age for women forecast by Nellie McClung in *In Times Like These:*

> The time will come, we hope, when women will be economically free, and mentally and spiritually independent enough to refuse to have their food paid for by men; when women will receive equal pay for equal work, and have all avenues of activity open to them; and will be free to choose their own mates, without shame, or indelicacy; when men will not be afraid of marriage because of the financial burden, but free men and free women will marry for love, and work together for the sustenance of their families. It is not too ideal a thought. It is coming, and the new movement among women who are crying out for a larger humanity, is going to bring it about.[45]

[45] Nellie McClung, *In Times Like These* (Toronto, 1972) p. 85.

Appendix

Women's Centres, Women's Newspapers and Regional Contacts

This list first appeared in the September 1975 issue of *Status of Women News* (published by National Action Committee on the Status of Women, Toronto) and was up to date at that time.

Women's Centres

British Columbia:

Women's Centre & Bookstore
804 Richards St.
Vancouver, B.C.

Women's Centre
P.O. Box 521
Nelson, B.C.

Women's Centre
522 Pandora Ave.
Victoria, B.C.

Women's Resource Centre
2961 — 272 St.
Aldergrove, B.C.

Vernon Women's Centre
Ste. 6
3000 — 30th St.
Vernon, B.C.

Alberta:

Women's Centre
11812 — 95th St.
Edmonton, Alta.

Edmonton Women's Place
9917 — 116 St.
Edmonton, Alta.

YWCA Women's Centre
320 — 5th Ave.
Calgary, Alta.

Women's Centre
820 — 6th Ave.
Lethbridge, Alta.

Women's Information Centre
9904 — 100 St.
Grande Prairie, Alta.

Saskatchewan:

Saskatoon Women's Centre*
124A 2nd Ave. N.
Saskatoon, Sask.

Women's Centre
1 Angus St.
Regina, Sask.

Manitoba:

A Woman's Place
143 Walnut St.
Winnipeg, Man.

Women's Liberation
c/o Millie Lamb
Ste. 10 — 812 Wolseley Ave.
Winnipeg, Man.

Women's Place
300 Victor St.
Winnipeg, Man.

Women's Centre*
YWCA
447 Webb Place
Winnipeg, Man.

Women's Information Centre
YWCA
148 — 11th St.
Brandon, Man.

*Has a newsletter

Ontario:

Women's Centre*
581 O'Connor St.
Ottawa, Ont.

North Bay Women's Centre
2 — 236 Worthington St. W.
North Bay, Ont.

The Women's Place
968 University Ave. W.
Windsor, Ont.

Women's Place*
25 Dupont St.
Kitchener-Waterloo, Ont.

Guelph Women's Centre
35 Priory St.
P.O. Box 1162
Guelph, Ont.

Women's Resource Centre*
322 Queens Ave.
London, Ont.

Women's Resource Centre*
YWCA
56 Queen St.
St. Catharines, Ont.

Women's Place
262 Rubidge St.
Peterborough, Ont.

Toronto Women's Bookstore
85 Harbord St.
Toronto, Ont.

Women's Development Centre
15 Birch Ave.
Toronto, Ont.

Northern Women's Centre*
c/o YWCA
350 Arthur St.
Thunder Bay, Ont.

Quebec:

Women's Information & Referral
Centre
3595 St. Urbain
Montreal, P.Q. H2X 2N6

La Place des Femmes
3764 Boul. St. Laurent
Montreal, P.Q.

Nova Scotia:

Women's Centre (Halifax)*
5683 Brentan Place
Halifax, N.S.
Mailing Address:
P.O. Box 5052
Armdale, N.S.

Women's Centre
P.O. Box 894
Wolfville, N.S.

New Brunswick:

c/o Hilary Prince
YWCA
Women's Information & Referral
Centre
27 Wellington Row
St. John, N.B.

Fredericton Women's Centre
28 Saunders St.
Fredericton, N.B. E38 1N1

Women's Information Centre
St. John YWCA
27 Wellington Row
St. John, N.B. E2L 3H4

Prince Edward Island:

Women's Travelling Resource Centre
285 Kent St.
Charlottetown, P.E.I.

Newfoundland:

Women's Centre*
P.O. Box 6072
St. John's, Nfld.

Northwest Territories:

c/o Nellie Cournoyer
Inuvik, N.W.T.

Yukon:

Women's Centre*
4051 4th Ave.
Whitehorse, Yukon

*Has a newsletter

Women's Newspapers

British Columbia:

Women Can
704 Richards
Vancouver, B.C.

Kinesis
2029 W. 4th Ave.
Vancouver, B.C.

Priorities
3485 W. 15th Ave.
Vancouver, B.C.

B.C. Federation of Women Newsletter
1240 Doran Rd.
North Vancouver, B.C.

Alberta:

Branching Out
P.O. Box 4098
Edmonton, Alta.

Source
The Alberta Women's Newsletter
10006 — 107 St.
Edmonton, Alta.

Calgary Women's Newspaper
206 — 223 12th Ave. S.W.
Calgary, Alta.

Saskatchewan:

Network of Saskatchewan Women
P.O. Box 1525
Rosetown, Sask.

Manitoba:

Emergency Librarian
c/o Barbara Clubb
32 — 351 River Ave.
Winnipeg, Man.

Ontario:

Status of Women News
121 Avenue Rd.
Toronto, Ont.

The Other Woman
Box 928, Station Q
Toronto, Ont.

The Native Sisterhood
P.O. Box 515
Kingston, Ont.

Tightwire
(Women's Penitentiary Newspaper)
P.O. Box 515
Kingston, Ont.

Clearing House for Feminist Media
P.O. Box 207
Ancaster, Ont.

Canadian Newsletter of Research on Women
Dept. of Sociology
OISE
252 Bloor St. W.
Toronto, Ont.

The Northern Woman
P.O. Box 314
132 N. Archibald St.
Thunder Bay, Ont.

Windsor Woman
Room 603
76 University Ave. W.
Windsor, Ont.

Quebec:

Québécoises Debouttes
4319 St. Denis
Montreal, P.Q.

Feminist Communication Collective
P.O. Box 455
Montreal, P.Q.

Long Time Coming
Lesbian Feminist Paper
P.O. Box 161, Station E
Montreal, P.Q.

Prince Edward Island:

A Woman's Newsletter
P.O. Box 1816
Charlottetown, P.E.I.

Yukon:

Victoria Faulkner Newsletter
4051 4th Ave.
Whitehorse, Yukon

Regional Contacts

British Columbia:

Vancouver Status of Women
2029 W. 4th Ave.
Vancouver 9, B.C.

Victoria Status of Women Action
Group
766 Monterey Ave., Victoria, B.C.

Marilyn Cairnduff
Women's Rights Committee
B.C. Federation of Labour
210 — 517 E. Broadway,
Vancouver, B.C.

West Kootenay Status of Women
Council
Selkirk College
P.O. Box 1200
Castlegar, B.C.

B.C. Federation of Women
c/o Joy Bradbury
65 — 445 S.W. Marine Dr.
Vancouver, B.C.

Women's Bureau
c/o Christine Waddell
411 Dunsmuir Ave.
Vancouver, B.C.

Alberta:

Alberta Action Committee on the
Status of Women
Mrs. J.A. Durand, President
1453 — 106A Ave.
Edmonton, Alta.
Jean Marchton, Acting Secretary
9214 — 117 St.
Edmonton, Alta.

Calgary Status of Women Council
223 — 12th Ave. S.W.
Calgary, Alta.

Saskatchewan:

Action Committee on Status of
Women
c/o Jane Abramson, Chairperson
2004 — 14th St. E.
Saskatoon, Sask.
Gwen Lee, Vice-chairperson
209 St. Andrews Cres.
P.O. Box 1525
Rosetown, Sask.

Mary Helen Richards
Corresponding Secretary
1129 Elliot St.
Saskatoon, Sask.

Manitoba:

Manitoba Committee on the Status
of Women
c/o M. Smith
447 Webb Place Winnipeg, Man.

Manitoba Action Committee
(Brandon)
Women's Information Centre
YWCA
Brandon, Man.

Ontario:

Ontario Committee on Status of
Women
P.O. Box 188, Station Q
Toronto, Ont.

Wendy Lawrence
309A — 51 Grosvenor St.
Toronto, Ont. M5S 1B5

Quebec:

La Fédération des Femmes du
Quebec
Pat Buesson
75 12è Ave.
Vimont, P.Q.

Centre de Renseignements, F.F.Q.
45 rue est Jarry
Montreal, P.Q.

Nova Scotia:
Mary Wall
Provincial Council of Women
6851 Regina Terrace
Halifax, N.S.

Muriel Duckworth
Voice of Women — La Voix des
Femmes
6250 South St.
Halifax, N.S.

Judith Wouk
6299 Yale St.
Halifax, N.S.

Dr. Lois Vallely
Dept. of History
Acadia University
Wolfville, N.S.

New Brunswick:

Marjorie Laws
Business and Professional Women's
Club
595 Shediac Rd.
Moncton, N.B.

Janet Culinan
Human Rights Commission
P.O. Box 6000

Fredericton, N.B.
Hilary Prince (YWCA)
27 Wellington Row
St. John, N.B.

Norah Toole
824 George St.
Fredericton, N.B.

Prince Edward Island:

Status of Women Action Committee
Martha Practt, Acting Secretary
57 Newland Cres.
Charlottetown, P.E.I.

P.E.I. Council of Women
c/o Beatrice Reeves
R.R. 1
Charlottetown, P.E.I.

Newfoundland:

Newfoundland Status of Women
Council
Sally Davis, President
P.O. Box 6072
St. John's, Nfld.

Celia Griffith, Treasurer
P.O. Box 6072
St. John's, Nfld.

Northwest Territories:

NWT Status of Women Action Com-
mittee
Alison J. McAteer, Co-ordinator
P.O. Box 1225
Yellowknife, N.W.T. X0E 1H0

Ellen Binder
P.O. Box 1057
Inuvik, N.W.T.

Yukon:

Yukon Status of Women Council
4051 4th Ave.
Whitehorse, Yukon

**National Action Committee on
the Status of Women:**

Lorna Marsden, President
419 Markham St.
Toronto, Ont.

Grace Hartman, Immediate Past
President
Ste. 800 — 233 rue Gilmour
Ottawa, Ont.

Laura Sabia, Past President
29 Edgedale Rd.
St. Catharines, Ont.

Cathleen Morrison, Secretary
184 Moore Ave.
Toronto, Ont.

Moira Armour, Editor, Status of
Women News
121 Avenue Rd.
Toronto, Ont. M5R 2G3

Marjorie Robertson, Typesetter
Toronto, Ont.

Bibliography

The following is a partial list of books referred to in the text.

Baker, Elizabeth C. and Hess, Thomas B., ed. *Art and Sexual Politics.* Toronto: Macmillan Company of Canada, 1973.

Brown, R. Craig and Cook, Ramsay. *Canada, 1896-1921: A Nation Transformed.* Canadian Centenary series. Toronto: McClelland & Stewart, 1973.

Burnet, Jean R. *Ethnic Groups in Upper Canada.* Toronto: Ontario Historical Society, 1972.

Canadian Women's Educational Press. *Women at Work: Ontario, 1850-1930.* Toronto, 1974.

Canadian Women's Educational Press. *Women Unite!* Toronto, 1969.

Cleverdon, C.L. *The Woman Suffrage Movement in Canada.* Intro., Ramsay Cook. Social History of Canada series. Toronto: University of Toronto Press, 1973.

Creighton, Luella. *The Elegant Canadians.* Toronto: McClelland & Stuart, 1967.

Daly, Mary. *Beyond God the Father.* Boston: Beacon Press, 1974.

De Beauvoir, Simone. *The Second Sex.* New York, 1961.

Firestone, Shulamith. *The Dialectic of Sex.* New York: William Morrow & Co., 1970.

Flexner, E. *Century of Struggle: The Woman's Rights Movement in the United States.* Cambridge, Mass.: Harvard University Press, 1959.

Hanke, Lewis. *Aristotle and the American Indian.* Bloomington: Indiana University Press, 1970.

Harris, Paul, ed. *Brief to the Bishops.* Toronto: Longman, 1965.

Harshaw, J.P. *When Women Work Together.* Toronto: YWCA, 1966.

Hole, J. and Levine, Ellen. *The Rebirth of Feminism.* New York: Quadrangle, 1973.

Innis, Mary, ed. *The Clear Spirit: Twenty Canadian Women and Their Times.* Toronto: University of Toronto Press, 1966.

Jameson, Anna B. *Winter Studies and Summer Rambles in Canada.* New Canadian Library. Toronto: McClelland & Stewart, 1965.

Kanowitz, L. *Women and the Law: The Unfinished Revolution.* Albuquerque: University of New Mexico Press, 1969.

Kraditor, A.S. *Ideas of the Woman Suffrage Movement, 1890-1920.* New York: Columbia University Press, 1965.

McClung, Nellie, *Clearing in the West.* Toronto: Thomas Allen Ltd., 1964.

McClung, Nellie. *The Stream Runs Fast.* Toronto: Thomas Allen Ltd., 1965.

McClung, Nellie. *In Times Like These.* Intro., V. Strong-Boag. Social History of Canada series. Toronto: University of Toronto Press, 1972.

McLeod, T.H., ed. *Post Secondary Education in a Technological Society.* Montreal & London: McGill-Queen's University Press, 1973.

Millett, Kate. *Sexual Politics.* New York: Doubleday, 1970.

Moodie, Susanna. *Roughing It in the Bush.* New Canadian Library. Toronto: McClelland & Stewart, 1962.

O'Neill, W. *Everyone Was Brave.* New York: Quadrangle, 1969.

Pike, Robert M. *Who Doesn't Go to University—And Why: A Study on Accessibility to Higher Education in Canada.* Ottawa: A.U.C.C., 1970.

Porter, John. *The Vertical Mosaic: An Analysis of Social Class and Power in Canada.* Toronto: University of Toronto Press, 1965.

Roche, Anne. *The Gates of Hell.* Toronto: McClelland & Stewart, 1975.

Rowbotham, S. *Women Resistance and Revolution.* New York: Pantheon, 1973.

Ruskin, J. *Sesame and Lilies.* Everyman series. London: J.M. Dent & Sons.

Stephenson, Marylee, ed. *Women in Canada.* Toronto: New Press, 1973.

Vicinus, M., ed. *Suffer and Be Still: Women in the Victorian Age.* Bloomington: Indiana University Press, 1972.

Ward, Norman and Spafford, Duff, ed. *Politics in Saskatchewan.* Toronto: Longman, 1968.

Young, G.M. *Victorian England: Portrait of an Age.* London, 1936.

Zaremba, Eve, ed. *Privilege of Sex: A Century of Canadian Women.* Toronto: House of Anansi Press, 1974.

Zuker, Marvin A. and Callwood, June. *Canadian Women and the Law.* Toronto: Copp Clark, 1971.